Shakespeare's
English Kings,
the People,
and the Law

D0915286

Shakespeare's English Kings, the People, and the Law

A STUDY IN THE RELATIONSHIP BETWEEN THE TUDOR CONSTITUTION AND THE ENGLISH HISTORY PLAYS

Edna Zwick Boris

RUTHERFORD • MADISON • TEANECK
FAIRLEIGH DICKINSON UNIVERSITY PRESS
LONDON: ASSOCIATED UNIVERSITY PRESSES

Associated University Presses, Inc.
Cranbury, New Jersey 08512

Associated University Presses
Magdalen House
136–148 Tooley Street
London SE1 2TT, England

Library of Congress Cataloging in Publication Data

Boris, Edna Zwick, 1943–
    Shakespeare's English kings, the people, and the law.

    Based on the author's dissertation, Indiana, 1974.
    Bibliography: p.
    Includes index.
    1. Shakespeare, William, 1564–1616—Histories.
    2. Constitutional history in literature. 3. Great Britain—
Constitutional history. 4. Great Britain—Politics and government
—1558–1603. I. Title.
PR2982.B6   822.3'3   76-19838
ISBN 0-8386-1990-8

PRINTED IN THE UNITED STATES OF AMERICA

In memory of my father, Louis H. Zwick

Contents

Preface

Studies that draw on disciplines other than one's own are at best perilous undertakings. First, no amount of research in another field ever permits one to feel as secure in interpreting the material as one is in one's own field. Second, some of the greatest difficulties in interdisciplinary studies result from the volume of scholarship produced in the twentieth century; by the time a scholar's work becomes well enough known to be familiar in another discipline, more often than not it has already been successfully challenged by newer research not yet known outside the field.

Constitutional history, particularly in England, with its largely unwritten traditions, is especially ambiguous. To the extent that I have succeeded in the task of bringing to bear on Shakespeare's English history plays some knowledge of the constitutional structure of Elizabethan England, I owe a great debt to many people, one of whom must be singled out for mention here—Professor Morris Arnold of The University of Pennsylvania's School of Law. The willingness with which he shared both his unfailing knowledge of the documents and his critical perspective on matters of controversy among scholars has earned a debt of gratitude that I can never hope to repay. I also wish to thank Professor Leo Solt of the History Department and Professors Georges

Edelen, Roy Battenhouse, and Albert Wertheim of the English Department at Indiana University, who supervised the doctoral dissertation on which most of this book is based. Professor Willis Barnstone in the Comparative Literature Department first encouraged me to submit the dissertation for publication.

Richard Boris and Bernard Morris, political scientists, helped provide terms with which to discuss the constitutional relationships examined in this study. The word *societal,* which is used to mean "of or pertaining to the structure, organization, or functioning of society," may seem alien to literary students. I have not been able to find an adequate synonym in the vocabulary usually used in literary studies and have therefore preferred to borrow a term from the social sciences rather than risk inaccuracy. Charles Gray and Moody E. Prior very kindly read the text just prior to publication.

It was with considerable surprise that I first realized, after having completed years of undergraduate and graduate courses in Renaissance drama, that Edward Coke was speaker of the House of Commons in 1593. How differently might one perceive Shakespeare's English history plays, I wondered, if one took into account contemporary constitutional developments as distinct from political theory. I have no doubt that a scholar of more mature years than my own would be better suited to such an undertaking; but I am equally certain that such a scholar would know better than to attempt a study fraught with so many ambiguities. It is my hope, however, that others will further the investigations recorded here. The complexities of constitutional history, of the English history plays, and of the relationships between the two need to be considered and debated. Though there may be no easy answers, the discussion itself should enrich our understanding.

Introduction

This study, which developed out of my curiosity about the relationship between Shakespeare's English history plays and Tudor constitutional developments, has a dual purpose. The first, set out in the first chapter, is to demonstrate that knowledge of constitutional history can add to our understanding of the politics of these plays, for in the late sixteenth century, the English Crown was generally understood, despite disagreements over specific issues, to be limited by law and by Parliament. The second, to which the remaining chapters are devoted, is to suggest that the nine history plays written by Shakespeare before Elizabeth's death record a transformation in constitutional organization that captures the essence of historical constitutional developments as a movement not from simple to complex organization but from vague to more precise relationships.[1] Throughout this study I am less concerned with the correlation between specific events and dramatic representation than with the general thematic reflection in the plays of a changing constitutional structure.

Among political theorists in the sixteenth century, there was a great variety of opinions about the best theoretical underpinnings for the constitution. These ideological controversies are not my point of focus; I concentrate instead on the actual functioning of the Tudor constitution as illustrated in several events that historians have singled out as important; in addition, I rely to a great extent on the observations of Sir Thomas Smith, one of the few contemporary Elizabethan writers who deliberately set out to describe the actual functioning of the constitution as he saw it from the perspective of a trusted governmental servant, not to plead for any particular political ideology. Though he was, of course, not an impartial observer, his writings are among the most complete and least partisan contemporary documents analyzing the Elizabethan constitution.

Late sixteenth-century England was in the midst of many transitions. In legal terms, there was movement from moral to positive or man-made law; in economic terms there was a movement from vestiges of feudalism to nascent capitalism; in societal terms there was a movement from inherited status to implicit contract as the basis for position. All of these changes reflect an awareness of the need for more refined definitions of societal relationships than were provided by the Elizabethan heritage of medieval feudal ideals. The inadequacy of feudal ideals to sixteenth-century problems was particularly manifest in the increasing contention for sovereignty, as some critics have called it, among Crown, Parliament, and spokesmen for the common law traditions.

When Shakespeare and other playwrights dramatized English history and English institutions, they all devoted some attention to the figure of the king, to his relationship with his subjects, and to the functioning of the law. In so doing, they were giving dramatic representation to the three fundamental powers in England's unique governmental structure. Marlowe, Peele, Shakespeare, and the anonymous author of *Woodstock* share a common perspective on the English monarchy as a constitutionally limited one. Only by guarding their subects' well-being and by respecting specific provisions established by legal tradition do English kings reign well in the plays. When either subjects' best interests or long-standing traditions are disregarded, the kings consistently suffer the consequence of successful rebellion. Without drawing a strict correlation between issues in the plays and contemporary events, one can see in constitutional terms parallels between the treatment of English institutions in the plays and the contemporary functioning of those institutions. Some of these parallels are set out in this study's first chapter, which discusses the three branches in the government and how they are manifested in the plays.

Shakespeare more than any other Elizabethan playwright was drawn repeatedly to English history for his dramatic materials. Before Elizabeth's death he wrote nine English history plays, first covering in four plays the period leading up to the Tudor reign, then examining in another tetralogy the period before that, and taking time as well to devote one play to King John. In Shakespeare's *Henry VI* plays, in terms of constitutional themes, attention is paid to meetings of parliament, to meetings of councils, and to the administration of justice; in addition, however, consideration is given to essentially medieval feudal concerns in both the making and breaking of fealty oaths and in references to status. In Shakespeare's plays dramatizing the reigns from Richard II through Henry V, the council, parliaments, and the administration of justice are all focused on, but feudal relationships are given almost no attention. I wish to suggest through the course of this study that one possible explanation for the absence of interest in feudal structure in the second four plays is Shakespeare's increased reflection of the contemporary constitution in English history plays the more he worked with historical materials. I can offer nothing more certain than a suggestion, however, largely because of the nature of English constitutional history.

From before the reign of Richard II through to today, there have been parliaments, kings, and justices. The language discussing those institutions often appears strangely modern and even similar over many years. Sir John Fortescue, for instance, Henry VI's onetime chief justice, wrote of the English that the people "assent unto the laws," while Thomas Smith wrote around a hundred years later

that "every man's consent is given to the laws in England."
We know that *every man* in the sixteenth century did not
mean universal franchise; similarly, between the writing of
the statements by Fortescue and Smith vast changes had
taken place in the procedure, functioning, and status of
Parliament and in particular of the Commons, which had
been transformed from an auxiliary element in the government to a unit of such strength that it could on occasion
challenge royal prerogative under Elizabeth. The monarchy,
too, varied widely in constitutional significance between the
time of Richard II and Elizabeth I. The Crown was very
strong for a time under Richard II, extremely weak under
Henry VI, temporarily strengthened by Edward IV, and
greatly strengthened by Henry VII. Yet had constitutional
provisions for the monarchy changed? The twentieth-century
American presidency can provide an analogous difficulty.
Woodrow Wilson had cause to lament the weakness of the
executive in comparison with a strong Congress in his *Congressional Government,* yet within half a century or so, the
situation would be clearly the reverse though the *constitution*
remained the same.

How is one then to regard the deposition of Richard II?
From one point of view, Bolingbroke's revolution was a
conservative one to lessen Richard's newly asserted strength
of the Crown in relationship to the lords and barons. From
another point of view, however, the Lancastrian revolution
was a modern experiment in which large bodies of nobles
were closely associated with the daily business of government, thus dispersing authority somewhat from the Crown
and involving consultation with the upper class. Since parliaments existed in the time of Richard II and Henry VI as
well as of Elizabeth I, deciding whether references to
consultation in Shakespeare's plays are contemporary in
character is one of the many difficulties in this study. The
difficulty is compounded, I might add, by the enormous
influence that Shakespeare's handling of this period has had
on even the best of constitutional historians, such as S. B.

Chrimes, particularly in his *Lancastrians, Yorkists, and Henry VII.*

I admit at the outset that this is a matter of interpretation and, hence, of possible disagreement, but I believe and hope to show that Shakespeare's treatment of constitutional relationships reveals a change that has its greatest meaning if viewed in reference to his own time. Though medieval kings, for instance, met with parliaments, they had much greater latitude than did sixteenth-century kings. Medieval kings could change enacted statutes by adding amendments that had not been assented to by Parliament, a practice that was no longer possible in the sixteenth century when even royal proclamations sometimes came under parliamentary scrutiny. To cite just one comparison where, in Shakespeare's plays, Henry VI only summons a parliament when there is actual civil war and not when he wishes to impose a tax, Henry V will include a pledge to summon Parliament in his first public address. There is only a difference in degree, but it is a significant one. Henry VI's actions illustrate the greater freedom from restraints that late medieval kings enjoyed in terms of the tripartite constitution. Henry V's *2 Henry IV* pledge, which he fulfills in *Henry V*, indicates, I think, the narrowing of the boundaries within which the late-sixteenth-century monarch was expected to operate rather than Shakespeare's accurately portraying the constitution as it existed in Henry V's time. The "narrowed boundaries" were, of course, still quite wide.

There is a paradox in the treatment of an earlier period to show later ideas. In preparing to write the first four plays, Shakespeare had to immerse himself in the events of an era universally regarded as disastrous for the nation. What he shows in his first four English history plays is the breakdown of feudalism: concepts of fealty prove inadequate and are abandoned in favor of concern with individual accountability commensurate with societal position. Claims for honor and respect because of inherited rank and references to a dynasty of sixty years' standing give way to such practical considerations as whether or not a king can enforce the laws and command obedience. In preparing to write the four plays in the second tetralogy, Shakespeare contemplated a period that culminated in a reign viewed as successful. Though Henry IV and Henry V predate Henry VI, as kings in Shakespeare's plays they do not rely on a system of fealty; rather, Shakespeare's Henry IV and Henry V depend upon their own careful governance and their ability to demonstrate, anachronistically, public allegiance to the traditions of the English constitution as it functioned in the late sixteenth century. A notable example of this allegiance would be Shakespeare's handling of the newly crowned Henry V's reconciliation with the Lord Chief Justice in *2 Henry IV*. I thus agree with such critics as Lily B. Campbell and David Bevington in believing that Shakespeare, unlike Ben Jonson, was less interested in accurate history than in using history to explore current political problems.[2]

Chapters 2, 3, and 4 analyze respectively plays of the first tetralogy, *King John,* and plays of the second tetralogy to show a movement away from feudal to modern societal structure, though the historical periods covered in those plays range from the Renaissance back to early medieval times. The discussion attempts to show that while Shakespeare shared with his contemporary playwrights a concern with the particular nature of the tripartite English constitution uniting Crown, law, and people in the governing structure, he went beyond the specific characteristics of the constitution to perceive a larger movement toward greater specificity in societal relationships. It is my hypothesis that Shakespeare, whether intentionally or accidentally, imposed a late-sixteenth-century political understanding upon his historical material so that the plays show chaos resulting from an imprecise relationship among the Crown, the people, and the law and then some success in governing resulting from a more explicit system of royal duties coupled with accountability. The plays seem to suggest that there is only one fruitful direction in which societal relations can develop. They do no more than suggest, however, for the consolidation achieved by Henry V was temporary and was directed at ends whose worth Shakespeare may have doubted. What value there is to subduing the French when so many domestic problems remain is a question that persists through all nine plays. This question provides a pessimistic counterpoint to Henry V's achievement that is repeatedly lauded in the first tetralogy and demonstrated in the second.

The thematic unity provided by historical material, by the movement toward increased precision in the constitutional relationship among Crown, people, and law, and by the accompanying reservation about the attainments of human society do not necessarily mean that Shakespeare wrote all nine plays to demonstrate the working of a constitutional principle. The plays, by and large, are distinct though related; I recognize that they do not constitute one vast literary work. Attention to governmental or constitutional structure is, nonetheless, apparent in all of these plays. I did not, however, perceive a coherent pattern in them until after I had alternated through many readings of the plays, the documents, and the history. Therefore, though Shakespeare might have begun work on these plays with a clearly formed master plan, I think it more likely that his perception of the constitutional significance of the periods covered was defined through the process of writing the plays and may not ever have been conscious. Even so, in choosing the clearest method for organizing this study, it seemed best to consider each branch of government as a unit through the four plays of each tetralogy. The alternative, of a discussion organized in terms of the three branches within each play, would have been too fragmented and would have necessitated a cumbersome amount of cross referencing. I leave to some future study an examination of the Stuart constitution and *Henry VIII*.

Chapter 1 begins with a survey of some of the literary scholarship on the plays that prompted my investigation into constitutional history. It then turns to a discussion of the three branches of the English constitution and their manifestation in the late-sixteenth-century drama.

NOTES TO INTRODUCTION

1. S. B. Chrimes begins his standard *English Constitutional Ideas in the Fifteenth Century* (Cambridge: At the University Press, 1936) with a discussion of this idea, which was first enunciated by F. W. Maitland.
2. Jonas A. Barish, ed., *Ben Jonson: Sejanus* (New Haven, Conn.: Yale University Press, 1965), pp. 3-4; Lily Bess Campbell, *Shakespeare's "Histories"—Mirrors of Elizabethan Policy* (San Marino, Calif.: Huntington Library, 1947), p. 125; David Bevington, *Tudor Drama and Politics, A Critical Approach to Topical Meaning* (Cambridge, Mass.: Harvard University Press, 1968), p. 5.

Shakespeare's
English Kings,
the People,
and the Law

Constitutional Background

A. Some Scholarship

In the many studies of Shakespeare's history plays that have been published in the twentieth century, one phrase appears repeatedly to describe Shakespeare's main pre-occupation in these plays; the phrase is *order and degree.* For example, in his 1918 study of *English History in Shake-speare,* J. A. R. Marriott wrote that Shakespeare "believed in order, degree, subordination."[1] Arthur Sewell, in his 1951 study called *Character and Society in Shakespeare,* concluded that "in the histories, even where disorder most threatens, we have a sure expectation that it will not tri-umph. . . . The ideal of political order remains constant."[2] M. M. Reese wrote in 1961 that Shakespeare affirms "order and degree" in these plays.[3] Andrew Cairncross, in his intro-ductions to the new Arden editions of *Henry VI,* which appeared between 1957 and 1964, describes the plays as part of a "pageant in which England and man himself work out the expiation of an original crime towards the final reassertion of a divinely controlled universal order."[4] Ron-ald Berman in 1967 wrote of *Richard III* and *King John*

that "the natural order" reasserts its "own laws," that
Faulconbridge concludes with "devout submission to the
'lineal state' of the land," and that "both plays end with a
kind of apotheosis in which history is visualized as the
servant of law."[5]

As one can see from Cairncross and Berman, in the view
of many critics, Shakespeare's use of "order and degree"
has become linked with another idea. This is the belief that
there was a moral myth of Tudor succession, expounded
particularly by Edward Hall, in which the deposition of
Richard II was a crime that could be expiated only by the
suffering of civil war, which ended when the Tudors came
to the throne. E. M. W. Tillyard, in his *Shakespeare's
History Plays* (1944), was the most influential proponent
of the theory that Hall's moral pattern is evinced in Shakespeare's two tetralogies.[6] An underlying assumption of that
theory is that the English Crown must descend lineally so
that any interruption in that lineal descent, such as through
deposition, would be a crime against cosmic order.

Emphasis on lineal descent in interpreting the plays was
accompanied by a belief that the plays celebrate a divinely
ordained social structure that will ultimately triumph over
all internal challenges. Alfred Hart's study (1934) of the
influence of homilies on Shakespeare's plays tended to reinforce this belief.[7] Two homilies in particular were often
cited for their relevance to the history plays, "An exhorta-
tion to obedience" and "An homily against disobedience and
wilfull rebellion," both of which inculcate absolute obedience
to the powers-that-be as divinely ordained.[8] Curiously, the
lines most often cited to illustrate the fact that a rigid
hierarchical social structure was the basic assumption governing Shakespeare's plays occur not in the English history
plays but in *Troilus and Cressida,* in Ulysses' speech on
order and degree (see in particular Tillyard, *Shakespeare's
History Plays,* p. 17). L. C. Knights's warning in a 1957
lecture to the British Academy against this application of a
speech that is not unquestioned even within its own play to
the histories went largely unheeded.[9] Even though as early

as 1948 W. Gordon Zeeveld had warned that "the classical concept of a fixed social order . . . was being inevitably and permanently destroyed even while Tudor theorists praised with one voice the traditional principle of degree," Arthur Colby Sprague, in 1964, wrote (that the view) "that the sovereign was God's deputy in a 'wonderful order' of 'angels and men' would have been accepted without question by Elizabethan readers of Shakespeare's works."[10] George W. Keeton stated in 1967 that "Shakespeare accepts without qualification this general conception of the State, and of the order which is achieved by each degree following its own vocation. . . . Shakespeare's conception of the right to rule England is fundamentally dynastic . . . , and he has the best claim who can prove priority of descent. All others are usurpers. This is a view which is reflected in all the Histories."[11]

In the last decade a few works have appeared as harbingers of challenge to some of these long-held assumptions. H. S. Richmond in his 1967 book entitled *Shakespeare's Political Plays* discusses the presence of several "sanctions that vindicate authority" in the plays, though he does not offer an overview that would link his separate discussions of the plays.[12] The fact that his essays succeed in escaping the preoccupation with lineality is significant. Henry Ansgar Kelly in 1970 challenged an essential element to Tillyard's thesis—the premise that there was a Renaissance conception of God who would punish innocent descendants for several generations in an entire nation.[13] Robert Ornstein in 1972 pointed out that scholarship on Elizabethan thought has created the impression that there were only two categories of Renaissance thought and art—the orthodox and the deviant—so that most critics have been busy showing that Shakespeare either wholeheartedly affirmed authority or subtly challenged it, when, in fact, thought on government and society was diverse and that diversity was reflected in art. Finally Moody Prior, in *The Drama of Power*, wisely observes, "we can be reasonably certain that if we read the history plays with official pronouncements on disobedience

as the primary gloss and chief touchstone, we will miss out
very badly."[14]

I would like to suggest that preoccupation among critics
of Shakespeare's plays with lineality and with divinely structured order and degree as sanctions for the Crown is related
to an inaccurate assumption about the nature of Elizabethan
government. Alfred Hart stated, for example, that "no
monarch of England ever exercised such absolute power
as 'good Queen Bess.' Autocracy was in her blood and the
very breath of her nostrils. The term 'contrary to law' had
no meaning when law came into conflict with her royal prerogative" (Hart, *Shakespeare and the Homilies,* pp. 11-12).
John Dover Wilson wrote in a study of "The Political
Background of Shakespeare's *Richard II* and *Henry IV*"
that "the constitution in which [Elizabethans] rejoiced was
not a democracy with a party system and the paraphernalia
of parliamentary government, but a monarchy . . . divinely
ordained, strong, absolute, unchallenged, and entirely popular."[15] Tillyard similarly insisted that the Tudors inspired a
religious respect "that caused the English to accept and even
to approve the drastic curtailments of their old liberties
made definitive by Henry VIII and continued by Elizabeth,
her Parliament admitting that her prerogative could override any laws made by them . . ." (Tillyard, *Shakespeare's
History Plays,* pp. 66-67).

All these statements create the impression that the
English lived under an absolute monarchy comparable to
that in France. Yet the English monarchy differed significantly from that in France, a fact that was vividly perceived
by Englishmen at least as far back as the days of John
Fortescue and kept current by the Hundred Years' War and
the Catholic encirclement of Protestant England. Fortescue
had written that the "French king reigns over his people
Dominio Regali," by which he meant as absolute monarch,
and that his people are so abused by his taxation that "they
go crooked, and are feeble, not able to fight nor to defend
the realm." England on the contrary is "ruled under a better
law," and her people are more prosperous; they are ruled

"by such laws as they all assent unto," for the English king rules *Dominio Politico et Regali*, by which he meant something approaching limited or constitutional monarchy.[16] Thomas Smith, during Elizabeth's reign, also contrasted Englishmen with Frenchmen, saying, "our ancient princes and legislators have nourished [citizens of our nation] as to make them stout-hearted, courageous and soldiers, not villaines and slaves, and that is the scope almost of all our policy."[17]

English constitutional history shows that not the Crown alone but the Crown, Parliament, and the common law were the three fundamental branches of the sixteenth-century English constitution. Constitutional history comprehends a complex system of governmental authority and a multiplicity of sanctions for rule not taken sufficiently into account thus far in studying the plays. In order to compensate for the preoccupation with the Crown that has marked even such fine studies of the plays as Una Ellis-Fermor's essay "Shakespeare's Political Plays," each chapter in my study is divided into three sections—on the Parliament, the Crown, and the law—which are arranged to follow the order observed by Thomas Smith, the principal Elizabethan constitutional observer, in his *De Republica Anglorum*. The sections on Parliament and the law in the present chapter both concentrate on the strength of those two branches of government as restraints upon the Crown, while the section on the Crown emphasizes the problems and uncertainties surrounding the English Crown. For lineal descent was by no means the only path leading to the Crown, nor was absolute acceptance of an extant order and degree the only behavior permitted by the continually developing constitution. Once the constitution as it had evolved by the end of Elizabeth's reign is generally understood, I think one will be in a better position to recognize in Shakespeare's plays the attention he gives to the sanctions of lawful rule, general consent, and dedication to the common good. Where Henry VI succeeds to the throne only as his father's son, Henry V feels it necessary to give public demonstration of his commitment to the three other sanctions, so that the movement from *1 Henry VI* to *Henry V* is, I believe, a movement away from feudal heritage toward late-sixteenth-century constitutional realities. While it is true that the Crown was central to the government, since one could not be unaware of Elizabeth, the Crown had defined limits to its power that have been largely underestimated in studies of the kings in English history plays.

I wish to state at the outset, however, that attention to the forces limiting the power of kings within the plays does not result in interpretations that radically differ from those by generations of scholars: there can be no denying the importance of kings in the plays. But reconstructing as best one can the constitutional context of the times within which these plays were written enriches one's understanding by filling in significant background details for the main configurations of which one is already aware. After all, England would again be torn by civil war not many years after these plays were written. Events as profoundly disruptive as war are never sudden developments but result from stresses present long before. Since those stresses were evident in Elizabethan society, one should also expect to find some indication of them in the literature of Elizabethan writers.

B. *Parliament and the People*

Parliament in the sixteenth century embodied two dichotomous constitutional principles. It was summoned and dissolved by the king and therefore dependent upon him as a "High Court" of the king.[18] It was at the same time a representative assembly whose authority was separate from and independent of the king because

> every Englishman is entended to be there present, either in person or by procuration and attorneys, of what preeminence, state, dignity, or quality soever he be, from the Prince (be he King or Queen) to the lowest person of England. And the consent of the Parliament is taken to be every man's consent. [Smith, *De Republica Anglorum,* pp. 48–49]

Every man did not mean what it would mean today. Franchise was limited to substantial citizens. But what Thomas Smith is describing is the recognition that delegates considered themselves to be representatives of the whole nation, not merely of separate localities, and their decisions were binding upon everyone.[19] This distinction between a Parliament whose authority stemmed from the king and a representative body whose authority stemmed from the people was delineated in historical documents by the terms "Parliament" and "Estates" or the "three estates" or by naming the groups. When delegates of the realm were summoned by a king to join with him in passing legislation, such sessions were called meetings of "Parliament." But when there was any irregularity in succession that complicated the designation of the assembly being summoned by a particular king, then the body was called the "Estates." For example, the transition from the reign of Richard II to Henry IV was authorized in documents where the name "Parliament" was never mentioned. The sanctioning body was referred to as the "Estates" (Chrimes, *Constitutional Ideas,* p. 107). When Lord Burghley in 1585 contemplated the possibility of an interregnum caused by Elizabeth's assassination, he referred to the Parliament to be summoned after her death as the "Three Estates" (see the conclusion to this section). Shakespeare seems to have maintained the same distinction in the text and in the stage directions of his plays, since he only refers to Parliament in scenes where there is no question as to who is king (in *1H6, 2H6,* and *H5*). The deposition scene in *Richard II,* on the other hand, contains no mention of Parliament except in a stage direction added by later editors, "Enter as to the Parliament." The two labels thus signify that English tradition provided for the people's assuming independent constitutional authority, a fact that Shakespeare recognized in preserving the distinction. Shakespeare, in fact, has Henry V mention both "Parliament" and "all his state" in his first appearance as king at the end of *2 Henry IV.*

During the sixteenth century Parliament matured as a

legislative body, achieving many small gains that can be seen as signposts toward the development of a sovereign Parliament able to make law independent of the Crown. Constitutional history is not lineal, however, so that each step toward parliamentary independence was sometimes accompanied by a step in the other direction. Nonetheless, the century as a whole does record significant progress toward Parliament's achieving independence from the Crown.[20] That ultimate goal was not reached, but on many occasions in the plays the "commons" have power far beyond that actually enjoyed by the lower house in either the fourteenth or fifteenth centuries (see particularly the discussion of "commons" in chapter 2, below). Elizabethan playwrights may have seen foreshadowing in the many symbolic steps that were taken toward independence, such as the one evidenced in Ferrers' Case in 1543. The House of Commons refused an offer of support from the Lord Chancellor and ordered on its own authority that the sheriff of London release a member of Parliament who had been arrested for debt. Members of Parliament decided that "all commandments and other acts of proceeding from the nether house, were to be done and executed by their sergeant without writ [i.e. Crown authority], only by show of his mace, which was his warrant [i.e. Parliamentary authority]."[21]

Though it is somewhat artificial to designate the Reformation Parliament as a point of division, and there is some disagreement as to whether the legislation passed by that Parliament marked a revolution or an evolution in legislative powers of the king-in-parliament, there is agreement as to the importance of legislation in the years following the Reformation Parliament. G. R. Elton, who is the main spokesman for the revolutionary theory, writes that

> the sixteenth century witnessed the extension of parliamentary control to every aspect of life in the realm, so that for the first time, a truly omnicompetent legislative organ emerged.

And Penry Williams, who takes issue with the usefulness of

the concept of sovereignty in describing the power of king-in-parliament, nonetheless recognizes that statutes are different in the post-Reformation years.

[It might be better to say] that the state, in its legislation, came to have a far greater dynamic than before: statutes were more precise and came to be more respectfully regarded by the judges; they were in more constant occupation of fields that had only occasionally been entered before; and the notion of changing, or at least of saving, society by statutory action came to be widely held.[22]

Within Parliament, the Reformation contributed to the developing importance of the lower house. Since bishops and abbots were powerful members of the House of Lords, in attacking the Church, Henry VIII worked through the Commons. In so doing Henry could give the impression that he was responding to the "popular will" as expressed in the representative assembly.[23] Elton suggests that, in fact, Parliament reflected widespread anticlericalism and was encouraged to take action more by the withdrawal of royal restraint than by positive prodding.[24] The new status of the Commons after the Reformation is symbolized by their acquisition of St. Stephen's Chapel as a meeting place within the Palace of Westminster. Thenceforth they were the equals of the House of Lords as an accepted part of Parliament (Elton, ed., *Tudor Constitution,* p. 242). In fact, the lower house became the more important of the two as the place where most bills were introduced and political issues were debated.[25]

It is striking that the gentry, which expanded its ranks after the Reformation thanks to the secularization of Church lands, in the following decades became enormously interested in Parliament. Many new parliamentary seats were created to be occupied by the country gentry in what has been called an "invasion of Parliament."

Instead of one gentleman to four townsmen, Elizabeth's later parliaments contained four gentlemen to every townsman. The country gentleman and his cousin, the lawyer, had captured the House of Commons. [Neale, *Elizabethan House of Commons*, p. 372]

The implications of this fact are two-fold. Knowledge of the status of Parliament was not confined to the immediate environs of Westminster. The demand for more parliamentary seats, which resulted in its almost doubling during the century, indicates that constitutional issues and crises were being reported back to more people than ever before. Even Shakespeare's Joan of Arc, in mocking Talbot after her victory at Rouen, calls out to the English officers in conference, "God speed the parliament! Who shall be the Speaker?" (*1H6*, 3.2.60).[26] The dominance by the gentry in the House of Commons, coupled with the new constitutional importance of the lower house, meant that "by the reign of Elizabeth the House of Commons . . . at long last represented the dominant section of the community . . . [and] could also fairly claim to speak for the political nation, a role which down to the Wars of Roses had been more properly filled by the Lords" (Elton, ed., *Tudor Constitution*, p. 244).

During the historical periods dramatized in all of the English history plays written in the sixteenth century, the House of Commons had little constitutional importance. Parliament as the House of Lords did, however, play a political role. Therefore, scenes such as 3.1 of *1 Henry VI* and 1.1 of *3 Henry VI*, which are both set in "London, The Parliament House," correctly dramatize an assembly of Lords meeting with the King. There are some references in the plays to the "commons," for example in *Henry V* when the Archbishop of Canterbury and the Bishop of Ely discuss the bill urged by the Commons that would deprive the Church of half its wealth. In the deposition scene of *Richard II* Northumberland twice cites the "commons" as authority for proceeding against Richard (4.1.154, 272); in *2 Henry VI* Lord Salisbury says that the "commons" demand Suffolk's banishment for Gloucester's death (3.2.

242). However, while it is probable that "commons" in *Richard II* and *2 Henry VI* means the lower house, one cannot be absolutely certain, since, according to the *OED*, "commons" could also signify those substantial citizens who formed the constituency of the House of Commons. Therefore, *Parliament* in the plays usually means the House of Lords. But as Elton has observed, a parallel can be drawn between the political power of the lords and the ascendancy of the House of Lords and the later political power of the gentry and the ascendancy of the House of Commons. The importance of relations between Parliament and Crown remains constant for medieval through Elizabethan times. Dramatizing of key meetings of the king-in-Parliament would be both topical and historically accurate. *Crown-in-Parliament* or *King-in-Parliament* was a catchphrase often used to symbolize the concept of general consent described by Smith.

It was well known to Elizabethans that Parliament had jurisdiction over life, limb, and land. Individual actions in a play against any of these three by any single character, whether king, noble, or commoner, would readily be perceived as unconstitutional. William Harrison in his *Description of England* had written that without Parliament

> no forfeiture of life, member, or lands of any Englishman, where no law is ordained for the same beforehand, is available or can take place amongst us.[27]

The positive powers of Parliament, as Thomas Smith detailed, are that it

> gives forms of succession to the crown, defines of doubtful rights, whereof is no law already made, appoints subsidies, tailes, taxes, and impositions, gives most free pardons and absolutions, restores in blood and name as the highest court, condemns or absolves them whom the Prince will put to that trial. [Smith, *De Republica Anglorum,* pp. 48-49]

Only Shakespeare, so far as I know, dramatizes meetings of

Parliament, and he accords to the decisions taken there great moral weight.

In *2 Henry VI*, for example, York's social position is restored in Parliament, which has authority to "define of doubtful rights," as Smith noted above. Thereafter no one dares mock his standing in society as Somerset had done in the rose-plucking scene before the meeting of Parliament where he said, "We grace the yeoman by conversing with him" (*1H6*, 2.4.81). Winchester's contempt for Parliament, evidenced when he tears Gloucester's bill and disclaims his reconciliation with Gloucester in an aside to the audience, marks him unquestionably as the evil councilor and isolates him more profoundly than does his personal rivalry with Gloucester. If there had been any question as to which of the two the audience was to favor, this scene in Parliament determines their moral status.

Similarly, when matters falling within areas that traditionally required general approval by king and Parliament are decided upon by individuals acting on their own, such decisions consistently have unfortunate consequences. The individuals who act on their own are shown to be acting willfully or foolishly and not in the best interest of the commonweal. From the plays there emerges an underlying theme of respect for the common wisdom as embodied in the consultative process of Parliament and a correlative reservation about the value of independent action. Henry VI, for instance, had agreed to marry the daughter of the Earl of Armagnac in a meeting with his councilors but decided, with only Suffolk's prodding, to break that treaty by marrying Lady Margaret. When Henry then authorized Suffolk to impose a tax of a tenth to pay for the voyage and wedding, he was overstepping his authority as king, an ill omen for Henry's rule. The principle that direct taxation could be levied only by assent of Parliament was established by the middle of the fourteenth century, well before Henry VI's reign (Elton, ed., *Tudor Constitution,* p. 42). The individual determinations by Warwick, Northumberland, Buckingham, and others in various plays as to whom they will accept as king contribute to their diminishing moral stature in each play. Richard II's seizing John of Gaunt's possessions even though he does so to finance the English cause in the Irish Wars contributes to his undoing as king because it represents an act of tyranny imposed without consent of his Parliament.

It would have been impractical, however, to dramatize a meeting between Parliament and king each time the principle arose that a king was accountable to his people. Parliament, therefore, is represented on very few occasions. But in addition to meetings between Parliament and king, Shakespeare's kings are shown meeting with the nobles either in council or other groups. Whether or not he heeds the advice given him on such occasions usually reflects how well a king rules and suggests how long he will continue to rule. The expediencies of the stage impose a departure from reality in that the council seems to function less as an administrative aide to the king than as a place where the peers can make their views known. The council and other groups of peers thus supplement the Parliament as vehicle for the tradition that not the Crown alone but the Crown-in-Parliament is the sovereign body in the realm.

Recognition of the importance of Parliament was not confined to members of Parliament; those associated with the Crown also recognized the status of Parliament during Elizabeth's reign. Lord Burghley in January 1585 drafted a bill suggesting that Parliament temporarily become the sovereign power in the interregnum if Elizabeth were assassinated. First, privy councilors and royal officers would search for all those involved in the assassination. Then the council was to summon the same Parliament that had last met during Elizabeth's reign. The "Three Estates" were to become the sovereign body of the country with power to continue, alter, or cease the council's authority. Each house would name ten members to a committee that would control finances. Once those involved in the Queen's murder had been dealt with, the "Three Estates" were

to hear and determine all claims to the succession to the Crown, choosing the person who appeared 'to have best right . . . in blood by the royal laws of the realm'; and its decision was to be announced by proclamation under the Great Seal, in the form of an Act of Parliament. All other claims were then to cease under pain of treason, and the interregnum was to end.[28]

Burghley decided against presenting the bill in Parliament. But the fact that he even penned it is a significant acknowledgement of the importance of Parliament as representative agent in the constitutional structure of the realm. Nobles and commoners in the plays are often shown to enjoy comparable importance as dramatic embodiments of the constitutional principle of popular voice in the government of England. For the opinion of the "commons," as will be shown in chapter 2, usually anticipates military success and defeat, and approval from the lords, whether obtained from Parliament, council, or from groups of individuals, is an essential element in stabilizing a king's reign in Shakespeare's plays.

C. The Crown

While the Crown-in-Parliament might have been the primary power in England as the main lawmaking body, the king alone was responsible for the day-to-day governance of the realm. It was in the king's name that law was enforced, peace kept, and justice administered. At this practical level, Tudor government was relatively stable and efficient. The council acting for the Crown developed into an effective administrative body able to assure that political transactions were enforced throughout the realm. Despite parliamentary developments, at no time could an Elizabethan forget that the state in which he lived was a monarchy. All the English history plays show that the primary force in maintaining or disrupting the prosperity of the realm is the king himself.

To be short the prince is the life, the head, and the authority of all things that be done in the realm of England. And to no prince is done more honor and reverence . . . , [Smith, *De Republica Anglorum*, p. 63] wrote Thomas Smith while he was ambassador to France, a position that facilitated his making a comparative assessment.

The strength of Parliament did not prevent England's developing a strong monarchy that had much in common with those in France and Spain. Smith, having first described the powers of the English Parliament, quickly countered with his tribute to the English prince, no doubt to correct any impression that Parliament's strength weakened the monarchy. That a monarchy could be strong despite a strong representative body was unthinkable in France, where kings succeeded in almost eliminating the national assembly. This contrast between the French and English monarchies enters the plays in the person of Margaret, Henry VI's French wife, who constantly chafes at the restraints imposed on Henry by council members and Parliament (see below, chap. 2D). She had grown up under the French monarchy, "which was a model to monarchists in its theory, its power, and its unconfined freedom of action; it was also a byword for tyranny."[29] Though in part disingenuous, York's sons Richard and Edward blame Margaret's French interpretation of the royal powers for the civil wars.

> For what hath broach'd this tumult but thy pride?
> Hadst thou been meek, our title still had slept;
> And we, in pity of the gentle King,
> Had slipp'd our claim until another age.
>
> (*3H6*, 2.2.159–62)

I will consider three aspects of the English Crown that were important in the sixteenth century and are important in the plays: the problem of succession, the right of rebellion, and the parameters of royal prerogative. All three issues are intertwined with both Parliament and the law, which limited the sphere of Crown activity.

1. Succession. That Elizabethans were governed by a monarch is the only certainty among the many uncertainties surrounding the sixteenth-century Crown. Who becomes king and by what procedure were two of the major problems. Since succession falls within the sphere of public law, the answers should have been determined by custom and statute. But, as Elizabethans were well aware, neither statute nor custom had yet established one set procedure. There was a strong belief in heredity as the determining factor in choosing a king.[30] A precedent favoring heredity as sole determinant was established when Edward II's reign was dated from the death of his predecessor, not from the date of his coronation as had hitherto been the custom.[31] But this precedent was greatly weakened by Edward's subsequent deposition. There was also no certain rule entailing the crown to males, for if there had been, the Mortimer family would have been excluded and Henry IV would have been the lawful successor to Richard II (*Taswell,* p. 497, and see below in chapter 4). The dynastic struggle between York and Lancaster would in that case have had to have been legitimated by appeal to other issues than heredity. The long list of possible successors to Elizabeth is ample evidence that England lacked a consensus acknowledging order of ascent.

It is probably no coincidence that each of Shakespeare's English history plays raises the issue of succession, from Richard II right through to Henry VII. While heredity is often emphasized, the plays also explore the importance of popular support, military strength, and administrative abilities. My subsequent chapters will show that the relative importance of these factors shifts from heredity to other bases for legitimacy.

Elizabeth herself was the grandchild of Henry VII, whose claim, despite all other colorations, was based on possession recognized by Parliament

> To the pleasure of Almighty God, the wealth, prosperity, and surety of this Realm of England, to the singular comfort of all the King's subjects of the same, and *in avoiding of all ambiguities and questions,* be it ordained, established, and enacted, by authority of this present Parliament, that the inheritance of the Crowns of the Realms of England and of France, with all the preeminence

and dignity Royal to the same pertaining . . . *be, rest,* remain, and abide in the most Royal person of our now sovereign Lord King Harry the VIIth, and in the heirs of his body lawfully come; perpetually with the grace of God so to endure, and in none other.[32]

Parliament notably evaded all questions of Henry's ancestry and means of achievement. The careful wording included only the then current state of affairs. This recognition was not entirely perfunctory: if Parliament had not recognized Henry as king, there could have been a complete breakdown in government with no one having authority to rule. Elizabeth's own title was a parliamentary one, as were the titles of the other Tudors as determined by the Succession Acts of 1534, 1536, and 1543.[33] Thomas Smith stated that Parliament gives the "forms of succession to the crown." Father Parsons, although representing a point of view radically different from Smith's had argued that confirmation by Parliament makes possession of the Crown lawful, citing the examples of the successive kings during the Wars of the Roses.[34] But the fact of a parliamentary title was devoid of any modern implications. Legislative determination of succession in fact ceased for a time after the Tudors. James ascended the throne not through the terms of Henry VIII's will as allowed by Parliament but by hereditary right and considerations of political expediency (Levine, "A Parliamentary Title . . . ," pp. 126-27). The 1559 edition of the *Mirror for Magistrates* contains in the concluding section called "To the Reader" a statement that summarizes several theoretically possible means of succeeding to the throne. The statement, in addition, reflects the fear of civil war that so marked the post-York-Lancaster period:

. . . whatsoever man, woman or child, is by the consent of the whole realm established in the royal seat, so it have not been injuriously procured by rigor of sword and open force, but quietly by title either of inheritance, succession, lawful bequest, common consent, or election, is undoubtedly chosen by God to be his deputy.[35]

The essential element in the *Mirror* passage is not the particular means of access to the title but the acceptance of the candidate by the realm. In the case of Henry VII the "consent of the whole realm" was won on the battlefield, then was symbolized by the enactment of Parliament that the Crown "rested" in him. Both the evidence of history and the actual situation, therefore, indicated to Elizabethans that succession was determined by politics more than law when the choice of a successor was complicated by the absence of a direct and competent heir. (Chrimes, *Lancastrians*, p. 77).

Shakespeare accurately reflects the politics involved in determining the succession. He shows Parliament as the place where questions of succession are discussed, particularly in *2 Henry VI* when Prince Edward is excluded from the succession to Henry VI in favor of York and his heirs. He also shows that Parliament, in fact, can do little more than confirm battlefield decisions; it has no power of its own to enforce a succession different from that determined by military strength. Despite the frequent appearance of foreign mercenary troops in the plays, however, military strength is closely tied to support by the general populace, so that military victory comes to have a sanction similar to that of a parliamentary meeting. While the deposition of Richard II, for example, is too complex to admit of easy generalization, the only argument that could be made for its legitimacy would have to be based on the fact that Richard's ouster reflected the wishes of a considerable portion of the population. This fact is communicated in the play by Richard's almost total lack of support from both the people and the army and by his resignation's being insisted upon in a meeting between Lords and King. The deposition is further confirmed by York's report of Londoners' welcoming Henry, while scorning Richard. Power politics complexly intertwines with the traditional sanctions of a unified commonweal. The intertwining will be discussed in detail in the chapters on Shakespeare's two tetralogies.

2. *Rebellion.* A question arises about the basis on which "the realm" would withhold or accord consent initially

and subsequently, meaning the right to rebel against and depose a king. To judge from successions and depositions, expressed in the most general terms, the determining factor was the expectation of competent governance. However, there were differences of opinion as to the meaning of "competent governance." For religious militants of all persuasions, good governance was a matter of right religion. Peter Wentworth was willing to risk imprisonment each time he sought parliamentary support in pressuring Elizabeth to establish the succession: Wentworth wanted to be certain that she would have a Protestant successor. Robert Parsons, meanwhile, in 1594 dedicated to Essex a huge volume, *A Conference About the Next Succession to the Crowne of Ingland,* in which he argued the case for a Catholic, the Infanta of Spain. But for the vast majority who had already accepted the Henrician Reformation, the Marian Restoration, and the Elizabethan Settlement, good governance evidently manifested itself on a less spiritual plane, in the administration of justice, the enforcement of law, and the maintenance of peace and prosperity.

Though official propagandists, particularly the homilists, denied subjects the right to rebel and depose a monarch, the frequency and vehemence of such denials are evidence that the idea of rebellion was in the air. Thomas Smith raised the question and warned only that "it is always a doubtful and hazardous matter to meddle with the changing of the laws and government" (Smith, *De Republica Anglorum,* p. 13). When considered as a group, the English history plays dramatize many rebellions, involving different groups of people, different circumstances, and different justifications too numerous to be more than glanced at here though they will be analyzed in subsequent chapters. Jack Cade, York, Margaret, Bolingbroke, Edward IV, the Percies, Richmond, Mortimer Junior in *Edward II,* and Salisbury and Pembroke in *King John* are some of the leaders of factions.

In general, all playwrights show that a contender for the throne will gain popular support when it appears that he can contribute to national prosperity and well-being. The reverse is also true, that a king who cannot or does not so contribute will lose support. In Marlowe's *Edward II,* for instance, the commons "murmur" against the king when his infatuation with Gaveston becomes all-consuming to the neglect of his other subjects (2.2.160).[36] The people instead support Mortimer Junior while he is identified with the common good, as shown by his sympathizing with soldiers who are underpaid while gifts are lavished upon Gaveston. Support soon shifts from Mortimer, though, when his seeking Edward II's death and his own establishment as protector make it clear that he will be a tyrant. In Shakespeare's *3 Henry VI* support shifts from the Lancastrians, who have lost many possessions in France, to the Yorkists, who seem better able to secure military victory and repossess lost territories. When Edward IV, however, marries Lady Gray for his own pleasure rather than make a French alliance that would benefit the realm, the "common people by numbers swarm" to support the Lancastrians (4.2.2) for lack of any better alternative. "The commons rebel" (1.2.249) against Richard II in *Woodstock* as long as he allows his flatterers to tax his countrymen unjustly. Though the ending of the play is missing, Richard's repentance seems to be leading to a reconciliation between a king newly dedicated to the well-being of his realm and the general populace.

Shakespeare was the only playwright who dramatized a sufficient number of rebellions to provide basis enough for comparison between successful and abortive revolts. He shows a fairly consistent pattern for success. For example, both temporary and more permanent possession of the Crown is achieved by those kings who are publicly committed to specific constitutional principles such as the obligation to consult with representatives of the estates and to see that the laws are impartially enforced. As king, Henry IV is most often shown to be meeting with his peers and listening to their reports and advice on governing the realm. Henry V pledges in his first public appearance after the coronation to meet with his Parliament and all the estates of his realm. A king's disregarding such principles or his inability to observe such principles consistently results in his losing public support, which is reflected in military defeat leading to deposition. Once crowned, Henry VI, for instance, usually leaves his council to its own devices, barely interceding when quarrels among the council members disrupt the effective governance of the realm. When Edward IV chooses a wife without consulting Warwick as he had pledged to do (*3H6*. 2.6.99-102), he is temporarily ousted from the throne. When Richard II, in seizing Gaunt's estate, ignores the best advice of the highest-ranking nobility (York and Gaunt), he is permanently deprived of his throne. A king's most potent weapon against rebellion, therefore, would seem to be fulfilling the definitions of the English Crown provided by English traditions, that is, by ruling in accord with constitutionally established obligations. What made this difficult, however, was the unwritten nature of the English constitution.

3. Prerogative. The Crown was simultaneously a repository of power and an agent to assure the well-being of the realm. Prerogative was the means to effect the king's duty sworn at the coronation—"to do justice in mercy and in truth, and to maintain the laws" (Chrimes, *Constitutional Ideas*, p. 19). In the plays, as in the sixteenth century, the monarch needed to tread a careful line between maintaining his rights and fulfilling his obligations. Both the historical record and the plays show that when a ruler cannot assure the prosperity of the realm, no assertion of royal prerogative will secure the Crown its rights.

Common law delineated the areas of royal prerogative. According to Smith these included power of war and peace, power to choose the privy council, power of martial law in wartime and insurrection, power in coining money, power of pardon if no one objected against the offender, giving of offices, and receipt of the tenths of all ecclesiastical promotions. Writs are done in the king's name, justice is done in his name; he has "wardships and first marriage of all who hold lands of him in chief," plus divers other rights called prerogatives royal, or the prerogative of the king, which be declared particularly in the books of the common laws of England. [Smith, *De Republica Anglorum,* pp. 58–63]

The history of relations between Elizabeth and her Parliaments shows a continuing struggle over the prerogative. The Commons desired that their opinions on matters falling within Crown prerogative be considered, and Elizabeth desired to preserve her royal prerogatives intact. The record shows that when pressure on her was strong enough and when she was convinced that the Commons were right, Elizabeth would yield. Two notable examples resulted from the Commons' anger at abuses by royal purveyors and by holders of royal patents or monopolies. In the first instance she allowed members of the Commons to join councilors in a committee to devise regulations for purveyors, and in the second she agreed to let patent holders be judged in the common-law courts. Similarly, Shakespeare shows that when "the commons" are reported to be outraged at the murder of Humphrey, Duke of Gloucester, and are reported to insist that Suffolk be executed or banished, Henry VI replies in language not unlike Elizabeth's when pressured,

> I thank them for their tender loving care:
> And had I not been cited so by them,
> Yet did I purpose as they do entreat.
>
> (2H6, 3.2.279–81)

Both the Elizabethan and the Lancastrian concessions to popular pressure reflect the necessity that the monarch be sensitive to public opinion when it questions the monarch's fulfilling his constitutional obligation to assure that justice in the form of equity be carried out in the land.

When, on the other hand, Elizabeth was convinced that an officially designated successor would cause unnecessary danger to herself and the realm, she remained adamant—this was not a matter for the Commons to act upon. Constitutional history of the previous hundred or so years shows however that the succession was an area in which Parliament had played a role. The more important occasions, all dramatized in Shakespeare's plays, in which Parliament or the "Estates" had intervened were in accepting Richard II's resignation and Henry IV as successor, in designating York and then Edward IV as successors to Henry VI, in accepting Richard III as successor to Edward IV, and in recognizing Henry VII and his descendants. Elizabethans, with many protests, among which Shakespeare's plays might possibly be included, allowed their queen to have her way on the succession because in most other respects she was a responsible and effective ruler.

Elizabeth took care that her responses to parliamentary pressure, at least in form, did not weaken royal prerogative. She acted as the Commons wished but not by joining with them in passing a statute. Avoiding statutory restraint nonetheless meant that she had to allow equally effective restraint from other sources. It will be seen in the plays, too, that to reign well kings must take into account the unique constitutionally limited nature of the English Crown. Not to do so is consistently hazardous, as, for instance, Richard II discovers when he disregards the advice of his lords in seizing John of Gaunt's property, or, as King John discovers when Prince Arthur is found dead despite pleas by his lords for Arthur's safety.

In sum, the sixteenth-century English monarchy was complex. The many dynastic changes of the previous century had made apparent that in England a distinction could be drawn between an individual monarch and the institution of the monarchy. The prince was indeed the "life" of all things done in the realm, as Thomas Smith had said. But a particular prince who consistently disregarded the constitutional limitations on his power or did not effectively carry out his duty to maintain peace and enforce the law would before long find himself in difficulty, as did the Stuarts. It is a tribute to the strong respect for the institution of the monarchy and the desire to avoid "hazardous matters" that the Stuarts endured as long as they did. The precarious union of the Crown-in-Parliament ceased at Elizabeth's death, leaving it to the subsequent generations to resolve the question of which was sovereign when they did not agree.

> It was only gradually, during the Tudor period, that the idea of sovereignty rose to prominence. Even then, it was not yet the concept of a single agent, such as the monarch, endowed with absolute authority, but rather the sovereignty of the "King in Parliament." The actions of the king and the representatives of the people, jointly, were allowed to be sovereign in the name of the law of reason. . . . Once the idea of a sovereignty had supplanted medieval concept of a commonwealth, a struggle for power was almost inevitable.[37]

From the perspective of the twentieth century, one might see in the Commons' suit against Richard II and Henry V's reconciliation with the Lord Chief Justice suggestions that Shakespeare was directly responding to the struggle for power among the branches of government, but there is not enough internal evidence in the plays. There is a great deal of evidence, however, to indicate that king and people "jointly," in Mosse's words, "were allowed to be sovereign in the name of the law of reason," as I shall show in the remaining chapters.

D. The Law

Particular developments in sixteenth-century law are not treated extensively in the English history plays. However, a great deal of attention *is* given to the enforcement of law and the administration of justice, no doubt reflecting the importance of law and justice in Elizabethan, as in any, society. Unlike Spain and France, England was able to forge an independent state under the strong monarchy without significant damage done to the legal rights of her citizens. It has often been theorized that the secret of England's distinction was the continuity in and nature of her law.

Medieval England had enjoyed the unusual benefits of a compact territory and, by medieval standards, an exceptionally powerful and effective monarchy. . . . Above all, it obeyed one law—the common law of England, developed since the twelfth century. . . . It provided unity in the realm on a foundation of sectional and personal rights, while elsewhere unification with the help of the monarchical Roman law led to absolutism.[38]

The significance of the distinction between legal systems was not lost to sixteenth-century observers. Thomas Smith concluded his description of the English government with the following personal statement:

I have declared summarily as it were in a chart or map, . . . the form and manner of the government of England, and the policy thereof, and set before your eyes the principal points wherein it does differ from the policy or government at this time used in France, Italy, Spain, Germany and all other countries, which do follow the civil law of the Romans compiled by *Justinian* into his pandects and code. . . . [Smith, *De Republica Anglorum*, pp. 142–43]

In all countries that adopted civil or Roman law, the legal system was based on an authoritative text, Justinian's code, and the commentaries of the legal profession.[39] England had no such text but rather, a system of case law and a procedure for changing law that required participation by both Crown and Parliament.

The difference was remarkable. Both in the making and enforcing of law, continental monarchies became all-powerful—proclaiming and administering law with no restraint. In France in the sixteenth century, for example, while regional assemblies retained some strength, the national Etats Generaux declined in importance; in Spain no national Cortès was called until 1709, and even then not all regions participated.[40] In England, Parliament not only persisted from the Middle Ages but greatly increased in strength through an inextricable relationship with the continuity and

strength of the law. The common law grew in importance
with the expansion of the legal profession, the increased
size of Parliament, and the importance of Parliament in
the constitutional structure.[41] It had become fashionable, for
instance, to finish one's education with study of the law. By
1593, according to Neale, forty-three percent of the House
of Commons possessed a legal education (*Elizabethan
House of Commons,* pp. 307-8).

Law resembling civil law did exist in England. It had the
status of extraordinary law administered in prerogative
courts, such as the court of Chancery, but not in the common
law courts. Chancery in the sixteenth century was "essentially an administrative tribunal seeing that justice was done
where there was no law."[42] In the Middle Ages, Chancery
had often been the place of recourse for common citizens
with complaints against the nobility. But by the time of
Elizabeth, Chancery's jurisdiction extended to a wide range
of situations that arose in a nascent international capitalist
economy, particularly cases involving merchants, problems
of fraud, and duress.

There were conflicts between prerogative and Common
Law courts.

> The issue was the rule of law versus rule by administrative fiat.
> As such it was to be a political dispute between the men who
> staffed the common law benches and their brethren in the House
> of Commons versus the crown and its agents in the prerogative
> courts. [Prall, "Development of Equity," p. 19]

The monopoly issue, for instance, resulted in the victory for
common law courts when the queen, in responding to pressure from the House of Commons, agreed to allow test
cases to go to trial there rather than in prerogative courts.
Victory for the common law courts, of course, was not
always the case. Cawdrey in 1591 sought to have common
law judges override a decision by the High Commission, a
"prerogative" court. He lost his case, and the decision confirmed the authority of the ecclesiastical judges of the Court

of High Commission (Elton, ed., *Tudor Constitution*, pp. 220-21, 226-27). There is a parallel distinction between common and administrative law in Shakespeare's plays that appears in judicial decisions reached by reference to tradition and decisions determined solely by a king's response to the pressures of a particular situation. King John's opinion on Faulconbridge's bastardy would be an example of the first possibility, and Richard II's halting the Mowbray-Bolingbroke combat would illustrate the second.

The law administered in Chancery always remained separate from the common law, yet, nonetheless, "the law administered in the court was more like that of England than that of Rome," no doubt because from 1529 on, beginning with Sir Thomas More, common lawyers held the office (Elton, ed., *Tudor Constitution*, p. 152). Thus, even in the development of a system of administrative law and justice under the Tudors resembling that on the continent, the persistence of a parallel common law facilitated the growth of an administrative law that was closely tied to medieval notions of justice and the king's obligation to protect his subjects' rights.

Within the law itself, as in the relationship between the Crown and Parliament, the precise constitutional balance was not established with certainty. So long as the Tudors remained in power, however, greater weight rested on the side of English tradition and the common law than on the side of administrative law. But there were some tense moments. One particularly difficult situation occurred because of Elizabeth's reaction to Mary's execution. She alleged that Secretary Davidson had forwarded the order to execute without authorization. Elizabeth wanted to have him beheaded and sought opinions on her right to order this on her own authority. When he heard that Mr. Justice Anderson had agreed with her,

Burleigh was almost aghast. He wrote in cipher to an unnamed correspondent, urging him to warn the judges secretly to be very careful how they replied. He said: "I would be loath to live, to see a woman of such wisdom as she is, to be wrongly advised, for fear or other infirmity . . . with an opinion gotten from the judges that her prerogative is above her law.[43]

Davidson was not beheaded, and the longstanding tradition remained intact, which gave jurisdiction over life to Crown-in-Parliament, meaning in this instance common law courts as an extension of that principle, and not to the queen alone.

From Bracton to Hooker the belief persisted that the king is under the law, meaning that all the king's proceedings must be limited by the law.[44]

I cannot choose but commend highly their wisdom, by whom the foundations of this commonwealth have been laid; wherein though no manner person or cause be unsubject to the king's power, yet so is the power of the king over all and in all limited, that unto all his proceedings the law itself is a rule.[45]

Respect for the law is a constant theme emphasized strongly through all the English history plays of this period. Dramatists may have anticipated the efforts by some seventeenth-century common lawyers, particularly Edward Coke, to use the common law as codification of the common wisdom and heritage to mediate between royal and parliamentary extremists in the struggle for sovereignty.

Both in Shakespeare's plays and plays by other playwrights a character's attitude toward the law is a touchstone against which to measure his moral stature. And the effectiveness with which he maintains law and order is an indication of the quality of the reign and a basis to predict the longevity of a king on the throne. Suffolk, for instance, declares in the rose-plucking scene of *1 Henry VI* that he "frames the law unto his will" (2.4.9). The threat that such an attitude poses to the commonwealth may not be readily apparent, but subsequent actions reveal how much damage someone with Suffolk's notion of law can do. He persuades Henry to break a negotiated treaty by marrying Margaret of Anjou, not because this will benefit the realm but because it will give Suffolk greater power as *eminence grise.* Later Suffolk helps arrange the assassination of Gloucester, uncle to the king. For his actions he is roundly condemned by the "commons" who demand his banishment and death (*2H6*, 3.2.242-52) and by pirates who order his execution after citing his crimes against the nation (4.1.100-102).

Gloucester, on the contrary, is a mainstay of the law. He prepares a bill to submit to Parliament following proper legal procedure to resolve the dispute between Winchester and himself, while Winchester's contempt for legal order is readily apparent when he rips Gloucester's bill. Gloucester accepts the banishment of his wife because of his respect for the law and agrees to let the law take its course when he is accused of treason. So long, in fact, as Gloucester is protector, the law in Henry VI's government functions with some effectiveness, such as in exposing the Simpcox miracle as fraudulent and in appointing trial by combat to decide whether Peter or Horner is lying. This identification between Gloucester and the law is partly what marks him as the good councilor. When he is no longer protector, however, justice is no longer properly administered, as evidenced by his own death and Suffolk's at the hands of pirates. Henry VI's inability to assure that justice is done constitutes one of his greatest failings as king. Abandoning Gloucester to his accusers marks a moral low point in Henry's reign, and his subsequent inaction after Gloucester's death provokes the "commons" to remind Henry of his responsibilities to rule. In the portraits of other kings, too, their ability to administer justice is given particular attention. John's knowledge of the law regarding bastardy is one of the few positive aspects of his reign, and that early scene with Faulconbridge shows him at his best in the play, while his worse moments involve his disregard of Arthur's essential rights to life and limb. Richard II seizes Gaunt's wealth in what Shakespeare shows to be blatant disregard of legal procedure; that act is dramatized as the key to Richard's subsequent downfall. Once they are kings, both of his successors, in contrast, are extremely careful about the functioning of the law as evidenced by their official agents from the local sheriff, who immediately pursues Falstaff to Eastcheap after the double robbery, to the Lord Chief Justice who is accorded a prominent position.

In plays by other playwrights law and justice are consistent clues to a king's stature. Peele's encomium to the monarchy in the person of Edward I contains a scene in which Edward instructs his Spanish wife that in England the law includes the king. She wants Englishmen's beards cut and one breast removed from English women. Longshanks begins with his own hair to her horror. He explains,

> Madam, pardon me and pardon all,
> No justice but the great runs with the small.
> .   .   .   .
> Here must the law begin. . . .
> Else Princes ought no other do,
> Fair lady, then they would be done unto.
>
> (scene 10, lines 1668–77)[46]

The anonymous *Woodstock* portrays a king who allows his ministers to use legal tricks to deprive Englishmen of their liberty and wealth, while the moral hero of the play consistently supports "justice" and "ancient liberties." The abusive Chief Justice is finally betrayed by his own servant who becomes nervous about his own actions after "plodding in *Plowden*" where he could not find any law to justify his past actions (5.6.32-5). Marlowe's *Edward II* ends on a positive note when the young king warns his mother,

> . . . you are suspected for his death,
> And therefore we commit you to the Tower,
> Till further trial may be made thereof;
> If you be guilty, though I be your son,
> Think not to find me slack or pitiful.
>
> (5.6.78–82)

Unlike both Edward II and Mortimer, Jr., the new king intends to enforce the law impartially.

While the Tudors reigned, English institutions prospered to reach maturity—the Crown in its administrative capacity, the Parliament in its representative character, and the lawyers and judges of the common law in their function as preservers of ancient rights. But signs of disagreement between the Crown and the Parliament were apparent. With continental examples readily available of governments less respectful of peoples' rights than Tudor government, Elizabethans could not help but be uneasy at the prospect of the end of Elizabeth's reign. So very much depended upon the quality of the ruler. England's main safeguard, as John Aylmer, Bishop of London, had written in 1559 when he defended Elizabeth's right to rule, is that it is not the king alone who rules:

> If . . . the regiment were such, as all hanged upon the King's or Queen's will, and not upon the laws written: if she might decree and make laws alone, without her senate. If she judged offenses according to her wisdom, and not by limitation of statutes and laws: . . . if to be short she were a mere monarch, and not a mixed ruler, you might peradventure make me to fear the matter the more.[47]

And Elizabeth did, regardless of any personal royalist sentiments she may have felt to the contrary, give every appearance of standing by the constitution. But if her successors were to proceed differently, what then? This constitutional dilemma is one of the many aspects of men of society explored in Shakespeare's plays about English history.

The next chapter follows the same tripartite division into the people, the Crown, and the law in discussing the first tetralogy. The role of the commons, of the nobles, of hereditary class standing, of hereditary legitimacy, of *Realpolitik* in determining legitimacy are some of the aspects of the plays that will be discussed. While these early English history plays are less well focused than the later ones, it will be seen that they contain suggestions for the basic ideas further developed in the later plays.

NOTES TO CHAPTER 1

1. J. A. R. Marriott, *English History in Shakespeare* (London: Chapman and Hall, 1918), p. 28.
2. Arthur Sewell, *Character and Society in Shakespeare* (Oxford: Clarendon Press, 1951), p. 74.
3. M. M. Reese, *The Cease of Majesty, A Study of Shakespeare's History Plays* (New York: St. Martin's Press, 1961), pp. 102-3.
4. Andrew Cairncross, ed., *The Third Part of King Henry VI* (Cambridge, Mass.: Harvard University Press, 1964), p. lxvi.
5. Ronald Berman, "Anarchy and Order in *Richard III* and *King John*," *Shakespeare Survey* 20 (1967):59.
6. E. M. W. Tillyard, *Shakespeare's History Plays* (London: Chatto and Windus, 1956).
7. Alfred Hart, *Shakespeare and the Homilies* (Melbourne, Australia: Melbourne University Press, 1934).
8. See, for example, Lily Bess Campbell, *Shakespeare's "Histories"—Mirrors of Elizabethan Policy* (San Marino, Calif.: Huntington Library, 1947), p. 216; and Irving Ribner, *The English History Play in the Age of Shakespeare* (Princeton, N.J.: Princeton University Press, 1957), p. 255.
9. L. C. Knights, "Shakespeare's Politics with some Reflections on the Nature of Tradition," *Proceedings of the British Academy* 43 (1957): 119.
10. W. Gordon Zeeveld, *Foundations of Tudor Policy* (Cambridge, Mass.: Harvard University Press, 1948), p. 190; Arthur Colby Sprague, *Shakespeare's Histories, Plays for the Stage* (London: Society for Theatre Research, 1964), p. 9.
11. George W. Keeton, *Shakespeare's Legal and Political Background* (New York: Barnes and Noble, 1968), pp. 242, 249.
12. H. S. Richmond, *Shakespeare's Political Plays* (New York: Random House, 1967), p. 63.
13. Henry Ansgar Kelly, *Divine Providence in the England of Shakespeare's Histories* (Cambridge, Mass.: Harvard University Press, 1970), pp. 299-300.
14. Robert Ornstein, *A Kingdom for a Stage, The Achievement of Shakespeare's History Plays* (Cambridge, Mass.: Harvard University Press, 1972), p. 4; Moody Prior, *The Drama of Power* (Evanston, Ill.: Northwestern University Press, 1973), p. 100.
15. John Dover Wilson, "The Political Background of Shakespeare's *Richard II* and *Henry IV*," *Shakespeare Jahrbuch* 75 (1939):40.
16. John Fortescue, *The Governance of England: Otherwise Called the Difference Between an Absolute and a Limited Monarchy,* ed. Charles Plummer (Oxford: Clarendon Press, 1885), pp. 113, 114, 115, 112-13.
   Spelling and punctuation have been silently normalized in all quotations cited. Obsolete words have, however, been left as is.

17. Thomas Smith, *De Republica Anglorum,* ed. L. Alston (Cambridge: At the University Press, 1906), p. 106.
18. R. W. K. Hinton, "English Constitutional Theories from Sir John Fortescue to Sir John Eliot," *English Historical Review* 75 (1960) :425.
19. S. B. Chrimes, *English Constitutional Ideas in the Fifteenth Century* (Cambridge: At the University Press, 1936), p. 131.
20. Kenneth Pickthorn, *Early Tudor Government—Henry VII* (Cambridge: At the University Press, 1934), discusses the evolution of the "commons" from petitioners—see pp. 119-25; see also Chrimes, *Constitutional Ideas,* pp. 141, 164.
21. Raphael Holinshed, *Chronicles of England, Scotland, and Ireland,* vol. 3 [ed. Henry Ellis] (London: J. Johnson et al, 1808) :825.
22. G. R. Elton, "The Tudor Revolution: A Reply," *Past and Present* 29 (December 1964) :42; Penry Williams, "The Tudor State," *Past and Present* 25 (July 1963) :44.
23. J. E. Neale, *Elizabeth I and Her Parliaments 1559–1581* (London: Jonathan Cape, 1953), pp. 20-21.
24. G. R. Elton, ed., *The Tudor Constitution, Documents and Commentary* (Cambridge: At the University Press, 1960), pp. 320-21; and see also, on anticlericalism, J. P. Cooper, "The Supplication Against the Ordinaries Reconsidered," *English Historical Review* 72 (1957) :641.
25. J. E. Neale, *The Elizabethan House of Commons* (New Haven, Conn.: Yale University Press, 1950), pp. 372-73.
26. References to Shakespeare are based on the New Arden editions of the plays with the exception of *Richard III,* for which references are based on the edition by John Dover Wilson for the University Press (Cambridge, 1968).
27. William Harrison, *Description of England,* ed. Georges Edelen (Ithaca, N.Y.: Cornell University Press, 1968), p. 154.
28. J. E. Neale, *Elizabeth I and Her Parliaments 1584–1601* (London: Jonathan Cape, 1957), pp. 45-46. The Draft Bill is in *State Papers, Dom. Eliz. 176/22. Calendar of State Papers, Domestic Series, of the Reign of Elizabeth 1581–1590* lists a provision to be added to the Bill for the Queen's safety, corrected by Burghley. Ed. Robert Lemon, reprint (Nendeln, Liechtenstein: Kraus Reprint, 1967), 2:224.
29. Paraphrased. G. R. Elton, "Constitutional Development and Political Thought in Western Europe," in *The Reformation 1520–1559,* vol. 2 of *The New Cambridge Modern History,* ed. G. R. Elton (Cambridge: At the University Press, 1958), p. 439.
30. S. B. Chrimes, *Lancastrians, Yorkists, and Henry VII,* 2d ed. (London: Macmillan, 1966), p. 77.
31. *Taswell-Langmead's English Constitutional History,* 11th ed., ed. Theodore F. T. Plucknett (London: Sweet and Maxwell, 1960), p. 478.
32. *Rotuli Parliamentorum ut et Petitiones, et Placita in Parliamento Tempore 1278–1532,* [ed. John Strachey; London: n.p., 1777?], 6:270. My italics.

33. Mortimer Levine, "A Parliamentary Title to the Crown in Tudor England," *Huntington Library Quarterly* 25 (1961-62):121.
34. Robert Parsons, *A Conference About the Next Succession to the Crowne of Ingland* [1594], in *English Books Before 1640*, University Microfilms, Reel 387, S.T.C. no. 19398, Huntington Library, San Marino, Calif., pt. 1, pp. 58-59.
35. *Mirror for Magistrates* [1559-87], ed. Lily B. Campbell, reprint (New York: Barnes and Noble, 1970), pp. 420-21.
36. References to *Edward II* are based on W. Moelwyn Merchant's edition in the New Mermaids series (London: Ernest Benn, 1967); references to *Woodstock* are to the edition by A. P. Rossiter (London: Chatto and Windus, 1946).
37. George L. Mosse, *The Struggle for Sovereignty in England, From the Reign of Queen Elizabeth to the Petition of Right* (East Lansing, Mich.: Michigan State College Press, 1950), p. 6.
38. Elton, "Constitutional Development," pp. 441-42. Brian Manning argues in "The Nobles, the People, and the Constitution," in *Crisis in Europe 1560-1660,* ed. Trevor Aston (New York: Basic Books, 1965), p. 247 that Henry VII inaugurated absolute monarchy in England. I find this doubtful.
39. W. S. Holdsworth, *A History of English Law* (Boston: Little, Brown, 1924), 4:220, 225.
40. Russell Major, *Representative Institutions in Renaissance France, 1421-1559* (Madison, Wis.: University of Wisconsin Press, 1960), pp. 126-47; Manuel De Bofarull Y Romañá, *Las Antiguas Cortès El Moderno Parlamento El Regimen Representativo Organico* (Alcala De Henares, 1945), pp. 87-97.
41. F. W. Maitland's theory that English law was threatened by a reception of Roman law in the second quarter of the sixteenth century has been successfully countered by E. S. Thorne's argument that a reception was never urged. F. W. Maitland, *English Law and the Rennaissance* (Cambridge: At the University Press, 1901); E. S. Thorne, *English Law and the Renaissance* (Florence, Italy: Leo S. Olschki, 1966).
42. Stuart E. Prall, "The Development of Equity in Tudor England," *American Journal of Legal History* 8 (1964):18. Actually, Mr. Prall may be making more positive a description than current knowledge will allow. According to Charles Gray, "we remain ignorant of a lot of Chancery's really practical activity, and on the other hand it was a pretty well established part of the judicial system with a recognized sphere and jurisprudence, which rather tends to pull it away from 'prerogative courts'—whatever a 'prerogative court' is—an over-used and ill-understood category, because each body so classified has its own history and function, indeed its unique relation to the 'prerogative.'" Quoted from a letter to me. As W. J. Jones wrote, "England was a network, a jigsaw puzzle of courts constructed on different levels. At every stage there was a struggle to assert authority." "The Crown and the Courts

in England 1603–1625," in *The Reign of James VI and I*, ed. Alan G. R. Smith (London: Macmillan, 1973), p. 181. This was also true under the Tudors.

43. Elizabeth Jenkins, *Elizabeth the Great* (New York: Coward-McCann, 1959), p. 280.

44. Charles Howard McIlwain, *Constitutionalism Ancient and Modern* (Ithaca, N.Y.: Cornell University Press, 1940), pp. 113–14.

45. Richard Hooker, *Of the Laws of Ecclesiastical Polity*, VIII, ii, 13, in *The Works*, 7th ed., ed. J. Keble, rev. R. W. Church and F. Paget (Oxford: Clarendon Press, 1888), 3:353.

46. References to *King Edward the First* are based on the edition by Frank S. Hook in *The Dramatic Works of George Peele* (New Haven, Conn.: Yale University Press, 1961).

47. John Aylmer, *An Harborowe for Faithfull and Trewe Subjectes* [1559], facsimile reprint (Amsterdam, the Netherlands: Theatrum Orbis Terrarum, 1972), sig. H4^r.

2

The First Tetralogy

The first tetralogy comprehends many more characters and incidents than the second, diffusing conflicts that are better defined in the second group of plays. There are many more lords, many more commoners, and even many more kings portrayed, which makes economical discussion difficult, particularly for the first group to be examined, the people. Following a division already present in the plays, I shall discuss the commons and lords separately beginning with the lower classes.

A. The Commons

With the possible exception of Cade, who is closely associated with York and is in fact claimed by York to be his instrument, the lower classes are consistently shown to be well aware of the condition of the realm, to be independent minded and critical of those in decision-making positions, to be loyal to the commonwealth, to be preoccupied with traditional rights and roles, and to be supportive of those who respect them. Thus by the end of the first tetralogy the opinion of the commoners has considerable moral value and their support of a leader justifies his achieving power, that is, contributes a legitimating sanction analogous to the support of the "estates." All four of the plays give some consideration to the lower classes, but the one that gives them greatest attention is *2 Henry VI*, which emphasizes relationships between upper and lower classes. I shall, however, discuss the plays in the order of their historical chronology and start with *1 Henry VI*.

In the very first scene a messenger indicates that even soldiers in the French fields are aware of difficulties at home and accurately place the blame on the nobles.

> Amongst the soldiers this is muttered—
> That . . .
> You are disputing of your generals;
>
> .   .   .   .
> Awake, awake, English nobility!
>
> > (*1H6*, 1.1.70–78)

The soldiers are, in fact, near mutiny (1.1.170) at being asked to defend Orleans without resupply because of a breakdown in command at home after Henry V's death. They do not mutiny, however, thus implying that they are more willing than the nobles to subordinate their particular needs to the general requirements of the commonweal. A similar contrast between the virtues of commoners and abuses by the nobles emerges when the Mayor of London has great difficulty in getting Gloucester and Winchester to stop fighting at the Tower Gate. Once the two lords and their followers have left, he points up the contrast between those lords and himself as a common citizen.

> Good God, these nobles should such stomachs bear!
> I myself fight not once in forty year.
>
> > (*1H6*, 1.3.89–90)

The servants of Winchester and Gloucester continue the strife, even going so far as to skirmish before the king in the Parliament House. Though their weapons were only stones, according to tradition dating back at least as far as King Alfred's time, it was illegal to use weapons or even to have weapons at-the-ready in the king's presence. Henry's response is to charge them to keep the peace by reminding them of their fundamental feudal obligation, which was to the king. A typical feudal oath, according to Bracton, indicated that primary allegiance was to the king: "in body and goods and earthly honor I will bear you fealty against all men . . . saving the fealty owed the lord king and his heirs."[1] Theoretically there would be no conflict for a subordinate between following commands of his lord or commands of his king.

> We charge you, on allegiance to ourself,
> To hold your slaughtering hands and keep the peace.
>
> (*1H6*, 3.1.86–87)

The next line is also Henry's, and it is an appeal to the protector. "Pray, Uncle Gloucester, mitigate this strife" (3.1.88). Evidently the servants of Winchester and Gloucester do not recognize either their feudal obligation to the king or the traditional respect for the royal presence, for they continue to fight. "Nay, if we be forbidden stones, we'll fall to it with our teeth" (3.1.90). This incident is unique, so far as I know, in all the history plays. A direct order from a king to a servant is directly refused obedience.

Gloucester's servants' justification for insubordination is to cite the commonweal in the first of many such citations by members of the lower classes.

> My lord, we know your Grace to be a man
> Just and upright, and, for your royal birth,
> Inferior to none but to his Majesty;
> And ere that we will suffer such a prince,
> So kind a father to the commonweal,
> To be disgraced by an inkhorn mate,
> We and our wives and children all will fight
> And have our bodies slaughter'd by thy foes.
>
> (*1H6*, 3.1.94–101)

The servants are relying on the most basic analysis of feudal structure as a series of obligations to those who are in higher social positions in exchange for protection by those social superiors. As the servant points out, the only one above Gloucester is the king himself, who is evidently not preventing Winchester from "disgracing" him. Therefore Gloucester's servants are disregarding strict feudal lines to see to it that the fundamental obligation of protection is carried out. In *Richard III* Edward IV will have cause to lament the lack of such action when no one steps in to protect his brother Clarence as a lord protects his servant by pleading for his life after he had killed a gentleman. No one except the king could have protected Clarence, and so he died (see *R3*, 2.1.100-102, 119-31). The reference to feudal obligations by both Henry and the servants is one example of a recurring preoccupation with a system of automatic fealty and protection that distinguishes the first tetralogy from the second.

Henry's first appearance on stage betrays his lack of authority over servants or lords. His sole leverage over Winchester is based on public shame by which he can effect only a hypocritical reconciliation that is immediately renounced in an aside by Winchester: "So help me God, as I intend it not!" Henry accepts the reconciliation, as do the servants, thereby restoring a semblance of order.

> KING.   Away, my masters! trouble us no more,
>   But join in friendship, as your lords have done.
> 1 SERV. Content; I'll to the surgeon's.
> 2 SERV. And so will I.
>
> (*1H6*, 3.1.144-47)

The servants' taking matters into their own hands thus seems to have gained the result they had wished. The young king and the quarreling lords were horrified enough at the specter of civil broils to pay lip service to the requirements of civil order; the king intervened, then the lords and servants obeyed. The scene does not tend to the glory of the servants, however. That first "Nay" to the king's charge that they keep the peace, and their exiting line, "I will see what physic the tavern affords" (3.1.148) make them seem to be little better than rabble who use lords' quarrels to excuse their own tumults. Though their spoken intentions are for the best, the tenor of the scene is that it is unfortunate that the servants should have to intervene. The emphasis is on the problem in the highest level of government: weakness in the king and quarrelsomeness among the peers. Shakespeare does not glorify the lower classes and disparage the upper but presents a critical portrait of both.

One curious aspect of Shakespeare's English history plays is his almost total neglect of those substantial citizens who formed the constituency of the House of Commons. There are no characters developed with very much attention who would constitute those middle ranks between Winchester and Gloucester's servants and, for instance, the Earl of Salisbury or Lord Say. In *1 Henry VI* there is a lawyer who appears briefly in the rose-plucking scene where he sides with York against Somerset. In *2 Henry VI* there is a clerk who is executed by Cade. But even these two possibly did not have an income sufficient to qualify them for franchise. Many lower-class citizens appear in the plays, however, which creates the impression that the concept of representation was much more modern than it actually was. It is odd to see the allegiance of a butcher and weaver being actively sought by king and rebel alike while no gentry or merchants merit even a passing reference. So while the country gentry and the lawyers had power in the House of Commons, they do not appear in the plays except indirectly, behind references to the citizens in *Richard III* or to the "commons" in *2 Henry VI*, such as when Humphrey, the Duke of Gloucester's death is announced.

As soon as news of Gloucester's death becomes public, Salisbury and "the commons" enter the room of state where King and council members were meeting. Salisbury acts as spokesman:

> Dread lord, the commons sends you word by me,
> Unless false Suffolk straight be done to death,

Or banished fair England's territories,
They will by violence tear him from your palace
And torture him with grievous ling'ring death.

(3.2.242–46)

Cognizant of their seeming insubordination, Salisbury emphasizes that this action is a result of "mere instinct of love and loyalty" (3.2.249) "in care of Henry's most royal person" (3.2.253). He compares their present action with protecting a sleeping ruler from a serpent:

And therefore do they cry, though you forbid,
That they will guard you, whe'r you will or no . . .

(3.2.263–64)

Though Salisbury's strong language makes the "commons" sound like a lynch mob, their information is accurate and their judgment is appropriate, substantiating the moral stature of the "commons" as political arbiters. As Bevington suggests, Humphrey's removal does not excuse the uprisings, but it places blame on the country's leaders. The audience had learned in the previous scene that Suffolk was responsible for Gloucester's death: "I'll see it truly done" (3.1.330). Against such a dangerous lord, only immediate, decisive action would be effective. This is a "crucial turning point between orderly appeal for redress of grievances and mob rule."[2] The commons speak but one line: "An answer from the king, or we will all break in!" (3.2.277) Yet Henry's response is instantaneous

. . . by His Majesty I swear,
Whose far unworthy deputy I am,
He shall not breathe infection in this air
But three days longer, on the pain of death.

(3.2.284–87)

Henry's handling of the whole Gloucester business will be discussed in the section on the Crown. Here I wish to point out that Henry seems to fear the commons' displeasure more than he feared the loss of his uncle or the rancor of his lords. When the council accused Gloucester and Henry recognized his endangered innocence, the King did not intervene. But now when the commons threaten to act, Henry responds immediately and in terms that they have defined for him. The horror of Gloucester's death might possibly have spurred Henry to act on his own; but to judge from his weakness in other confrontations, it is unlikely that he would have been this forceful without the incentive provided by the commons' insistence. One also wonders how much the acceptance by Suffolk, lords, and commons of the sentence owes to the fact that Henry decreed it and how much to the knowledge that it was demanded by and would be supported by the "commons." There is thus a suggestion here of the sanction that general support provides to authority.

Not everyone, however, is as respectful of the lower orders as Henry. Suffolk is captured by pirate-seamen who accuse him as follows:

> The commons here in Kent are up in arms;
> And to conclude, reproach and beggary
> Is crept into the palace of our King,
> And all by thee.

> (4.1.99–102)

Suffolk's response embodies the concept of privilege without responsibility and, even worse, contempt for those inferiors who are necessary to his own rank.

> O! that I were a god, to shoot forth thunder
> Upon these paltry, servile, abject drudges.
> .   .   .   .
> It is impossible that I should die
> By such a lowly vassal as thyself.

> (4.1.103–10)

The pirate-captain and Whitmore do not accept Suffolk's dismissing them as "jaded grooms" (4.1.52) or "base slaves" (4.1.67). They claim to be gentlemen (4.1.31) whose lives have as great a value as Suffolk's.

> What! think you much to pay two thousand crowns,
> And bear the name and port of gentlemen?
> Cut both the villains' throats—for die you shall:
> The lives of those which we have lost in fight
> Be counterpois'd with such a petty sum!
>
> (4.1.18–22)

The Captain's assessment of the position of gentleman is similar to Thomas Smith's, who felt that "it is not amiss" for gentlemen to be taxed according to their position, since they "be made good cheap in England." He who "can live idly and without manual labor, and will bear the port, charge, and countenance of a gentleman, he shall be called master. . . ."[3] The title, however, would not go without the charge and countenance.

The nobly born, ambitious Suffolk thinks of nothing but his own advancement and sees his social responsibility as limited to a sort of public performance.

> . . . Rather let my head
> Stoop to the block . . .
> And sooner dance upon a bloody pole
> Than stand uncover'd to the vulgar groom.
> True nobility is exempt from fear. . . .
>
> (4.1.124–29)

The seamen execute Suffolk after citing his crimes against the commonweal: kissing the Queen, selling French territories, matching Henry beneath his estate, and so on. They thereby forego the large ransom Suffolk could have brought and provide a sharp contrast with Suffolk. Despite the vigilante justice they apply, the seamen emerge from this scene more responsive to the common good than the gentlemen. Few would feel that the pirates did wrong in executing Suffolk, for his behavior deserved no indulgence, regardless of his rank; respect for rank should only be accorded to those whose actions, not inherited status, merit respect. It is perhaps important to note that Elizabethan "pirates" were not of the Captain Hook variety but were seamen waging unofficial guerrilla warfare against Spain at sea.

They were called pirates only because their raids against Spanish treasure ships usually had to be publicly disapproved.

The surviving gentleman resolves to bring the body to the king, adding, "If he revenge it not, yet will his friends" (4.1.146). Thus both "commons" and "gentlemen" recognized the failure in traditional law and order and respond by taking matters into their own hands. There is a difference, however, in that the individual members of the lower classes thus far do not stand to profit personally from their actions, which they can therefore cast in a mold of the common good. The gentleman, on the contrary, in referring to revenge by friends recognizes that their motivation will be personal and private. The sanction of support by the "commons" is given greater moral value than the sanction of support by personally ambitious aristocrats.

Within the context of Elizabethan parliamentary developments and the notable power of the House of Commons, it may be misleading to costume the "commons," who enter Parliament to demand Suffolk's banishment, and the pirates as rabble, which was done, for example, in Joseph Papp's *Wars of the Roses* production for the New York Shakespeare Festival in the summer of 1970. Decent clothing and comportment by the "commons" and "pirates" would coincide better with the preoccupations with which Shakespeare endows these characters. Many students of Shakespeare have been so conditioned by such sartorial decisions to be prejudiced in their assessment of Shakespeare's attitude toward the commons.[4] He shows the citizens, particularly in the first tetralogy, to be more concerned with the realm and with moral behavior than most of the aristocrats, a fact that also holds true for the followers of Cade.

The next scene contains Cade's first appearance. It begins with a brief prologue in which one of Cade's followers, George Bevis, exclaims,

> Oh, miserable age! Virtue is not regarded in handicraftsmen.

John
HOLLAND.   The nobility think scorn to go in leather aprons.
BEV.   Nay, more; the King's Council are no good
            workmen.
HOL.   True; and yet it is said, "Labour in thy vocation":
            which is as much to say as, "Let the magistrates
            be labouring men"; and therefore should we be
            magistrates.

                                          (4.2.10–19)

Holland's syllogism, which turns on a double sense of
"labouring," is a non sequitur, yet it is an accurate description of what has happened. Just as servants in *1 Henry VI*
sought to protect a lord who was second to the king, so in
2 Henry VI "commons" and pirates determine what is just
while king and council tend to their personal concerns rather
than to commonwealth affairs. The feet and hands of the
realm would appear to be functioning properly, but not the
head.

Cade's pedigree with accompanying commentary by Dick
the butcher and Smith the weaver is a parody of that inherited position which Suffolk stood upon, while the prejudice against lawyers and clerks that Cade and his followers
evidence is an inversion of Suffolk's contempt of social inferiors. An even wider breach between upper and lower
classes becomes apparent when Sir Humphrey Stafford
enters. He greets Cade's followers with this salutation:
"Rebellious hinds, the filth and scum of Kent, / Mark'd for
the gallows" (4.2.116-17). Cade meanwhile addresses his
followers as "you, good people" (4.2.69). When Stafford
asks Cade if he is a cloth shearer, Cade answers that "Adam
was a gardener" (4.2.128). But the lesson is lost upon
Stafford. Only soldiers choose to side with Stafford and the
king. Cade's appeal—"You that love the commons, follow
me" (4.2.175)—keeps his following for him, and they
enjoy great success, taking London Bridge and causing the
king to flee the court. Here Cade seems to be using *commons*
to refer neither to the Lower House nor its constituency but

to "the lower order, as distinguished from those of noble or knightly or gentle rank" (*OED,* s.v. *commons*).

The breakdown in communications between the classes and the greater responsibility of the educated for that failure is further emphasized in the "trial" of Lord Say. Instead of drawing upon his learning to help him communicate with his listeners through adaptation to their comprehension, at Say's first chance to speak in his own defense he quotes a Latin sentence that betrays his unfavorable judgment of his accusers. Next he cites not a contemporary reference but Caesar's opinion of Kent. And though he goes on to plead eloquently by citing his dedication to the realm, he cannot overcome the breach he helped create when he was unable to resist the temptation to flaunt his knowledge. His integrity is not quite "flawless," as Bevington asserts, but his error by no means warrants his fate (Bevington, *Tudor Drama and Politics,* p. 240). Cade orders Say's execution, and his followers carry it out, another indication that Shakespeare is not romanticizing the judgment of the lower orders. But Cade's followers desert him in the very next scene in favor of the first royal emissaries who treat them with respect. For just as Holland and Bevis were aware of failings within the government, failings that caused them to join with other Kentish commoners in rebelling, so Dick the butcher and Smith the weaver were aware of Cade's pretensions. The failure in leadership but the instinct for survival in the people extends downward even as far as Cade and his commons. His followers desert him when his autocratic rule no longer appears to hold much promise of improvement over Henry's weak rule. There is a similarity of theme between the pirates and commons' feeling that they must take matters into their own hands and Cade's followers' deserting him.

Buckingham and Clifford present themselves much differently from Stafford.

> BUC.   . . . we come ambassadors from the King
> Unto the commons, whom thou hast misled.

(4.8.7–8)

To the King's offer of pardon, the commons reply, "God save the King!" (4.8.19). Cade, curiously, is forced into the position of holding his followers in contempt, with predictable results.

> What, Buckingham and Clifford, are ye so brave?
> And you, base peasants, do ye believe him?
>
> (4.8.20–21)

Cade reminds them of their "ancient freedom" (4.8.27) and of their being slaves to the nobility (4.8.28), with the effect that they return to his support. But Clifford continues the appeal to their better nature by asking them to spare England and take their quarrels to France. They desert the Cade who called them "base peasants" and resolve to "follow the king and Clifford" (4.8.54).

Despite the fickleness of Cade's mob, the stupidity and ruthlessness that Cade's followers evidence may ultimately be less repulsive than the stupidity and ruthlessness evidenced in high places.[5] And, I would add, the principles governing their behavior are less self-serving and more closely related to the general good than the principles governing the king and most of the aristocracy. Cade's followers do not really challenge the concept of hierarchy: good magistrates would not provoke rebellion. But they challenge the right to obedience of inadequate princes. The commoners are, as Robert Ornstein writes, victims seeking to survive;[6] they are almost innocent in comparison with the aristocrats.

As *2 Henry VI* ends, Henry's forces lose the battle of St. Alban's to York's army. Following Margaret's advice, Henry flees to London where she says he is "lov'd"(5.2.81). When *3 Henry VI* opens in London with York seated on the throne in the Parliament House, however, Henry does not try to remove York from the seat of state because

> Ah, know you not the city favours them,
>
> .   .   .   .
>
> Far be the thought of this from Henry's heart,
> To make a shambles of the parliament-house!
>
> (1.1.67–71)

What Henry does not perceive is the connection between these two statements. Londoners favor York because they know that their king lacks the quality of leadership. The disfavor of the people is not a permanent given that Henry must learn to accept. The real problem is his failure to rule. The emphasis in this scene is on Henry's wrongs in not governing well rather than on York's right to the throne.[7] Decisive action on Henry's part would win back the people's allegiance, but this is a lesson Henry does not acknowledge until the moments before his death. When forces representing the king are in the field and there is no longer a rival contender for the throne after York's death, Warwick reports that his soldiers "had no heart to fight" (2.1.135). And when King Edward foolishly alienates most of his supporters by marrying Lady Gray, the "common people by numbers swarm" to support the forces in the field representing Henry's cause. Had Henry exerted even minimal authority, the implication is clear that his people would have supported him. But forceful action by Henry was the exception rather than the rule, and many references appear in this play to the people's supporting the Yorkists, who retain final possession of the crown.

After the Towton battle, when Henry sits on a molehill while the terrible suffering of his people unrolls before him, Young Clifford comments that

> The common people swarm like summer flies;
> And whither fly the gnats but to the sun?
> And who shines now but Henry's enemies?

(2.6.8–10)

When Henry has fled to Scotland and Margaret is pleading for King Lewis to support his cause, she says that "our people and our peers are both misled" (3.3.35), meaning that no one then supports the absent claimant. Though Henry is briefly restored through the efforts of Warwick and Clarence, he is only a figurehead, and before long Warwick reports that "many giddy people flock to" Edward

(4.8.5). The relationship is a circular one. Common men, as Henry learns from the keepers who capture him, support the power-that-is. But the power-that-is became such by winning general support and will only remain the power-that-is as long as it can retain that support. This seems to be a primary lesson of this first group of plays, and it is a lesson perfected by Richard III in the concluding play of the tetralogy.

If Richard is to be king, he must eliminate rival heirs and win the support of the Mayor and Londoners. He therefore stages an elaborate business to convince the Mayor that he acted for the safety of the nation in executing Hastings. He sends Buckingham to the Guildhall, in hot pursuit behind the Mayor, to play the orator by maligning Edward's children. But the citizens, like the scrivener who wrote Hastings's indictment, are aware.

> Who is so gross,
> That cannot see this palpable device?
>
> (3.6.10–11)

Buckingham comes back to report that "the citizens are mum" (3.7.3) and that only his own followers, a sort of claque, cried, "God save King Richard!" (3.7.36). In the actual meeting between Mayor, citizens, and future king, Shakespeare limits their approval to the minimum that could not be avoided without changing historical fact. To Gloucester's elaborate disclaimer of any desire for the crown, the Mayor replies, "God bless your Grace! We see it, and will say it" (3.7.237), but he does not say that they will take the reproach upon themselves as Richard had urged. Buckingham salutes him as "England's worthy king!" but the Mayor and citizens say simply, "Amen" (3.7.240-41). Richmond can legitimately say that Richard's soldiers "Had rather have us win than him they follow" (5.3.244), and he does win. Aside from the necessity for a young playwright to flatter the ruling house, an important factor in this ending of *Richard III,* there is an acknowledgment that decisive action is not sufficient to gain and retain popular support. Richard was the most vigorous of all contenders in the first tetralogy, perhaps in all the English history plays. But he did not remain in power long. The factors necessary for a long reign remain to be explored in the subsequent English history plays.

B.   The Lords

While the lords' perception of the constitutional structure of the realm in the first tetralogy is presented as a series of individual views, there are several themes closely related to feudal structure that unify the diverse actions of the many lords portrayed in these four plays. One such theme is the authority assumed by the hereditary aristocracy during the king's minority. A second is the preoccupation most lords evidence with class distinctions. A third, most developed, theme is the younger generation's abandoning their elders' concern with hereditary legitimacy in order to satisfy personal ambitions; subsequently, the new lords reluctantly recognize that a king must have specific abilities and fulfill specific requirements in order to rule.

The presence of a child on the throne, while it would mean the lack of any meaningful leadership from the person possessing the crown, would not cause any formal change in societal organization. The aristocracy could continue intact because the Crown continued through all circumstances as a symbol for the unity of the realm—that is, "the King never dies."[8] Thus, even before his coronation, the young Henry can exact a feudal pledge of obedience from Richard Plantagenet and in return establish him as Duke of York once Parliament has approved the action.

> KING. If Richard will be true, . . .
> . . . all the whole inheritance I give
> That doth belong unto the house of York
>
> PLAN. Thy humble servant vows obedience
> And humble service till the point of death.

> KING. Stoop then and set your knee against my foot;
> And in reguerdon of that duty done
> I gird thee with the valiant sword of York.
>
> (*1H6*, 3.1.164–71)

Similarly, Talbot, also before the coronation, comes to do his "duty" to his "sovereign" (3.4.4) and

> Lets fall his sword before your Highness' feet;
> And with submissive loyalty of heart
> Ascribes the glory of his conquest got
> First to my God, and next unto your Grace.
>
> (3.4.9–12)

These two essentially feudal ceremonies illustrate the preoccupation with feudal structure in Shakespeare's first written history plays, a structure that will receive no mention at all in his last English history plays.

The notion of continuity of the Crown despite minority of the king was not without its difficulties. The king, though a child, was still responsible for the governance of the land. But administration was complicated by the "notion of the impossibility of a dichotomy of royal person and royal authority—that is, of any alienation or delegation of sovereignty"[9] even to a protector. During Henry VI's minority, Parliament decided that the position of protector would entitle its holder only to rights of patronage over minor offices. The important powers were reserved to the council as a whole (p. 148), a majority of which could remove any office-holder including the protector (p. 136). The protector functioned, in effect, as chairman to a corporate board of directors. In practice, what the lords were proclaiming was a "peerage doctrine"—that "if the king himself were unable to execute his authority, then to them alone and as a whole belonged the function of doing it for him" (p. 151). When Henry calls his uncles "The special watchmen of our English weal" (*1H6*, 3.1.66), he is referring to this doctrine of government by the aristocracy. Whether in practice such a government is possible is examined through the first tetralogy.

The council was supposed to act as a body, but Shakespeare shows each member determining his actions for himself. In act 1, scene 1, Bedford, who is regent of France, announces that he will take 10,000 soldiers to rescue Talbot (1.1.155). Gloucester, who is protector, decides to examine the weapons in the Tower.[10] Exeter, who is governor of the king, announces that he will see to his safety. Left alone, Winchester announces that he intends to steal the king and be "chief steersman" (1.1.177). While historically Winchester acted in behalf of the council in disagreeing with Gloucester, whose interpretation of the role of protector encompassed more power than suited the council, Shakespeare makes their quarrel a personal one. Winchester's denying Gloucester access to the Tower thus appears to be his own decision in act 1, scene 3. The later accusations by the council members against Gloucester are made to seem the contrivance of individual lords and the queen, who were all tired of the legal restraints imposed upon them by Gloucester's dedication to law and tradition. The historical council, on the contrary, had found reason to rebuke Gloucester because of his pretentious claims to the regency that they felt were not supported by precedent or law.[11] Though constitutionally Gloucester was the "villain," he was personally popular with the people who preferred to dissociate king and would-be protector from the injustices resulting from the less than ideal government of Henry's minority.[12] Shakespeare chose the popular view of Gloucester rather than the lords' view. Instead of making Gloucester the culprit, Shakespeare shows him to be too weak a bulwark against lords whose authority, when not limited by royal guidance, degenerates into a hydra-headed power struggle. Once the apex of the feudal pyramid was absent or too weak to function, the powerful lords one level below the top inevitably, as Shakespeare shows, engaged in struggle to fill that gap.

Henry, even when he comes of age and formally assumes control of the government by accepting Gloucester's staff of office, is not strong enough to restrain his lords. The habits of independence that they had developed as regents in his minority continue in his majority. When Cardinal Beaufort (former Bishop of Winchester) wants York to put down the Irish rebellion, and York in orthodox fashion replies that he will, "so please His Majesty" (*2H6*, 3.1.315), Suffolk replies,

> Why, our authority is his consent,
> And what we do establish he confirms.
>
> (3.1.316–17)

Later York, before his open break with the king, claims that he brings an army "to remove proud Somerset from the King, / Seditious to his Grace and to the state" (5.1.36-7).

With government in the hands of the highest ranking aristocracy, there follows a preoccupation with social position and privilege as a means of distinguishing those with traditional access to power. Insistence on the privileges of status would be an important means for the aristocracy to preserve the feudal societal structure against internal challenges from the lower ranks. Somerset calls Richard Plantagenet a "yeoman" before Henry has restored his rights. Plantagenet knows that he cannot speak in Parliament until he is restored.

> Plantagenet, I see, must hold his tongue,
> Lest it be said, "Speak, sirrah, when you should;
> Must your bold verdict enter talk with lords?"
>
> (*1H6*, 3.1.61–63)

Both Cardinal Beaufort and the Duke of Buckingham reproach the Earl of Warwick for advising Henry that York would be a better regent than Somerset.

> CAR.   Ambitious Warwick, let thy betters speak.
> WAR.   The Cardinal's not my better in the field.
> BUCK. All in this presence are thy betters, Warwick.
>
> (*2H6*, 1.3.109–11)

Suffolk's argument that Henry renounce the Earl of Armagnac's daughter in favor of Margaret hinges on the distinction in rank between earl and king, that an oath to an earl's daughter may be broken because a king should be matched with a king's daughter (*1H6*, 5.5.34, 66).

Amidst the repeated changes in dynasty, such distinctions in rank blur in *3 Henry VI*. Warwick, who was deemed unworthy to speak in the previous play, is declared a suitable father to a possible queen when his daughter is pledged to Prince Edward (*3H6*, 3.3.245). The same Warwick is able to give away crowns and dukedoms (5.1.27-31), determining by withholding or according his support whether Henry or Edward should be king. Lady Gray, who thinks herself too base to be so honored, becomes the wife of Edward IV. But in *Richard III* there are reassertions of the privileges of rank. Richard, as a duke, orders the lords accompanying Lady Anne to set down Henry's corpse.

> Unmannered dog! stand thou when I command:
> Advance thy halberd higher than my breast,
> Or, by Saint Paul, I'll strike thee to my foot,
> And spurn upon thee, beggar, for thy boldness.
>
> (*R3*, 1.2.39-42)

Later the Dukes of Gloucester and Buckingham are able to imprison Lords Rivers, Gray, and Vaughan (2.4.43-45) then win the Mayor's acceptance of Hastings's death largely because of their rank.

> Mayor. . . . do not doubt, right noble princes both,
>   But I'll acquaint our duteous citizens
>   With all your just proceedings in this cause.
>
> (3.5.63-65)

Privileges of position within feudal social structure do not enter into the second tetralogy with anything approaching the intensity in the first tetralogy even though historically the lines should have been more sharply drawn in the days of Richard II than in the days of Henry VI, one of the paradoxes evidenced in the later-written plays about the

earlier period. Though there may be a psychological explanation—that in times of cultural instability people place a
compensating stress on title to emphasize that about which
they feel insecure—I suggest throughout this study an explanation that presumes Shakespeare's use of historical
material to reflect upon current political problems.

Beyond these few general ideas governing most of the
lords in the first tetralogy, their constitutional position in
the plays is represented by diverse individuals. They divide
into two basic groups, those who remain from the days of
Henry V and those who come to power during the tenure of
Henry VI. Differences in age and attitudes toward traditional values and order are the criteria for distinguishing
the two groups. Gloucester, Talbot, and the two Earls of
Salisbury represent the older group, Suffolk, Warwick, and
young Clifford the newer. The portraits of the older lords
detail failings in feudal aristocracy in general. The portraits of the younger lords show them achieving an increas-
ingly specific definition of the role of king.

Old Salisbury trained Henry V in the art of warfare. He
won respect from French and English alike. Talbot called
him "mirror of all martial men" (*1H6*, 1.4.73), while
Reignier, fearing his prowess, called him "madbrain'd"
and a "desperate homicide" (1.2.15, 25). It is reported of
him that even under the most trying of circumstances, when
his men are outnumbered and cut off from supply, he can
keep them from mutiny (1.1.160). His actual appearance is
very brief, just time enough to seek the opinions of two
lords on the best sites for the next assault on Orleans when
a cannon shot fired by a French master gunner's son hits him.
This brief incident emblematizes two moral lessons about
leadership that recur throughout the English histories. One
is that the best leaders do not presume to act solely on the
basis of their own views but regularly consult with and heed
the advice of others. Though this lesson was also true in
feudal times, in the context of late-sixteenth-century parliamentary development, it could assume ideological significance. The second is that in this war as in all others there

is no special divinity that hedges the lives of the upper classes. A mere boy can kill an Earl of Salisbury. In another example, York reports that "the Great Lord of Northumberland," Lord Clifford, and Lord Stafford "were by the swords of common soldiers slain" (*3H6*, 1.1.9), though, in fact, York himself killed Clifford in *2H6*, 5.2.28. Status alone afforded no protection or security. Salisbury's appearance is too brief for any major flaws in his character to be brought out. For two other survivors from Henry V's reign, ample attention is given to their virtues and their failings, which reflect on the aristocracy as a whole and government by an aristocracy.

Talbot, after Salisbury's death, is the mainstay of English forces in France. He is at his best when he acts in concert with his soldiers, a lesson that he teaches the Countess of Auvergne by blowing a horn, at which sound his soldiers enter.

> How say you, madam? Are you now persuaded
> That Talbot is but shadow of himself?
> These are his substance, sinews, arms, and strength,
> With which he yoketh your rebellious necks. . . .
>
> (*1H6*, 2.3.60–63)

But he is limited. His only standards of behavior are martial, such as when he thinks that the warlike Salisbury must merit heavenly favor for no other reason than his military ability:

> Heaven, be thou gracious to none alive,
> If Salisbury wants mercy at thy hands!
>
> (1.4.84–85)

And he is proud, for he "disdained" to be ransomed by exchange with someone of rank inferior to his own (1.4.29-33). He chose to remain a prisoner longer than necessary, unable to aid the English against the French. He calls the battle with the French "my wars" (3.4.3) when he salutes his young king:

I have awhile given truce unto my wars
To do my duty to my sovereign. . . .

(3.4.3–4)

In his anger at Fastolfe's cowardice, he first strips the garter
from his leg, explains his reasons for so doing, then finally
asks the lords at the coronation to judge his action (4.1.15–
29). In his last action, he puts greater value on the reputation of his name than on the good of his country by refusing
to escape from the encirclement in order to be able to return
another time and seek vengeance on the French. Though his
not wanting to desert his men is commendable, that motive
is accorded only one line (4.5.45); far greater attention is
given to his preoccupation with the name Talbot. This preoccupation is his son's sole heritage, too. Young Talbot
makes the same choice as his father by preferring to die in
defense of his name than to flee for the possible good of his
country. Talbot and son die together and neither voices any
reproach of the king whose failure to lead contributed to
their dilemma. Talbot assumes that he will go to heaven
though he dies in pride. "Soul with soul from France to
heaven fly" (4.5.55); "commendable prouv'd, let's die in
pride" (4.5.57). Personal pride and willful actions have
little place in the successful leadership of a commonweal;
these two lessons will be shown repeatedly throughout the
histories. The glorious, martial Talbot, after all, remains
only as a "stinking and fly-blown" corpse (4.7.76). The
territories he fought to conquer and retain are soon lost. He
leaves no child to carry on the tradition he embodied. While
it is true that the specific circumstances of his death were
caused by York and Somerset's rancor, which kept them both
from coming to his aid, Talbot decided against the escape
or surrender that would have allowed him another chance.

Only one lord in all the four plays is consistently favored
by the commons, a distinction made more noticeable when
it is reported by his personal enemy, Cardinal Beaufort.

What though the common people favour him,
Calling him "Humphrey, the good Duke of Gloucester,"

> Clapping their hands, and crying with loud voice,
> "Jesu maintain your royal Excellence!"
> With "God preserve the good Duke Humphrey!"
>> (2H6, 1.1.157–61)

Petitioners wait to see him, "for he's a good man! Jesu bless him!" (1.3.5). At his death the commons are sufficiently enraged to intervene directly by demanding Suffolk's banishment. Popular approval of Gloucester even survives long after his death, when following the death of Edward IV a citizen comforts another at the prospect of a child king by remembering Henry VI's infancy.

> . . . God wot;
> For then this land was famously enriched
> With politic grave counsel; then the king
> Had virtuous uncles to protect his grace.
>> (R3, 2.3.18–21)

This good memory persists despite Henry VI's attempt, when he was threatened with deposition, at discrediting Gloucester by blaming him for losing France:

> The Lord Protector lost it, and not I:
> When I was crown'd I was but nine months old.
>> (3H6, 1.1.111–12)

The reasons for the commons' devotion to Humphrey are not hard to find. In his every appearance he associates himself with the well-being of the realm and the offices and traditions guarding that well-being. These include the Mayor, Parliament, the King, the law, and so on. He consistently puts the needs of the realm before his own, as when he suppresses his rage at Winchester's denying him access to the Tower. When the Mayor of London and his officers command him to leave, he tells Winchester, "I'll be no breaker of the law" (1H6, 1.3.79). As he departs he acknowledges the Mayor's office: "Mayor, farewell: thou dost but what thou may'st" (1.3.86). He prepares a written statement of his grievances against Winchester for Parliament to act upon; despite Winchester's apparently tearing it up, Humphrey restrains himself from further fighting because he is in the presence of the King. (*1H6*, 3.1.8).

He sees himself as "Protector of the realm" (*2H6*, 1.3.120), whose services are needed until the King determines that they are no longer necessary. If the well-being of the realm requires that he suppress his personal anger at the council in order to continue serving as the adviser to the King, he will do so. When faced with the accusations by Margaret, Suffolk, Winchester, Somerset, and Buckingham, Humphrey leaves the council meeting without saying a word, then returns explaining,

> Now, lords, my choler being over-blown
> With walking once about the quadrangle,
> I come to talk of commonwealth affairs.
> As for your spiteful false objections,
> Prove them, and I lie open to the law. . . .
> (*2H6*, 1.3.152–56)

The King does still need his advice, for he is immediately faced with the problems of choosing between Peter's quoting his master as saying that York is the rightful heir and Horner's denial. Henry's solution is to turn to Humphrey, "Uncle, what shall we say to this in law?" (1.3.203).

The unfavorable terms of the marriage treaty so disturb Humphrey that he cannot finish reading the document. He extends his reaction to include all the realm when he says,

> . . . Duke Humphrey must unload his grief—
> Your grief, the common grief of all the land.
> (*2H6*, 1.1.75–76)

On another occasion he says that he would willingly die for the happiness of England (3.1.150). Thus Humphrey is an incarnation of the ideal feudal aristocrat. Were all the other lords to share his views, even Henry VI's feudal government could survive. Unfortunately, Humphrey is wrong to

assume that others share his views. While he thinks that the
English peers are the brave "pillars of the state" (1.1.74)
and that "honor and virtue" are the distinguishing characteristics of nobility (2.1.186-89), in fact most of the peers are
not supporting the state but struggling for its control with
means that are far from honorable. Humphrey not only
misjudges the peers, he is also mistaken about the law and
about his wife's character. Though she gives him many
warnings of her ambitions, Humphrey retreats from reproaching his wife at the first sign of her anger. "Nay, be
not angry; I am pleas'd again" (1.2.55). He cannot imagine
the lengths to which she will go in obtaining her ambitions.
He lulls himself into a false security by accepting the mere
semblance or trappings of order, such as Eleanor's saying
that in the future she will seek to avoid being rebuked by
her husband (1.2.53-54). He allows himself to be deceived
by his own virtue. Left to her own devices, his ambitious
wife threatens to scratch the Queen's face (1.3.141-42) and
consults with conjurers. When unrestrained by a king, the
peers conspire to systematically eliminate powerful rivals.
Left to enforce itself, the law cannot function, for a king
who did not know the law while Humphrey was protector
cannot see to its effective functioning when he is removed
from office. Though Humphrey knows that Henry is not
prepared to govern, his commitment to the feudal hierarchy
that made him subordinate to the King is so strong that his
reproach to Henry is mild.

> Ah! thus King Henry throws away his crutch
> Before his legs be firm to bear his body.
>
> .   .   .   .
>
> Ah! that my fear were false; ah! that it were;
> For, good King Henry, thy decay I fear.
>
> (2H6, 3.1.189–94)

The result is that Humphrey is assassinated, and the one
responsible for his death is sentenced at the demand of a
mob, not a jury, then executed by a pirate, not a hangman.
The chaotic aftermath to his death reflects unfavorably on
his close-chested control of the administration. The King

was not trained to carry on in his tradition. Gloucester left no offspring in the play to carry on either. This failure will be echoed at the end of *Henry V*, for Henry's fate and the fate of the realm are similar. He leaves no competent heir to further unify the realm, which thus disintegrates.

None of the leaders who remain from the days of Henry V can keep the country united. They are all killed either by foreign troops or domestic rivals, or they stand by, like Exeter, helplessly observing the degeneration into rivalry. With Talbot gone, there is no one to maintain the French conquests, and with Humphrey gone, there is no one to restrain the forces of civil unrest (Hamilton, *The Early Shakespeare,* p. 38). Though all the specific references to Henry V are favorable, as will be shown in the Crown section below, this legacy of failure in leadership reflects unfavorably on his rule and on the inadequacy of a series of oaths obligating duty upward to assure the stability of the realm when there is no one at the top of the chain to enforce the required protection for those beneath, that is, on the inadequacy of feudal structure to maintain order when the king is weak. Henry V's example of French conquest served only to win back the commons lured by the prospect of gaining more wealth than offered by Cade with his talk of domestic reforms; Henry V's example did nothing to secure a self-perpetuating domestic harmony.

The senior Clifford, who had helped to woo the commons back to allegiance to Henry VI by citing his legitimacy as son of Henry V, is killed defending his king against York's forces. Thereafter his son dismisses even a shred of dedication to anything other than personal revenge. On discovering his father's body, Young Clifford resolves, "In cruelty will I seek out my fame" (*2H6*, 5.1.60). He chooses to support Henry VI against the House of York with no reference to the realm.

> King Henry, be thy title right or wrong,
> Lord Clifford vows to fight in thy defense:
> May that ground gape and swallow me alive,
> Where I shall kneel to him that slew my father!
>
> (*3H6*, 1.1.163–66)

In his fury he stabs York's young son Rutland and, after joining the Queen in torturing York, stabs him too. In the moments before his death when he is wounded in the Towton battle, he analyzes the situation his country is in and places the blame on his king's not having fulfilled the requirements of his office.

> . . . Henry, hadst thou sway'd as kings should do,
> Or as thy father, and his father did,
> Giving no ground unto the House of York,
> They never then had sprung like summer flies;
> I, and ten thousand in this luckless realm
> Had left no mourning widows for our death;
> And thou this day hadst kept thy chair in peace.
> For what doth cherish weeds but gentle air?
>
> (2.6.14–21)

Young Clifford does not see that not only the Yorkists but he, too, is a weed not kept in check by leadership from his king. The lesson that a king must rule is not necessarily discredited through its being spoken by a doubtful moralist. The Cliffords father and son embody a movement away from hereditary legitimacy, which Clifford Senior cited in winning back the commons' allegiance, to recognition that specific abilities are needed in a king, for he must fulfill specific duties. This movement toward greater precision in specifying the expected behavior of a king will, in the second tetralogy, result in Henry IV and Henry V's acting according to late-sixteenth-century constitutional principles of royal conduct. At this point in the nine plays, however, one has yet to learn the exact meaning of "sway."

Another son who comes to power during the reign of Henry VI will further specify the duties required by the office of king. The Earl of Warwick, as son of the second man to bear the title of Earl of Salisbury in these plays, hears from his father such advice as the following:

> Join we together for the public good,
> In what we can, to bridle and suppress

The pride of Suffolk and the Cardinal,
With Somerset's and Buckingham's ambition;
And, as we may, cherish Duke Humphrey's deeds,
While they do tend the profit of the land.

(2H6, 1.1.200–205)

His response to such ennobling sentiments is equally selfless:

So God help Warwick, as he loves the land,
And common profit of his country!

(1.1.206–7)

Humphrey's benefit for England had been forcefully portrayed when he exposed the fraudulent miracle of Simpcox's recovery from blindness and worked a "miracle" of his own in curing Simpcox's lameness with a whip. This comic scene was interrupted by news of Humphrey's wife's treason and imprisonment, actions that foretold Humphrey's own fall from power. In the scene immediately following this preparation for Humphrey's absence, Salisbury and Warwick learn from the Duke of York that he has a better claim to the throne than the weak Henry VI, as a descendent of Edward III's third son where Henry descends from the fourth son.

So, if the issue of the elder son
Succeed before the younger, I am King.

(2H6, 2.2.50–51)

Thereupon both Salisbury and Warwick salute him as sovereign. However, it is far more likely that they accept the legitimacy of York's lineage because they prefer York as a more capable ruler than that he has provided them with new information that causes their sudden switch in allegiance (Ornstein, *A Kingdom for a Stage*, p. 51). They then stand by in silence while Gloucester is accused of treason and remain silent until Salisbury, true to his earlier concern for the public good, acts as spokesman for the commons in their anger at Gloucester's death.

Salisbury makes an open break with Henry along with York. But unlike York's personal disgust with Henry, which will be discussed in the Crown section, Salisbury's renunciation of allegiance is couched in traditional hierarchical terms and is thus consistent with his previous view of his societal position, only he extends that hierarchy one step beyond the Crown to God and a cosmic scheme of allegiance. His exchange of views with Henry is important as the first serious mention in these plays of a law known variously as higher law, natural law, or law of reason.

> SAL.   My lord, I have consider'd with myself
>   The title of this most renowned duke;
>   And in my conscience do repute his Grace
>   The rightful heir to England's royal seat.
> KING.   Hast thou not sworn allegiance unto me?
> SAL.   I have.
> KING.   Canst thou dispense with heaven for such an oath?
> SAL.   It is great sin to swear unto a sin,
>   But greater sin to keep a sinful oath.
>
> (*2H6*, 5.1.175–83)

The pious Henry's silence on this issue is an apparent admission of his weak position. None of the Lancastrians try to dissuade Salisbury, and so there is no discussion of the issue of higher law, how it is determined, the function of individual conscience, and so on (these issues are not raised until act 1 scene 4 of *Richard III*; see 2 D below). Old Salisbury survives the battle of St. Alban's but thereafter disappears from the plays, leaving his son to carry on in his place.

Warwick was the greatest landowner in England, controlling more land than the kings he installed and deposed (Marriott, *English History in Shakespeare,* p. 199). This fact is not mentioned in the plays but was the source of his power to determine the succession for a time. Sir John Fortescue, who was chief justice of the King's Bench during the reign of Henry VI and was closely identified with the

Lancastrian party, wrote in *The Governance of England,* one of the earliest English constitutional treatises, that

> the people will go with him that best may sustain and reward them. . . . We have also seen lately in our realm, some of the king's subjects give him battle, by occasion that their livelihood and offices were the greatest of the land, and else they would not have done so. . . . But this is written only to the intent that it be well understood, how necessary it is that the king have great possessions, and particular livelihood for his own suirte [security]; namely, when any of his lords should happen to be so excessively great, as there might thereby grow peril to his estate. For certainly there may no greater peril grow to a prince, than to have a subject equepolent [equally powerful] to himself.[13]

When Warwick first learns of York's claim to the throne, he assures him "that the Earl of Warwick / Shall one day make the Duke of York a king" (*2H6*, 2.2.77-78). In exchange, York pledges to "make the Earl of Warwick / The greatest man in England but the king" (2.2.80-81), at which point the scene ends. York has thus appealed to Warwick's personal ambition and Warwick has made no disclaimer to such a motive. He, therefore, like young Clifford and young Talbot, has abandoned even the rhetoric of his father's dedication to the common good. At the meeting of Parliament summoned by Henry to determine the rival York / Lancaster claims to the throne, he tells York to "possess" the crown, "for this is thine" (*3H6*, 1.1.26-27).

> Neither the King, nor he that loves him best,
> The proudest he that holds up Lancaster,
> Dares stir a wing if Warwick shake his bells.
> I'll plant Plantagenet, root him up who dares.
> (*3H6*, 1.1.45–48)

He labels Henry a usurper whom they defeated in the field and who abandoned his rights as Henry V's heir by losing all his French conquests (1.1.81, 90, 110). He orders the proceedings to be followed in Parliament, determining that Henry shall speak first, then demanding that York be treated fairly:

> Or I will fill the house with armed men,
> And o'er the chair of state, where now [York] sits,
> Write up his title with [Lancastrian] blood.
>
> (1.1.171–73)

When in the field with Edward, the new Duke of York, he vows he'll behead all who do not accept him as king (2.1.196-97). Edward pledges never to "undertake the thing / Wherein thy counsel and consent is wanting" (2.6.101-2), and he allows Warwick to arrange a marriage with Lady Bona of France.

Edward disregards his pledge, however, in marrying Lady Grey; Warwick, who learns this in the presence of King Lewis, renounces his support:

> No more my King, for he dishonours me
>
> .   .   .   .
>
> . . . for my desert is honour;
> And to repair my honour lost for him
> I here renounce him and return to Henry.
>
> (3.3.184–94)

As Young Clifford had allowed his allegiance to be determined by personal revenge, so Warwick allows his to be determined by personal honor. They both find, moreover, that they have chosen poorly, for neither king that they follow is adequate to the task. Clifford realizes that Henry did not rule as he should. Warwick is more specific in his reproaches to Edward. After Humphrey's fear of Henry's unreadiness to rule, Shakespeare has detailed first Clifford's accusation that Henry did not rule as he should have and now Warwick's catalogue of the qualities he thinks necessary in a king.

> . . . I degraded you from being King,
> And come now to create you Duke of York.
> Alas, how should you govern any kingdom
> That know not how to use ambassadors,
> Nor how to be contented with one wife,
> Nor how to use your brothers brotherly,
> Nor how to study for the people's welfare,
> Nor how to shroud yourself from enemies?
>
> (*3H6*, 4.3.33–40)

But Warwick dies in defense of the House of Lancaster, another victim to the mortality of the nobility. His role of kingmaker is temporarily filled by Buckingham in *Richard III*, where he and Gloucester use a divided council (3.1.179; 3.2.12, 76) to manipulate the aristocracy into supporting Gloucester. Buckingham, as did Warwick before him, finds the role of kingmaker to be a thankless one ("made I him king for this?" [4.2.117]). He is denied the promised wealth and later executed. The man he personally made king with no reference to any legitimating sanctions whether of heredity, ability, or popular support, is defeated shortly after attaining the throne. Henry Tudor will claim to embody all three sanctions.

The progression or degeneration from the first Earl of Salisbury through the Talbots and Cliffords to Warwick and Buckingham is a cumulative demonstration that feudal aristocrats acting singly or in groups cannot see to the effective governance of the land. What the Earl of Warwick determines is good for himself is demonstrated not to be good for the country. But not only respect for the common wisdom and common traditions in the form of popular support and following the law are needed to secure the effective governance of the realm, as the people show. The realization by Clifford, then Warwick, is that specific qualities and actions are needed in and from a king. Thus, in terms of the people's perception, the first tetralogy records a movement away from the ceremonies of allegiance, away from the references by lords and commoners to their feudal obligations, with an accompanying movement toward definition of the qualities needed in a king before commons and lords will accord their support, that is, a transition toward an implicit contract.

C.   The Crown

In both historic and dramatic terms, the Crown was a composite body. The Crown coincided with the king as head of the body politic, with the heir to a particular dynasty, and with those responsible for maintaining the inalienable rights of the Crown and the kingdom (Kantorowicz, *The King's Two Bodies,* p. 381). In dramatic terms this composite relationship could be expressed by a king's triple function as a man, as head of a family, and as head of state. The "Elizabethan habit of finding correspondences among all levels of existence" facilitated this multiple function of the person of the king in drama.[14] Personal feelings and strengths in a king thus would also have societal significance.

Ten interpretations of the Crown are presented in these four plays (eleven if we count Cade) : Henry V's indirectly in the many references to his example, Henry VI's, Margaret's as a spokesman for the Lancastrian cause, her son Edward's, York and Edward IV's, the French King Lewis's, the young Edward V's, Richard III's, and Henry VII's. Of the ten there are three kings—Henry VI, Edward IV, and Richard III—who are given full-scale treatment covering the several facets of their roles as king. The other rulers serve to illustrate one or two aspects of the Crown. Hereditary legitimacy, possession, popular support, and ability to maintain stability at home and possessions abroad are the sanctions for royalty that are explored through the several kings and their reigns. The kings will be discussed in the order more or less of their appearance in the plays.

King Henry VI is the most important king of these four plays. Not only does his reign span three of the plays so that they are named for him, but his personality, abilities, and failings determine the nature of events that take place. As the center of government or, in Thomas Smith's words, as the "life, the head, and the authority" of all that transpires in England, Henry directly or indirectly is responsible for much of what happens in these plays.

The scene of Henry's coronation begins with the actual placing of the crown on his head and thus omits the series of questions and answers by which the king-to-be pledges that he will maintain peace and the laws, and by which representatives of the people indicate that they will accept him as king.[15] Immediately after commanding that the crown be set on Henry's head, Humphrey demands an oath of allegiance from the Governor of Paris to the King. This pledge details a subject's duty under a feudal regime.

> Now, Governor of Paris, take your oath,
> That you elect no other king but him;
> Esteem none friends but such as are his friends,
> And none your foes but such as shall pretend
> Malicious practices against his state:
> This shall ye do, so help you righteous God!
>
> (*1H6*, 4.1.3–8)

The ceremony is interrupted by the sudden entrance of John Fastolfe before the Governor can reply. In terms of dramatic representation, therefore, there has been no exchange of pledged obligations either by king or subjects.

Upon seeing Fastolfe, Talbot rips the symbol of the Order of the Garter from his leg because he does not fulfill the requirements Talbot enumerates as traditionally associated with the position of knight.

> When first this Order was ordain'd, my lords,
> Knights of the Garter were of noble birth,
> Valiant and virtuous, full of haughty courage,
> Such as were grown to credit by the wars;
> Not fearing death nor shrinking for distress,
> But always resolute in most extremes.
>
> (4.1.33–38)

Talbot concludes that fulfilling the requirements of the position is a more valid criterion for respect than possession of the symbol or title. Therefore he declares Fastolfe a usurper:

> He then that is not furnish'd in this sort
> Doth but usurp the sacred name of knight,
> Profaning this most honourable Order,
> And should, if I were worthy to be judge,
> Be quite degraded, like a hedge-born swain
> That doth presume to boast of gentle blood.
>
> (4.1.39–44)

Henry agrees, since he banishes Fastolfe on pain of death (4.1.47).

This representation of Henry's coronation prefigures Henry's whole reign as dramatized by Shakespeare. Neither the specific responsibilities of the king nor acceptance by the people have been formalized at the outset. The removal of a knight from his office by another who has the will to act and the ability to persuade others to accept his definition of the previously unspecified requirements foreshadows precisely what will happen to Henry when challenged by York. The application of this scene to the Crown will not be enforced until much later; nonetheless the acceptance by all participants in the coronation of the principle that position and accountability or responsibility are inseparable establishes an important precedent.

Henry begins well enough, by sensing threats to the commonweal, by desiring cooperation among his peers to preserve their territories in France, and by agreeing to whatever benefits his country.

> [to Gloucester and Winchester]:
> Believe me, lords, my tender years can tell
> Civil dissension is a viperous worm
> That gnaws the bowels of the commonwealth.
>
> (1H6, 3.1.71–73)

[to York and Somerset] :
Go cheerfully together and digest
Your angry choler on your enemies.

(4.1.167–68)

[when asked to marry the Earl of Armagnac's daughter] :
I shall be well content with any choice
Tends to God's glory and my country's weal.

(5.1.26–27)

But from his first appearance, his weakness is also apparent. Henry has no command over servants, let alone lords, and he is too easily deceived by Winchester's hypocritical reconciliation with Gloucester. After dramatizing Henry's gesture of plucking a red rose to convince York and Somerset that their quarrel is over a trifle, Shakespeare shows York to be uneasy rather than charmed: "but yet I like it not, / In that he wears the badge of Somerset" (4.1.176-77). Henry would have done better to have worn both a red and a white rose rather than one or the other. Also Henry does not restrain Winchester's ambitions as had his father, who according to Exeter had prophesied that if Winchester became a cardinal he would "make his cap co-equal with the crown" (5.1.33), and so Winchester does become a cardinal. But by far Henry's most serious error is to allow himself to be persuaded by Suffolk, who thinks him a "wooden thing" (5.3.89), to marry Lady Margaret. The "sharp dissension" he feels in his breast as he impatiently awaits her arrival soon is mirrored by dissension within the royal family and then within the state.

Before long, Margaret publicly criticizes her husband: "all his mind is bent to holiness" (*2H6*, 1.3.55). In fact, however, his holiness is of a peculiar kind. He is quick to apply the rhetoric of piety, telling the Cardinal and Gloucester that Heaven is "the treasury of everlasting joy" (2.1.18). In asking his wife to stay out of the quarrel with Humphrey, he tells her, "blessed are the peacemakers on earth" (2.1.34). He assures Humphrey in removing him from office that

"God shall be my hope, / My stay, my guide, and lantern to my feet" (2.3.24-25). Without making any inquiry, he accepts the claim by Simpcox of a miracle: "Now, God be praised . . . !" (2.1.66). But he does almost nothing to fulfill his obligations as "vicar of God," as "vicegerent of Jesus Christ on earth," that is, his obligations as king (*Bracton*, p.33).

To take just one example, in his function as head of the judiciary, a king could not personally judge, yet he had "legal ubiquity" (Kantorowicz, *The King's Two Bodies*, pp. 4-5). It was his responsibility to "cause all judgments to be given with equity and mercy . . . in order that by his justice all men may enjoy unbroken peace" (*Bracton*, p. 304). But when members of the council accused Humphrey of treason, though Henry claimed, "My conscience tells me you are innocent" (*2H6*, 3.1.141), Henry abandoned Humphrey to his accusers:

> My lords, what to your wisdoms seemeth best,
> Do, or undo, as if ourself were here.
>
> (*2H6*, 3.1.195–96)

Though in the next scene he calls for Humphrey in order to try his case, it is too late. Thanks to Henry's ignorance of events transpiring in the council chamber, Humphrey's death can be plotted and executed without the king's interference.

In ordering Margaret to cease pleading for Suffolk when Henry has ordered him banished, Henry asserts,

> Had I but said, I would have kept my word;
> But when I swear, it is irrevocable.
>
> (3.2.292–93)

But his pledge to the daughter of the Earl of Armagnac had been of short duration, and his word sent to York that Somerset was imprisoned in the Tower endured even less time (4.9.38-40), for Somerset was in his presence when he went to meet York though Henry tried to get him to hide. York rages, "False King! Why hast thou broken faith with me" (5.1.91), and seizes the occasion to break openly with Henry:

> King did I call thee? No, thou are not king;
> Not fit to govern and rule multitudes.
> Which dar'st not, no, nor canst not rule a traitor.
>
> (5.1.93–95)

Henry thinks that his legacy to his son will be his "virtuous deeds" (*3H6*, 2.2.49), and in knighting the prince he bids him to "learn this . . . lesson: Draw thy sword in right" (2.2.62). But Henry's virtue (called "catastrophic" by Brockbank[16]) is little more than rhetoric employed on suitable occasions. As Pierce observed in *Shakespeare's History Plays*, Henry's asceticism vanished quickly at Suffolk's descriptions of Margaret in *1 Henry VI* (p. 37). When necessary Henry resorts to less than ideal means, such as in appealing to his lords' desire for vengeance in unseating York:

> Earl of Northumberland, he slew thy father,
> And thine, Lord Clifford, and you both have vow'd revenge
> On him, his sons, his favourites, and his friends.
>
> (1.1.54–56)

He is unprepared to deal with the Cade rebellion and plans only to "send some holy bishop to entreat" (*2H6*, 4.4.9); he cannot protect Lord Say, for he must flee. He is intimidated by everyone: by Warwick in Parliament (*3H6*, 1.1.), by Margaret who will not abide by his decisions and takes to the field, by Clifford who will not allow him to speak (*3H6*, 2.2.121-22), and finally by the very thought of governing, so that he names Warwick and Clarence to rule for him:

> I make you both Protectors of this land,
> While I myself will lead a private life.
>
> (4.6.41–42)

Though Henry comes to recognize his responsibility when he resolves to "learn to govern better" (*2H6*, 4.9.47) and regrets

> How will the country for these woeful chances
> Misthink the King and not be satisfied!
>
> (*3H6*, 2.5.107–8)

there is no apparent improvement. Where he had once been labeled "bookish" (*2H6*, 1.1.260) and "virtuous" (1.2.20), he comes to be labeled "base, fearful, and despairing" (*3H6*, 1.1.184), "faint-hearted and degenerate King" (1.1.189) with "no spark of honour" (1.1.190) when it becomes clear that there is no principle that he will enforce, not even family loyalty to his son whom he agrees to disinherit, nor responsibility for the land that he abandons to Warwick and Clarence.

Thus Henry's weaknesses as a man, as head of his family, and as head of state all become apparent in the three plays named for him. His downfall as king results from failings in each separate component of the composite function of king, so that at times retribution for sin seems to be an equally strong explanation for events as lack of leadership.[17] When Margaret tells Henry to feast his eyes on York's head, which is perched on the walls of his city, Henry prays,

> Withhold revenge, dear God! 'tis not my fault,
> Nor wittingly have I infring'd my vow.
>
> (*3H6*, 2.2.7–8)

But Henry's vow was broken through his failure to rule within his own household, and that also meant in this particular instance within his kingdom. In sum, Henry's version of the crown consisted of "gestures of royalty" and "political insights . . . as lessons learned by rote" with no base in the "political mastery" that could give substance to the gestures and enforce the insights.[18] Despite Henry's political failure, however, Shakespeare does manage "to arouse a measure of sympathy" for this man "as the conscience of his ravaged country."[19] But after a brief restoration made possible when Edward overconfidently relaxes his vigilance, Henry's version of the Crown is finally rejected by lords and commons alike.

The previous section has shown the progressive disenchantment of the commoners with Henry's inadequate rule —how they supported Henry while he was capable of responding to their pressure to temporarily reconcile Winchester and Gloucester and to banish Suffolk. Now it is seen that Henry is deserted when he disinherits his son and when he gives up all pretenses of ruling by making Warwick and Clifford the "protectors." As Henry Kelly points out, Polydore Vergil observed that "the command of a nation rarely follows after a person who flees from it."[20] Shakespeare's successive portraits of several lords records a similar disenchantment with Henry's regal model so that the support he commanded as a matter of course as heir to Henry V when the first play opened is thoroughly dissipated by the end of the third play. The discussion of the Yorkists below will further illustrate the disenchantment with Henry and the attention Shakespeare devoted to specifying the requirements necessary to be king.

Margaret, the other spokesman for the Lancastrian cause, does not provide a version of the Crown that is any more acceptable to her new countrymen than was Henry's. As woman, wife, and queen she is even more discredited than her husband. First at a personal level, the desire for vengeance that she manifests against Lady Eleanor (*2H6*, 1.3.82) persists through her horrible torturing of York, whom she needlessly stabs, to her ahistorical reappearance in *Richard III* where she calls effective curses down upon all who have crossed her in the past. As Henry's wife, her role was ill-fated from the beginning, a fact that she reveals by describing her difficult journey to England (*2H6*, 3.2.81ff.). She tells several lords that Henry is "too full of foolish pity" (3.1.225) and compares his favoring Humphrey with a child's not seeing the snake that will sting him because he is pleased by the flowers that hide it (3.1.228-30).

When Henry orders Suffolk's banishment, Margaret curses
Henry as soon as he leaves the room:

> Mischance and sorrow go along with you!
> Heart's Discontent and sour Affliction
> Be playfellows to keep you company!
> There's two of you; the Devil make a third!
>
> (*2H6*, 3.2.299–302)

The most serious rift within the royal family follows
Henry's agreeing to disinherit her son. Margaret asserts
her primary allegiance to the dynasty, not to the king or
kingdom, and "divorces" herself (*3H6*, 1.1.254) so that
she can be free to lead the Northern lords in battle against
the House of York. When asked to remain with Henry,
the prince chooses to follow his mother. When, before the
Towton battle, Henry rejoins Margaret despite his fear of
God's vengeance at Margaret's breaking his word given in
Parliament, Margaret orders Henry to "Defy them then,
or else hold close thy lips" (2.2.118).

As a queen, Margaret dismisses the petitioners to the
Lord Protector as "base cullions" (*2H6*, 1.3.40) and tears
their petition. She scorns the Lord Protector's wife whom
she disdains, from the lofty position of queen, as "base-
born" (1.3.83). She intervenes actively in the council, despite Henry's presence there, by beginning the accusations
against Humphrey (2.1.32). Rather than accepting a decision by king-in-parliament that disinherits her son, she takes
to the field with an army (*3H6*, 1.1.258–61). She does not
submit to the English Crown-in-Parliament as sovereign
power in the realm.

> . . . I here divorce myself
> Both from thy table, Henry, and thy bed,
> Until that act of parliament be repeal'd
> Whereby my son is disinherited.
> The northern lords, that have forsworn thy colours,
> Will follow mine. . . .
>
> (*3H6*, 1.1.254–59)

Her definition of sovereignty, like the absolutist French definitions, is that it lies solely in the Crown and is unlimited. "Art thou King, and wilt be forc'd?" (*3H6*, 1.1.237) she asks Henry on learning of the decision naming York as heir to the throne.

Despite the horror of her seeing her son stabbed, Margaret does not appear in a favorable light at the end of Henry's reign, because the memory of her crimes is too strong to be easily forgotten. It was she who first allowed the slaughtering of children in these wars and it was she who approved by her own example the torturing of their parents. So that from the narrowest personal level through the familial to the broadest national plane, Margaret's version of absolutist rule, because unrestrained by any laws whether constitutional or moral, is thoroughly discredited by her example.

Family unity within the ruling family is a theme that recurs through all Shakespeare's English history plays. In the first tetralogy both the Yorkist and Lancastrian families are disrupted by dissension. Margaret and her son both disagree with Henry, and he in turn is not pleased with their actions. Among the Yorkists, Clarence and Richard are both angered at Edward's marriage; Clarence temporarily deserts his brother, and Richard reveals his personal ambitions to "get a crown" (*3H6*, 3.2.194) despite the "many lives [that] stand between me and home" (3.2.173). The parallel disloyalties among families of the two factions explain in part why neither side is particularly attractive during the struggle in these plays. One does not find one family consistently presenting a united front against all challengers. There are alternations between the two families in terms of their internal harmony; victory or defeat tends to follow the alternations. Edward loses while Clarence is a member of the Lancastrian party, for example; Edward wins when his brothers stand united with him. Henry maintains his tenuous hold on the Crown so long as a semblance of family unity is maintained; but once Margaret and her son have deserted him, despite their technically representing the same side, they are subject to defeat first at Towton, then at Tewkesbury. One of the most horrible aspects of Richard as claimant to the throne is his disregard of family loyalty—brother, wife, mother, and nephews are all subject to his manipulation and, with the exception of his mother, his murdering reach. In the second tetralogy there will be a contrast between an essentially unified family and disunified challengers that leaves little doubt as to which is the preferable party to rule the country. Only once in both tetralogies is Shakespeare's audience (and the dramatis personae) faced with the dilemma of choosing between a well-unified rebel faction and a disunified royal family—just before York is killed. In the scene of his death, York wins sympathy from all who behold him (except Margaret and Clifford). Thus unity within the contending party comes to be associated with the right to the Crown.

Henry's failings as king are given greater urgency by the presence of a rival claimant to the throne, York. To the extent that he can do so, York emphasizes that he is strong in just those areas where Henry is most weak. Where Henry accepts the losses of French territories through the terms of the marriage treaty ("They please us well" [*2H6*, 1.1.62]), York is incensed. He compares the peers' agreeing to the loss of the territories to pirates' squandering their takings. Where Henry accepts the losses of French territories through revolt ("Cold news. . . , but God's will be done!" [3.1.86]), this loss spurs York to resolve, "Now, . . . or never" (3.1.332) for his claim to the throne. Though Shakespeare does not show York pledging that he will regain French territories, that hope is probably in Warwick's mind when he joins his father in supporting York, for Warwick reminds Henry in Parliament, "Talk not of France, sith thou has lost it all" (*3H6*, 1.1.110). York, moreover, wants to be king and to rule:

> Ah! Sancta majestas, who'd not buy thee dear?
> Let them obey that knows not how to rule,

> (*2H6*, 5.1.5–6)

while Henry is eager to surrender everything but the name of king throughout his reign, from his first relying on Humphrey's legal knowledge through his naming Clarence and Warwick protectors.

York offers another contrast to Henry in his reluctance to break his word. Henry cannot stop Margaret from breaking his pledge given in Parliament to make York his heir. York, however, refuses to break his oath until Richard argues that an oath given to a usurper has no value (this incident is further discussed in chapter 2 D). Since the audience knows during this exchange that Margaret's forces are already on their way, York's being persuaded to break his oath does not wholly discredit him; he remains slightly more honorable than Henry. York resolves to "trust not simple Henry nor his oaths" (*3H6*, 1.2.59). He is too late, however, to prepare adequately for his defense because Margaret has seized the initiative. York is captured, tortured, and killed in a scene that arouses pity for York even among the Lancastrians.

York had carefully prepared his approach to the throne. He first won the support of Salisbury and his son Warwick, the most powerful lord in the realm. Next he employed Jack Cade to masquerade as the deceased John Mortimer who named York his heir as claimant to the throne.

> By this I shall perceive the commons' mind,
> How they affect the house and claim of York.
>
> (*2H6*, 3.1.374–75)

The "commons" do respond to Cade though the revolt is short-lived, since Clifford and Buckingham win back their allegiance and Cade is killed. But York decides to press his claim even if he must dissemble until his strength is sufficient.

Upon seeing Somerset in Henry's presence after having been given Buckingham's word as Henry's agent that he was a prisoner, York announces his two motives before all the court for claiming the throne:

That head of thine doth not become a crown;
Thy hand is made to grasp a palmer's staff,
And not to grace an awful princely sceptre.
That gold must round engirt these brows of mine,
Whose smile and frown, like to Achilles' spear,
Is able with the change to kill and cure.
Here is a hand to hold a sceptre up,
And with the same to act controlling laws.

(*2H6*, 5.1.96–103)

York is offering himself as a contrast to Henry in terms of his presumed ability to maintain law and order. Once having assured himself of the sanction of some support by important lords and the commons, York declares that Henry was not made to be king and should not be king when there is another, namely himself, willing and able to enact and enforce law; he makes no mention of hereditary right. Then in immediate proof of the assertions that York has made contrasting Henry with himself when alone in the presence of the king's supporters, Henry allows York to call in men of his faction to substantiate his claim. First his sons Edward and Richard enter, then the Earls of Warwick and Salisbury. York's party is too substantial at the end of the scene for him to be seized as a traitor, whereas at the beginning he could have been overpowered despite his verbal refusal to be arrested.

At the confrontation with York in Parliament, Henry laments, "When I was crown'd I was but nine months old" (*3H6*, 1.1.112). But Richard counters with perhaps the key line in this dynastic struggle, "You are old enough now" (1.1.113). It is time that Henry, like Fastolfe before him, be held accountable for his failings and that Henry assume responsibility for his reign. But B. P. Wolffe, in a recent essay on the role of Henry VI, points out that "in the fifteenth century and for a long time afterwards there was still no machinery for changing the government when that government, the king, was adult and responsible for its own actions—except by the so-called 'Wars of the Roses.' "[21] The long period of grace accorded to Henry is now at an end. Henry feels powerless to resist York: "I know not what to say: my title's weak" (1.1.138), so he proposes making York his heir. However, Henry V, whose claim was even weaker because he was one generation closer than Henry VI to Richard II's deposition, would never have made such a concession. As Young Clifford points out, Henry V would not even have allowed a York to make a claim to the throne: "He durst not sit there [on the throne] had your father liv'd" (1.1.63).

The temporary solution agreed to by King and Parliament allows Henry to be king through his lifetime despite his weak title but specifies that he will be succeeded by York and his heirs despite their not being in current possession of the Crown. Thus, for the Crown-in-Parliament at this first ideological confrontation between York and Lancaster, Shakespeare shows that the primary criterion for wearing the crown is neither hereditary legitimacy nor possession but the ability to assure peace. Maintenance of order and stability in the realm is thus publicly acknowledged to be more important than possession or hereditary title in determining who is king. Those agreeing to the decision mistakenly believe that the Lancastrian supporters will be satisfied if Lancastrian rule ends with Henry VI and that the Yorkists will patiently mark time during Henry's inadequate rule so that this compromise will provide for an orderly succession. They will all learn, painfully, that to function effectively the Crown requires more support than can be provided by an isolated parliamentary agreement.

Edward wins the Crown as York's heir in the Towton battle. His first actions are majestical—his ordering that any surviver "be gently us'd" (*3H6*, 2.6.45), his agreeing to make a French alliance, and his pledging to consult with Warwick. But unlike his father, he shows little concern for the opinion of his commons or for the value of keeping his word and respecting the importance of the law in securing support. He breaks his pledge to marry Lady Bona by choosing instead Lady Grey. This choice blurs the distinction between the two houses of York and Lancaster, for

Edward is following Henry's example of marrying for his own pleasure rather than for the good of the realm. By breaking his word and disgracing his ambassador, Edward also severely undermines his ability to continue the Yorkist position as maintainers of law and order.

A sidelight on Edward's new interpretation of the Crown is provided by King Lewis's questions about the English king.

> Now, Warwick, tell me, even upon thy conscience,
> Is Edward your true king? for I were loath
> To link with him that were not lawful chosen.
>
> . . . .
> But is he gracious in the people's eyes?
>
> (*3H6*, 3.3.113–17)

He concludes, after Warwick's affirmative replies, that the Lancastrian title is weak, "As may appear by Edward's good success" (3.3.146). His criteria are those of the *Mirror for Magistrates* passage quoted in chapter 1—if a people accept their king and if he obtains the crown "lawfully," then there are no grounds for interference; furthermore, those two factors of lawfulness and acceptance add up to "good success." When news of Edward's marriage outrages Warwick, who then announces his own desertion of Edward and Clarence's impending defection, the tenuousness of Edward's lawfulness and acceptance is made apparent. King Lewis pledges to the newly allied Margaret and Warwick aid in unseating the very man he had been careful to respect not five minutes before, Edward, whom he now calls "false Edward, thy supposed king" (3.3.223). They all set about the business of restoring Henry VI to the English throne. His "pedigree / Of threescore and two years—a silly time" (3.3.93) is now considered to be adequate.

Edward compounds his error of marrying Lady Grey by repeatedly asserting his essential lawlessness:

> . . . I am Edward,

Your King and Warwick's, and must have my will.
(*3H6*, 4.1.15–16)

. . . it was my will and grant;
And for this once my will shall stand for law.
(4.1.48–49)

So that modified only by a slightly more elegant manner of expression, Edward's pronouncements sound like Cade's: "my mouth shall be the parliament of England" (*2H6*, 4.7.14).

Though Edward briefly loses the crown to Henry's forces, Henry's "pity," "mildness," and "mercy" (*3H6*, 4.8.41-43) are no match for the martial Yorkists. "Authority counts for more than good intentions," as H. S. Richmond suggests (*Shakespeare's Political Plays,* p. 72). Edward is quickly restored to the throne despite the fact that in Shakespeare's version he is not a very good king or strategist (p. 71). His first action after the battle of Tewkesbury is to stab the defenseless prince, and though his regret is almost immediate, "Hold, Richard, hold; for we have done too much" (5.5.42), it is too late to erase the horror of his impetuous action. His plans for the kingdom consist only of "stately triumphs, mirthful comic shows, / Such as befits the pleasure of the court?" (5.7.43-44), until he is on his deathbed, when he tries to reconcile his brothers with the new nobility, the relatives of the queen. So that as a man, as head of his family, and as head of his kingdom, Shakespeare's Edward IV is not an improvement over his Henry VI. But with the Lancastrian Prince Edward dead, there is no rival contender for the throne, so Edward IV ends his reign unchallenged. It is the absence of a rival contender rather than Edward's being lineal heir that wins him support in Shakespeare's play.

Edward's reconciliation between the new and old nobility is short-lived. After the several dynastic changes of the Lancastrian-Yorkist struggle, length of accomplishment as a goal to be striven for is a lesson understood even by the young prince, Edward's son.

That Julius Caesar was a famous man;
With what his valour did enrich his wit,
His wit set down to make his valour live:
Death makes no conquest of this conqueror,
For now he lives in fame, though not in life.

(*3H6*, 3.1.84–88)

Then he adds to his comment on the length of Caesar's fame a statement of his own intentions as future king:

An if I live until I be a man,
I'll win our ancient right in France again,
Or die a soldier, as I lived a king.

(3.1.91–93)

Within the context of the Wars of the Roses, the prince's desire to emulate Henry V by reconquering the territories he had conquered is misplaced. The juxtaposition of the longevity of Caesar's fame with the need to reaccomplish Henry V's achievements emphasizes Henry's failure.

As viewed from the chaos of the reigns of Henry VI and his immediate successors, the days of Henry V did appear to be golden. In the very first scene of *1 Henry VI*, when it would soon be revealed that soldiers were close to mutiny in France because of the quarreling nobility at home, Henry V was praised as "famous," "worthy," as someone who "commanded" and "conquered" (*1H6*, 1.1.6-16). Only old Mortimer remembered Henry as a bloody tyrant (2.5.100) because he imprisoned him to stop, for a time, the Mortimer claim to the throne. Most lords favorably remembered his conquest of the French and the firmness with which he kept his nobles in check. Winchester was not able to obtain the position of cardinal while he lived (5.1.28-33); rivals had no serious opportunity to claim the throne. When Prince Edward banished all cowards from their ranks before the battle of Tewkesbury, Oxford rejoiced at the reincarnation of Henry V:

O brave young Prince! thy famous grandfather

Doth live again in thee: long may'st thou live
To bear his image and renew his glories!

$$(3H6, 5.4.52\text{-}54)$$

The prince, however, does not live long. He is stabbed by the new King Edward IV after being defeated in battle. Edward V, who similarly emulates Henry V, also does not live long, for Shakespeare shows the newly crowned Richard immediately arranging for his assassination.

Richard acknowledges two sanctions as necessary to possession of the Crown; they are hereditary right and acceptance by the people. He manipulates both by arranging for the murder or discrediting of all those who are before him in line for the throne and by using his own and Buckingham's retainers to give the impression of popular support in being acclaimed king. These sanctions are his "ladder to the throne" (Prior, *The Drama of Power*, p. 120). But once king, he wants absolute obedience, for when Buckingham hesitates before agreeing to the death of the princes, Richard reveals, "None are for me / That look into me with considerate eyes" (*R3*, 4.2.29-30). As John Palmer points out in *Political and Comic Characters of Shakespeare*, "Buckingham lost his head the moment he claimed the right to think for himself" (p. 97).

Richard's tenure, however, despite his securing the semblance of hereditary and popular legitimacy, is brief. He had told Henry VI as he stabbed him, "For this, amongst the rest, was I ordain'd" (*3H6*, 5.6.58). In his path to the throne he executed all those still alive who had betrayed the commonwealth to serve their own ends—Clarence, Hastings, Rivers, Vaughan, Grey, and Buckingham. He can accomplish all this because

he gathers within himself Joan's duplicity, Eleanor's aspirations, Winchester's pride, Buckingham's and Somerset's ambition, Margaret's and Suffolk's scheming, Clifford's revengeful fury, and, above all, York's intense passion. [Hamilton, *The Early Shakespeare*, p. 187]

His rise to power and his elimination are dramatized less as constitutional than as moral phenomena. M. M. Reese has pointed out the lack of political interest in this play,[22] and Lily Bess Campbell has commented on the relative absence of political speeches.[23] Richard's reign in constitutional terms as dramatized by Shakespeare mainly provides a close to the parentheses opened and expounded in the earlier plays. Richmond is only briefly introduced so that his virtuous contrast to Richard is a given rather than a demonstrated fact. His taking arms with foreign troops against a wearer of the English crown is minimized. Emphasis is instead placed on his acting with popular approval. He calls his captains in, as in *1H6*, 1.4.61ff. did the old Earl of Salisbury; Richmond says, "Let us consult upon tomorrow's business" (*R3*, 5.3.45) while Richard plans alone the deposition of his troops (5.3.290ff.). Richmond considers his soldiers to be his "fellows in arms, and my most loving friends" (5.2.1), while Richard recognizes that "there is no creature loves me" (5.3.200). Above all, Richmond characterizes Richard not as his personal enemy but as England's enemy, a

> usurping boar,
> That spoils your summer fields . . . ,
> Swills your warm blood . . . , and makes his trough
> In your embowelled bosoms. . . .
>
> (5.2.7–10)

Richmond invokes God's name some twenty times in four brief appearances. Unlike Henry VI, however, his references to God do not keep him from acting on earth. In his concluding prayer for "smooth-faced peace, / With smiling plenty and fair prosperous days!" (5.5.33-34), Richmond for the first time in this tetralogy brings the sanction of active concern for the common good with his claim to the throne. Neither possession nor hereditary legitimacy have proved adequate without that concern. Richard becomes a scapegoat whose banishment carries with it the flaws of the participants in the dynastic feuds. Above all, Richard takes with him the relish for military conquests, thereby at last freeing the Crown from the martial criteria that diverted energies from domestic reform. We have come far from the praise for the conquering Henry V that opened the tetralogy to Henry VII's prayer for peace. I think, however, that Wilbur Sanders is correct in his skepticism about Richmond's curtain speech: ". . . the kind of human/critical awareness which Shakespeare has set in motion in the course of the play makes short work of the platitude with which he tries to wind it up. He has created an audience which is now too wary of simplifications to be fobbed off with this one."[24]

D. The Law

Law is dramatized with even less ease than lords and commoners, for it is more abstract. In the first tetralogy, in fact, sometimes *law* seems to be whatever individuals say it is. Cade would decree the laws of England from his lips; King Henry states that the law is what Humphrey says it is (*2H6*, 1.3.210)[25]; Edward IV would have his will stand for law; York demands the full "rigour" of the law for Horner (*2H6*, 1.3.196) without specifying what that means; Buckingham and Gloucester claim to respect the law but really do not (*R3*, 3.4.36-41). Some attention is given to the relationship between the individual and higher law when Clarence pleads with the murderers not to transgress the law of the "great King of kings" (*R3*, 1.4.200). But both murderers point out that Clarence has no right to make such a plea since he himself disregarded God's law in breaking his oath of loyalty to the House of Lancaster and in killing Prince Edward. Clarence admits that it is "commodity" that creates his newfound respect for God's law.

> Which of you, if you were a prince's son,
> Being pent from liberty, as I am now,

If two such murderers as yourselves came to you,
Would not entreat for life?

(*R3*, 1.4.257–60)

On that note the first murderer stabs him while the second
regrets and fears for his conscience, hardly an overwhelming
demonstration of the power of reason operating in each man
to maintain orderly societal relations. In their last moments
in *Richard III* many characters remember their lawless acts
in the Wars of the Roses; then in the highly artificial dream
sequences in which Richmond is blessed and Richard is
cursed for his misdeeds, Shakespeare emphasizes the ne-
glected law of conscience and shows it to be working in the
first tetralogy.

There are also brief references to equity, to the law of
arms, to officers of the law, to customary law. Yet amid
this diversity, it is possible to discern faint outlines of some
unifying themes—one, that the law most often cited concerns respect for certain places; two, that the law cannot
maintain itself and is therefore only as strong or as weak
as those responsible for enforcing it; three, that by far the
one legal aspect of societal relationships that is given the
greatest attention is the giving and renouncing of an oath
of fealty.

The custom of respecting certain public places appears
four times—in reference to the Tower of London, to the
Inns of Court, to the presence of the king, and to the House
of Parliament. The custom is more observed in the breach,
however. Winchester feels no compunctions about initiating
combat at the Tower, and Gloucester disregards the rule—
"Draw, men, for all this privileged place" (*1H6*, 1.3.46).
In the rose-plucking scene Plantaganet claims that Somerset
is "braving" him because he knows he is safe from fighting
there—"He bears him on the place's privilege" (2.4.86);
perhaps that is so, but it is curious that the law school is
the only place where the rule of noncombat is observed.
The King's presence is violated by the skirmish of Gloucester and Winchester's servants (3.1.85,91), and the Parlia-

ment House is threatened by Warwick's armed men in
3H6, 1.1.171.

In discussing Henry and Humphrey's handling of the
Peter/Horner incident, the "trials" and execution of Humphrey, Suffolk, and Say (and Hastings, which I did not
discuss), I have largely covered the second theme from
other perspectives, so there is no need to analyze these incidents again here. The pride that Thomas Smith evidenced
in the working of the English judicial system would not be
justified by what is seen in these plays. Only the trial of
judgment by battle, which Smith considered to be "in dis-
use" (*De Republica Anglorum,* p. 64), functioned effectively when the drunken Horner, who was defeated by his
terrified apprentice, called out, "Hold, Peter, hold! I confess, I confess treason" (*2H6*, 2.3.91), before he died.
Treason of high ranking noblemen such as Humphrey,
Suffolk, or Hastings should have been judged by Parliament
sitting as a court (Smith, *De Republica Anglorum,* p. 107).
Written evidence was to be shown, witnesses were to be
heard openly, and verdicts were to be unanimous (p. 80).
None of this was true for any of the condemnations in the
first tetralogy.

There can be little wonder at the inadequate functioning
of the law when so many in positions of leadership admit
to lack of legal knowledge. Suffolk is the first to reveal his
ignorance during the initial choosing of sides in the Wars of
the Roses. The choosing takes place in the garden alongside
Temple Hall, one of the Inns of Court that were the train-
ing centers of the legal profession. The quarrel is over a
point of law that is not explained or understood by the
participants in the quarrel.

> SUFFOLK. . . . I have been a truant in the law
> And never yet could frame my will to it;
> And therefore frame the law unto my will.
> (*1H6*, 2.4.7–9)

Warwick is next.

> . . . in these sharp quillets of the law,
> Good faith, I am no wiser than a daw.
>
> (2.4.17–18)

Henry is the third person who admits to ignorance of the law when he asks Humphrey, "Uncle, what shall we say to this in law?" (*2H6*, 1.3.203), when faced with the Peter/Horner incident.

Because of England's unique system of lawmaking, which required consent by Crown and Parliament for the enactment of law, especially because Parliament was considered to be a representative body so that consent of Parliament signified every man's consent, ignorance of the law was not justification for breaking it. Saint German said in the *Doctor and Student*:

> They that have taken upon them to have knowledge of the law, be not excused by ignorance of the law; nay no more are they that have a willful ignorance, and that would rather be ignorant than to know the truth, and therefore they will not dispose them to ask any counsel in it. And if it be of a thing that is against the law of God, or the law of reason, no man shall be excused of ignorance.[26]

Henry, despite his not knowing what specific remedies the law provides, says that justice is sure and right prevails:

> To-morrow toward London back again
> To look into this business thoroughly,
> And call these foul offenders to their answers;
> And poise the cause in Justice' equal scales,
> Whose beam stands sure, whose rightful cause prevails.
>
> (*2H6*, 2.1.193–97)

Yet one knows that during his reign the state of justice would not have been accurately pictured by Henry's description, and since he was sovereign, the fault was largely his own. As Saint German points out, also in *Doctor and Student*:

> our sovereign lord the king, at his coronation, among other things,

takes a solemn oath that he shall cause all the customs of his realm faithfully to be observed. [P. 19]

The two main references to feudal law, aside from the oaths of fealty, are in the Towton battle and at York. The son unknowingly kills his father because

> From London by the King was I press'd forth;
> My father, being the Earl of Warwick's man,
> Came on the part of York, press'd by his master. . . .
> <div align="right">(<i>3H6</i>, 2.5.64–66)</div>

As I have already indicated, in section 2A, feudal oaths placed service to the king above the obligation to serve one's lord, so that technically Warwick's man should not have followed him to battle against the king. There was one important exception to the feudal oath that possibly exempted Warwick and his man from duty to the king; this exception is mentioned in the exchange between King Edward and the Mayor of York. The gates of the city are closed to him when he arrives, so Edward reminds the Mayor, "if Henry be your king, Yet Edward, at the least, is Duke of York"; then he pledges, "Why, and I challenge nothing but my dukedom, / As being well content with that alone" (<i>3H6</i>, 4.7.21-24). In exchange for the keys to the city he promises that

> Edward will defend the town and thee
> And all those friends that deign to follow me.
> (4.7.38–39)

This promise of protection in exchange for loyalty was the key to the feudal arrangement, as Gloucester's servants were well aware. Despite the fact that none of the many oaths of fealty dramatized in the first tetralogy (two by York, one by Talbot, one by the Governor of Paris) make any mention of the lord's obligation, Shakespeare shows that that obligation was understood by every character in the play and provided the one means for a vassal to legally renounce his vassalage.

Dating from the eighth century in France and transferred to England with the introduction into England of feudalism after the Norman conquest, the oath of fealty became the means of confirming a feudal relationship between lord and vassal. "A man violating a sworn oath thereby rendered himself guilty of perjury, which was a mortal sin, and in an age of faith this would mean a good deal."[27] The Governor of Paris swears fealty to Henry VI at his coronation but eventually breaks that oath because by the end of Henry's reign the French territories are lost. Burgundy sends word to Henry at his coronation that he is no longer his vassal. Salisbury and Warwick also break their pledges to Henry in order to support York; then Warwick breaks his oath again in order to return to support of Henry.

In announcing his ending of fealty to Henry, Burgundy sends a message "To the King!" that accuses Henry of the first breach in their agreement.

> "I have, upon especial cause,
> Mov'd with compassion of my country's wrack,
> Together with the pitiful complaints
> Of such as your oppression feeds upon,
> Forsaken your pernicious faction
> And join'd with Charles, the rightful King of France."
>
> (*1H6*, 4.1.55–60)

Since "the vassal had not the right to denounce the contract that bound him to his lord, unless the latter had wilfully abused his power over him," Burgundy must claim that Henry's abuses relieve him of his feudal obligation so that Henry is no longer his sovereign (Ganshof, *Feudalism*, p. 98). Similarly, Salisbury breaks his oath to Henry only after repeated examples of his incompetent rule make further allegiance to him seem detrimental to the common good. Warwick renounces his allegiance to Edward after Edward first breaks several obligations to Warwick by disgracing his embassage in marrying Lady Grey.

Plantagenet vows obedience "And humble service till the point of death" (*1H6*, 3.1.168) to Henry in order to be created Duke of York. But as seen in the section on the Crown, York feels forced into breaking this oath because of Henry's incompetence, which is symbolized for him by the loss of French territories and by his lack of faith in not imprisoning Somerset as promised. In Parliament, York "willingly" takes another oath, pledging to Henry that he will honor Henry as

> king and sovereign;
> And neither by treason nor hostility
> To seek to put [him] down and reign [my]self,
> > (*3H6*, 1.1.204–6)

in exchange for promised inheritance of the Crown. This oath he is persuaded to break by his son Richard.

> An oath is of no moment, being not took
> Before a true and lawful magistrate
> That hath authority over him that swears.
> Henry had none, but did usurp the place;
> Then, seeing 'twas he that made you to depose,
> Your oath, my lord, is vain and frivolous.
> > (1.2.22–27)

Richard's argument is based on a technicality. An oath sworn to by two gentlemen in the presence of the Parliament should have remained binding under all circumstances. But Richard knows his father's at least public respect for the legal forms of feudal society—"God forbid your Grace should be forsworn" (1.2.18). Like Humphrey before him, York seems to recognize in the adhering to oaths the very foundation of society. "Hath he forgot he is his sovereign?" Humphrey had exclaimed in reading Burgundy's message at the coronation.

> O monstrous treachery! Can this be so—
> That in alliance, amity, and oaths,
> There should be found such false dissembling guile?
> > (*1H6*, 4.1.61–63)

All of them, Burgundy, Salisbury, Warwick, and York, publicly and solemnly renounce their obligations to their kings by placing the blame for the breach of engagement on the royal party to the agreements. They do not take their actions lightly. Renouncing an oath of fealty struck at a fundamental aspect of feudal structure. Penalty for such a breach, if it could be enforced, was forfeiture of land, because rights over land, that is, fiefs, were granted in return for loyalty, as one has seen in Plantagenet's pledge to Henry in exchange for the rights over the domain of York (see Ganshof, *Feudalism*, p. 98).

But for Henry, as shown in the Crown section, keeping an oath was not essential except when given in Parliament, for it was only the breaking of that parliamentary pledge to York that upset him, not the breaking of the marriage agreement with the daughter of the Earl of Armagnac nor his perjury in telling York that Somerset was imprisoned. This last caused Henry embarrassment but not enough distress to order that Somerset be sent to the Tower to keep his word. Even Edward shows greater reluctance than Henry to break an oath, for he must be threatened with loss of Montgomery's support before he will again claim the throne and thus renounce his pledge to the Mayor of York. Yet the relationship of vassal and lord obligated the lord to keep faith just as much as the vassal (Ganshof, *Feudalism*, p. 94). So that if the penalty for a vassal's breaking faith was the loss of his fiefdom, the penalty for the lord was rebellion by the vassal. The modern sense of "to defy" meaning "to challenge" developed out of the act of renunciation which was called *renunciare* or *diffiduciare* (Ganshof, *Feudalism*, p. 98).

The first tetralogy accordingly shows that progressive disenchantment follows Henry's oath-breaking, beginning with Humphrey's distress at the marriage with Margaret and ending with York's open break in which he denies Henry's right to rule after seeing the allegedly imprisoned Somerset in Henry's presence. So that for Henry, who does not live up to the obligations imposed on him by the law and his coronation oath, the consequence is rebellion. For Richard III, who is characterized as

> A bloody tyrant and a homicide;
> One raised in blood, and one in blood established;
> One that made means to come by what he hath,
> And slaughtered those that were the means to help him;
> A base, foul stone, made precious by the foil
> Of England's chair, where he is falsely set;
> One that hath ever been God's enemy,
>
> (*R3*, 5.3.246–52)

and for all other kings portrayed by Shakespeare, the process of reaching the decision to rebel is shortened from the two and a half plays required for Henry VI's nobles and commons to ultimately reject his leadership. Once having demonstrated that people do not rebel without sufficient cause, and after having dramatized many causes in great detail, in all his subsequent history plays Shakespeare will use a form of dramatic shorthand in which one or two errors will symbolize the cumulative royal mistakes detailed in the first tetralogy.

The next, shorter, chapter on *The Life and Death of King John* argues that *John,* when considered in constitutional terms, is probably an early play, perhaps contemporaneous with *1 Henry VI. King John* contains constitutional values that are absent from and, I therefore think, rejected by Shakespeare before the completion of the two tetralogies.

NOTES TO CHAPTER 2

1. *Bracton on the Laws and Customs of England,* ed. George E. Woodbine, trans. and rev. Samuel Thorne, 2 vols. (Cambridge, Mass.: Harvard University Press, Belknap Press, 1968), 2:232.

2. David Bevington, *Tudor Drama and Politics, A Critical Approach to Topical Meaning* (Cambridge, Mass.: Harvard University Press, 1968), pp. 238–39.

3. Thomas Smith, *De Republica Anglorum,* ed. L. Alston (Cambridge: At the University Press, 1906), pp. 39–40.

4. In this same production, no doubt because of budgetary concerns, the citizens who are asked to acclaim Richard III as king wear the same costumes and have the same demeanor as the group that heralds Simpcox and the group that supports Cade.

5. John Palmer, *Political and Comic Characters of Shakespeare* (London: Macmillan, 1965), pp. 317–18. *Political Characters of Shakespeare* was originally published separately in 1945.

6. Robert Ornstein, *A Kingdom for a Stage, The Achievement of Shakespeare's History Plays* (Cambridge, Mass.: Harvard University Press, 1972), p. 50.

7. Ornstein, *A Kingdom for a Stage*, p. 38, and A. C. Hamilton, *The Early Shakespeare* (San Marino, Calif.: The Huntington Library, 1967), p. 50, make this observation also.

8. Ernst H. Kantorowicz, *The King's Two Bodies, A Study in Mediaeval Political Theology* (Princeton, N.J.: Princeton University Press, 1957), p. 316.

9. S. B. Chrimes, *English Constitutional Ideas in the Fifteenth Century* (Cambridge: At the University Press, 1936), p. 37.

10. Actually, Bedford was protector, with Gloucester stepping in to fill that role only during Bedford's absences. See ibid.

11. *Rotuli Parliamentorum ut et Petitiones et Placita in Parliamento Tempore 1278–1532* [ed. John Strachey; London: n.p., 1777?], 4:326.

12. J. A. R. Marriott, *English History in Shakespeare* (London: Chapman and Hall, 1918), p. 178.

13. John Fortescue, *The Governance of England: Otherwise Called the Difference Between an Absolute and a Limited Monarchy*, ed. Charles Plummer (Oxford: Clarendon Press, 1885), pp. 129–30.

14. Robert B. Pierce, *Shakespeare's History Plays, The Family and the State* (Columbus, Ohio: Ohio State University Press, 1971), p. 242.

15. Reginald Maxwell Woolley, *Coronation Rites* (Cambridge: At the University Press, 1915), pp. 67–70.

16. J. P. Brockbank, "The Frame of Disorder—Henry VI," in *Early Shakespeare*, ed. John R. Brown and Bernard Harris, Stratford-Upon-Avon Studies 3 (New York: St. Martin's Press, 1961), p. 98; also available in *Shakespeare, The Histories, A Collection of Critical Essays*, ed. Eugene M. Waith (Englewood Cliffs, N.J.: Prentice-Hall, 1965), p. 64.

17. Derek A. Traversi, *An Approach to Shakespeare*, 3d ed. (Garden City, N.Y.: Doubleday, 1969), p. 17.

18. H. S. Richmond, *Shakespeare's Political Plays* (New York: Random House, 1967), pp. 33–34.

19. Moody Prior, *The Drama of Power* (Evanston, Ill.: Northwestern University Press, 1973), p. 42.

20. Henry Ansgar Kelly, *Divine Providence in the England of Shakespeare's Histories* (Cambridge, Mass.: Harvard University Press, 1970), p. 95.

21. B. P. Wolffe, "The Personal Rule of Henry VI," in *Fifteenth-century England 1399–1509, Studies in Politics and Society*, ed. S. B. Chrimes

et al. (Manchester: Manchester University Press, 1972), p. 45.

22. M. M. Reese, *The Cease of Majesty, A Study of Shakespeare's History Plays* (New York: St. Martin's Press, 1961), p. 224.

23. Lily Bess Campbell, *Shakespeare's "Histories"—Mirrors of Elizabethan Policy* (San Marino, Calif.: The Huntington Library, 1947), p. 332.

24. Wilbur Sanders, *The Dramatist and the Received Idea* (Cambridge: At the University Press, 1968), p. 72.

25. In G. B. Harrison, ed., *Shakespeare, The Complete Works* (New York: Harcourt, Brace and World, 1952), this line is attributed to Gloucester, who would thus be identifying his own view and the law.

26. Christopher Saint German or Germain, *Doctor and Student: Or, Dialogues Between a Doctor of Divinity and a Student in the Laws of England* [1518], reprint, ed. William Muchall, 17th ed. (London: A. Strahen and W. Woodfall, 1787), p. 79.

27. F. L. Ganshof, *Feudalism,* trans. Philip Grierson, 2d English ed. (New York: Harper and Row, 1961), pp. 28, 165.

3

King John

The Life and Death of King John has been dated from
1590 through 1596 by J. D. Wilson (1590 and 1594),
E. A. J. Honigmann (1590-91), D. F. Ash (1596), and
G. B. Harrison (1596?), dates that would place its composition anywhere from approximately contemporaneous with
the earliest *Henry VI* plays to just before or just after *Richard II*.[1] I have decided to discuss *John* between the two
tetralogies, so that the amplitude with which constitutional
issues were developed in the first tetralogy can provide a
substantial foundation of fact upon which to approach the
relatively meager development in *John*. From a constitutional
point of view, however, it would be possible to make a
strong case for *John*'s being among the earliest of Shakespeare's English history plays. Constitutional dilemmas in
John are presented as virtually abstract exercises, whereas
in the first tetralogy, such dilemmas are treated with the
complexity that personality and circumstances can provide;
furthermore, in the second tetralogy constitutional issues are
even more closely associated with choices between people
and parties. But in *John* choices are stripped of almost all

mitigating factors so that they are reduced to bald alternatives: which is to be honored, possession or hereditary title, for instance, is the dilemma faced by the citizens of Angiers. Moreover, constitutional solutions that are simplistic when compared with the solutions presented in the first tetralogy are seriously entertained in *John*.

A. The Commons

Except for the briefest of references to professions, no information is provided about the people in *John*. Shakespeare does not have them mention what economic grievances they have, as he does for Cade's followers and Simpcox, or what lords they respect, for instance. The "citizens" are basically abstractions, a fact that is reinforced by the rubric "1. citizen" used to designate a speaker. "Citizens" is the label used in this play for the occupants of the city of Angiers rather than "commons" of the first tetralogy. I doubt whether there is much significance to this change in terminology, since the preoccupations of the people so labeled are much the same—prosperity and peace. The main difference between the "citizens" of this play and the "commons" of the first tetralogy is that the citizens are eloquent, a fact commented on with characteristic exaggeration by Faulconbridge:

> What cannonneer begot this lusty blood?
> He speaks plain cannon fire, and smoke, and bounce;
> He gives the bastinado with his tongue;
> Our ears are cudgell'd; not a word of his
> But buffets better than a fist of France.
> Zounds! I was never so bethump'd with words
> Since I first call'd my brother's father dad.

> (2.1.461–67)

When asked to choose between King Philip, who presents Arthur's claim as lineal heir, and King John, who presents his own claim as possessor of the Crown, the citizens declare,

In brief, we are the king of England's subjects:
For him, and in his right, we hold this town.

. . . .

. . . he that proves the king,
To him will we prove loyal: till that time
Have we ramm'd up our gates against the world.

(2.1.267–72)

What will prove the king is military prowess, which will
signify the ability to protect the town. When the two armies
show themselves to be equally matched, the citizens persist
in their refusal to choose.

Blood hath bought blood and blows have answer'd blows;
Strength match'd with strength, and power confronted power:
Both are alike, and both alike we like.
One must prove greatest: while they weigh so even,
We hold our town for neither, yet for both.

(2.1.329–33)

There has been considerable difficulty for editors of this
play in assigning speech-headings in act 2, scene 1. As Wilson summarizes the problem,

at his earliest appearance (2.1.200) the First Citizen is abbrevi-
ated "Cit." in the speech-heading of the Folio text, but from l.325
onwards all his speeches are headed "Hub." except one at l.368
which is by accident attributed to "Fra." (= France, i.e. Philip
of France). [P. xlvi]

Various explanations and solutions have been adopted. It
has been suggested that the problem arose through the
same actor's doubling the two parts. Some editors, such as
Harrison, have rigorously separated the two parts so that
Hubert does not appear in this scene at all. Others, such as
Wilson, argue from John's gratitude (3.2.29-38) toward
Hubert that Hubert was the Angiers citizen who proposed
that Blanch and the Dauphin marry to avert the threatened
destruction of their city (p. xlvi). Though Wilson uses
"citizen" to designate the speaker in all of act 2, scene 1,

Honigmann replaces "citizen" in all speech headings by "Hubert." In that the Frenchman Melun reveals later that he knows Hubert but that Hubert is with John, one could argue either that Hubert was from Angiers or that he was always in service at the English court. I prefer the solution adopted by Wilson and Harrison in using "citizen" consistently throughout this scene so that Hubert remains an Englishman closely identified with English traditions and not an Angiers citizen who wins a place at the English court. But any interpretation of the play, such as my own, which is based in part on the editorial decision by Wilson and Harrison does have less than an absolutely secure foundation in textual history.

Thus far in the play there are several thematic similarities between *John* and the first tetralogy. By allowing the citizens a chance to choose between them, John and Philip seem to be elevating to a principle what is a recurring theme in the first tetralogy, that is, the power and importance of citizens' support for a king. John and Philip, like York and Henry VI, know that they cannot rule without citizens' support. And, like the commons in the first tetralogy, the citizens in *John* care less for the sanctions of lineality or possession than for ability, which here means military might. Were John and Philip unequally matched and were the citizens to prefer the claim of the weaker of the two, he could not guarantee their safety. Therefore, the citizens trust to trial by combat, which functions so effectively in the Peter/Horner dispute in the first tetralogy. In *John* the trials twice result in a draw, a verdict that the citizens (or Hubert) but not the kings accept.

> A greater power than we denies all this;
> And till it be undoubted, we do lock
> Our former scruple in our strong-barr'd gates:
> Kings of our fear, until our fears, resolv'd,
> Be by some certain king purg'd and depos'd.
>
> (2.1.368–72)

The kings, at Faulconbridge's suggestion, agree to wreck

the town that refuses to choose between them, thereby denying the respect they had earlier seemed to demonstrate for the right of the governed to choose their magistrate.

After proposing that Blanch and the Dauphin marry, a proposal that avoids war until Pandulph intervenes, citizens disappear from the play. Instead (in 4.2), there are a few references to the "people's" fears at the time of Arthur's death:

> FAUL. I find the people strangely fantasied;
> Possess'd with rumours, full of idle dreams,
> Not knowing what they fear, but full of fear.
>   (4.2.144–46)

Hubert similarly reports to John of rumors, of what "they say" (4.2.182), of "old men and beldams in the streets" (4.2.185), of a smith and tailor gossiping (4.2.193-95), of an "artificer" (4.2.201) talking about Arthur's death. These are descriptions of the people of England and would better fit the commons of the first tetralogy than the citizens of Angiers. Given the long tradition of Anglo-French rivalry often expressed in Elizabethan times and in Shakespeare's plays, it would be difficult to explain this change between the citizens of Angiers and the people of England as stemming from respect for Frenchmen and disparagement of Englishmen. It is more likely that the difference results from carelessness and lack of a unifying theme in this play that would focus the role of the people, rather than from a desire to show that the Angiers citizens are resourceful in the face of danger while English people are paralyzed by superstition.

B. The Lords

The lords in this play are better characterized than the commons only to the degree that they are given names. One never learns whose sons, husbands, fathers they are as one does for so many lords in the first tetralogy. The lords, except for Faulconbridge and Hubert, remain largely un-

developed as individuals so that their actions in choosing to
rebel against then to support John have the same abstract
quality as the choice offered to the Angiers citizens.

The Earls of Salisbury and Pembroke are the two spokesmen for the lords. They have few lines until act 4, scene 2,
when Salisbury expresses discontent with John's staging a
second coronation despite their advice to the contrary. He
calls the second investiture "wasteful and ridiculous excess"
(4.2.16), which, moreover, is dangerous:

> In this the antique and well-noted face
> Of plain old form is much disfigured;
> And, like a shifted wind unto a sail,
> It makes the course of thoughts to fetch about,
> Startles and frights consideration,
> Makes sound opinion sick and truth suspected,
> For putting on so new a fashion'd robe.
>
> (4.2.21–27)

Other names for that "plain old form" which Salisbury
reveres would be customary or common law. In Salisbury's
view, John respects neither law nor counsel but only his own
will; Salisbury seems angered at this to the point of sarcasm
when he says that John's disregarding their counsel leaves
them "well pleased":

> . . . before you were new crown'd,
> We breath'd our counsel: but it pleased your highness
> To overbear it, and we are all well pleas'd
> Since all and every part of what we would
> Doth make a stand at what your highness will.
>
> (4.2.35–39)

To this dual reproach, John makes a conciliatory gesture
containing the closest reference to the *Magna Carta* that
occurs in this play:

> . . . meantime but ask
> What you would have reform'd that is not well,
> And well shall you perceive how willingly

I will both hear and grant you your requests.

(4.2.43–46)

As S. C. Sen Gupta has pointed out, the *Magna Carta* does not enter into the play because the lords have no specific grievances of their own but express concern only for the well-being of Arthur and the realm.[2] There is actually no reason why the *Magna Carta* should be mentioned because it was not until the middle of the seventeenth century that the great charter became a strong enough myth for the "forces of liberalism" to rally around as "a symbol of successful opposition to the Crown which had resulted in a negotiated peace representing a reasonable compromise."[3]

Pembroke makes only one demand:

> let it be our suit
> That you have bid us ask his liberty;
> Which for our goods we do no further ask
> Then whereupon our weal, on you depending,
> Counts it your weal he have his liberty.

(4.2.62–66)

What the lords fear is that Arthur's continuing imprisonment will cause rebellion, since his restraint "Doth move the murmuring lips of discontent" (4.2.53). On hearing from John that Arthur is dead, Salisbury and Pembroke lead the other lords from the presence of the king. At their next appearance, Salisbury declares,

> The king hath dispossess'd himself of us:
> We will not line his thin bestained cloak
> With our pure honours, nor attend the foot
> That leaves the print of blood where'er it walks.
> Return and tell him so: we know the worst.

(4.3.23–27)

He is thereby making a solemn, public renunciation of his allegiance to a king who has abused his power just as Burgundy, Salisbury, and Warwick renounce their allegiance to kings in the first tetralogy. From the point of view of legal relationships between king and lords there is no change from the principles operating in the first tetralogy except that Salisbury's expression of the *reunuciare* in *John* sounds like an abstract formula: "the king hath dispossessed himself of us," placing all the blame on the king so that no defiance is necessary from the lords. They only need to vote with their feet, which they do in supporting Lewis, the Dauphin.

Yet the choice is not a happy one, for Salisbury is reduced to weeping in public at the thought of following a foreign flag.

> And is't not pity, O my grieved friends,
> That we, the sons and children of this isle,
> Were born to see so sad an hour as this;
> Wherein we step after a stranger, march
>
> .   .   .   .
>
> To grace the gentry of a land remote,
> And follow unacquainted colours here?
>
> (5.2.24–32)

When Melun, a Frenchman of English ancestry, warns the lords with his dying breath that Lewis will betray them, Salisbury welcomes the chance to return again to his native king, even if it is still John.

> We will untread the steps of damned flight,
> And, like a bated and retired flood,
> Leaving our rankness and irregular course,
> Stoop low within these bounds we have o'erlook'd
> And calmly run on in obedience
> Even to our ocean, to our great King John.
>
> (5.4.52–57)

Since this "great King John" is the same man of the "thin bestained cloak" whom they earlier deserted, and, since as far as one knows they have not learned of any transformation in John in the interim, I think one has no alternative but to conclude that the English lords have learned from

Melun to prefer any English king to a foreign leader. They evidently decide that a willful, lawless English king means less danger to them than a foreign king. The response to French intervention is nationalism, a uniting of all English forces that leaves the enemy no alternative but to send offers of peace (5.7.84). This same nationalism serves briefly in *1 Henry VI* to keep the English victorious over a disunified France. But once leaders like Talbot are gone, and once disunity disrupts the English nobility, the English eventually lose to a unified France, signified by Burgundy's defection from Henry (see Sen Gupta, *Shakespeare's Historical Plays*, p. 64).

Salisbury, Pembroke, and the other lords desert John on grounds that are similar to those in the first tetralogy, his disregard for law and for the opinions of his lords. They return to his support on grounds that are minimized in the first tetralogy, the danger from foreign troops and leaders. In the first tetralogy Henry VII, though he was educated abroad, wins the English Crown with some support by French troops, and the alternations between Henry VI and Edward IV are never tied to the fact that Henry's forces include men supplied by the French King Lewis. In *John* the most chauvinistic form of nationalism—my king right or wrong—is given the sanction of support by the lords as the play draws to a close, despite the lords' feeling quite differently about the king in the middle of the play. The lords are so anxions to be restored to John's good graces that they bring his son to intercede in their behalf (5.6.34–36).

Two men, Hubert and Faulconbridge, counter the general thrust of the allegiance, defection, and return to allegiance of the other lords by remaining loyal both to John and to principles of law. Interestingly, both of them enjoy the social status neither of lord nor commoner but somewhere between. Philip is the bastard brother of Robert Faulconbridge, and Hubert de Burgh's position is unspecified except by Lord Bigot, who considers him to be of lower rank than a nobleman: "Out, dunghill! Dar'st thou brave a nobleman?" (4.3.87). According to Owen Hood Phillips, Hubert was a "famous Chief Justiciar," but this is not mentioned in the play.[4] Hubert chooses not to injure Arthur as King John ordered. He claims that his mind is "fairer . . . / Than to be butcher of an innocent child" (4.2.258-59). When he seeks to defend himself from Salisbury's vigilantelike justice, he answers Lord Bigot's reproach by saying, "I dare defend / My innocent life against an emperor" (4.3.88-89). He thus becomes, after he has repented his temporarily agreeing to kill or maim Arthur, a moral touchstone embodying absolute values in a commodity-centered world. Melun claims that love for Hubert inspired his warning to the English lords, so that Hubert indirectly is England's salvation:

> Commend me to one Hubert with your king:
> The love of him, and this respect besides,
> For that my grandsire was an Englishman,
> Awakes my conscience to confess all this.
>
> (5.4.40–43)

It is only Hubert who seeks out Faulconbridge to warn him of John's death by poisoning so that

> you might
> The better arm you to the sudden time,
> Than if you had at leisure known of this.
>
> (5.6.25–27)

Though all the lords know of the king's death since they are there to witness it (5.7.64), the fact that Hubert thinks it essential that Faulconbridge be informed is an indication of the peculiar role that the Bastard fulfills in this play. For though the play is named for John, the Bastard is the central figure whose reactions are given the most attention and whose pronouncements contain more moral sentiments than those of anyone else.

To explain the disproportionate attention to the Bastard in a play named for King John, William Matchett has offered the suggestion that Hubert and the Bastard provide the main illustrations of the central theme in this play of "higher duty which true loyalty demands from the man of honour."[5] In order to derive this interpretation from the play, however, Matchett must assume that it is Hubert, a burgher from Angiers, who refuses to choose between John and Arthur.

> We have seen Hubert grow from his attempt at a coldly rational avoidance of the problem of choice between loyalties to a realization that a man is forced to commit himself and can only hope to do so honourably. We have seen the Bastard grow from a naive enthusiast following chance to a man of mature insight and ability. What Hubert brings the Bastard now is, in effect, an invitation to take the throne, to assume the role he has in fact been filling and for which the character he inherited from his father has proven so eminently fitted. It is all understated, but the implications are clear. . . . [P. 250]

Unfortunately, in this as in so many other details in this play, Shakespeare has relied too much on understatement, so that though Matchett's reading is an attractive one, it is by no means certain because it has to rely so heavily on implications rather than fact, on the evidence, as Matchett admits, that the play does "not contradict this thesis" rather than on evidence in the play which positively affirms it (p. 232).

Though he is technically not a bastard, since he was born after wedlock and was not denied by Lord Faulconbridge (both George W. Keeton[6] and Phillips, *Shakespeare and the Lawyers,* pp. 85-86 have concluded that John's decision is good law), Faulconbridge prefers to be known as the bastard son of Richard the Lionhearted rather than as the legitimate son of Lord Faulconbridge. Despite his claims at the end of act 2 that he is railing against "commodity" only because it has not yet wooed him, and he declares,

> Since kings break faith upon commodity,
> Gain, be my lord, for I will worship thee!
>
> (2.1.597–98)

Faulconbridge remains truer to selfless motives than anyone else except perhaps Hubert and young Arthur. On the
crucial issue of Arthur's death, the Bastard does not join
with the outraged lords in deserting John and in accusing
Hubert. Where Salisbury is eager to "rob the law"
(4.3.78), drawing his sword to execute Hubert summarily,
Faulconbridge intervenes to defend him. Faulconbridge acts
in his behalf not because he knows Hubert is innocent, for
once alone with Hubert, the Bastard reveals, "I do suspect
thee very grievously" (4.3.134), but to defend Hubert's
right to due process, part of his general dedication to the
"fair-play of the world" (5.2.118). Faulconbridge orders
the lords to "Keep the peace, I say" (4.3.93); then when
Salisbury refuses, he adds a personal threat:

> . . . Put up thy sword betime—
> Or I'll so maul you and your toasting-iron
> That you shall think the divel is come from hell.
>
> (4.3.98–100)

Both Hubert and Faulconbridge thus are willing to put their
lives on the line in defending principles of law—Hubert in
defying John's orders against Arthur and Faulconbridge in
defending Hubert against the outraged lords.

Not king nor lords but Faulconbridge, recognizing the
danger to the land, does what he can for England's defense
by encouraging John to "be stirring as the time" (5.1.48).
Later he is the first to pledge fealty to Prince Henry,
thereby assuring continuity of native rule before Salisbury
does so for the other lords (5.7.101-7). Though in fact the
lords report that Pandulph has negotiated a peace between
John and the Dauphin, this is quickly brushed over by Shakespeare in the last moments of the play—"Let it be so,"
says the Bastard (5.7.96). It is Faulconbridge who speaks
the following words:

> This England never did, nor never shall,
> Lie at the proud foot of a conqueror,

But when it first did help to wound itself.

. . . .

      Nought shall make us rue
If England to itself do rest but true!

                (5.7.112–18)

That it should be a Bastard who expresses this realization, not a Humphrey or an Exeter as in the first tetralogy, poses a difficult question of interpretation. It is not the royal blood coursing through his veins that provides an adequate explanation of Faulconbridge's behavior, for presumably John also has royal blood but with no noticeable effect on his slight dedication to the common good. Matchett concludes that in Shakespeare's having the Bastard pay homage to Henry, he has demonstrated through the play

> the moral complexity of the problem of loyalty which the Bastard (and to a lesser extent Hubert) has shown as the self-denying acceptance of a higher duty [in letting Henry be king] which true loyalty demands from a man of honour. ["Richard's Divided Heritage in *King John*," p. 253]

The Bastard would thus have earned the right during the course of the play to speak the concluding lines. While I find Matchett's reading an interesting one that goes a long way toward providing an analysis that unifies otherwise puzzling elements, I cannot agree with the idea that Hubert offers the throne to the Bastard and that the Bastard is consciously renouncing his claim in paying homage to Henry. For I feel that if Shakespeare intended this interpretation, he would have been more explicit. I would suggest as an alternative reading to Matchett's that Hubert fears danger to the realm during the transition to a new reign, so knowing how forcefully the Bastard worked for England's security, he hastens to prepare him for new danger. His respect for the Bastard's martial abilities would be all the stronger because Hubert has not yet been informed of the losses the Bastard suffered (5.6.39-40). The Bastard's homage to Prince Henry would then represent his efforts to strengthen the fledgling king in his position on the throne. My own suggestions in the following paragraph as to the Bastard's role in this play do not provide as comprehensive an analysis as Matchett's; this limited explanation is deliberate, for I believe that the play does not lend itself to entirely unified interpretations because of inconsistencies that I note in this chapter (see in particular the final paragraph).

Despite Faulconbridge's recognition of the influence of "commodity" on human behavior, his perception of events is essentially naive, or, as Matchett puts it, he remains "impulsive" throughout the play ("Richard's Divided Heritage in *King John*," p. 252). Similarly, the resolution of the dilemmas in *John* is simple in comparison with the resolution in the first tetralogy. In *John,* one Frenchman can convince the lords to rejoin their king, and, once Arthur is dead, John and then his son are the only native claimants to the throne (unless one accepts Matchett's suggestion of the Bastard as an alternative claimant). Against the background of the overly simplified context of the play, I venture to offer a tentative observation on the significance of the Bastard that occurs to me within the constitutional framework of this study. There might be a suggestion by Shakespeare, in his making the leader who is most consistently dedicated to the well-being of the realm an uncultured, rough and ready, picaresque hero, that the virtues of common sense are of greater value in securing the realm than noble birth. There would then be some relationship between this idea and the identification in the first tetralogy between the commons' support and a leader's effectiveness. No firm conclusion is possible, however, because Shakespeare has not provided enough material to confirm what he intended. Nonetheless, I find in the very confusion an indication that this is an early play, perhaps contemporaneous with *1 Henry VI,* for the themes of that play are most closely related to the Bastard's patriotic conclusion of *John.*

C. The Crown

According to *Taswell-Langmead's English Constitutional History,* John's election slowed for a time the development of a custom of inheritance by which the son would have priority over the brother.

> Even in private inheritances the doctrine of representation, by which the issues of a deceased elder brother would exclude the succession of the surviving younger brother, was as yet unsettled although it had in fact been making headway in private law until John's accession gave a check to it. In England there appears to have been an absence of any feeling in favour of the boy Arthur of Brittany, son of John's elder brother Geoffrey; while John's claim was supported by the death-bed recommendation of the late king, the influence of the queen-mother, and the adherence of a numerous and influential party among the barons. He was elected king without opposition. . . .[7]

As Shakespeare's play opens, the French ambassador to King John addresses him as "the borrow'd majesty, of England" (1.1.4) and says that he rules "usurpingly" (1.1.13) in the place of his brother's son, Arthur Plantagenet. The play thus begins with the information that there are conflicting claims to the Crown and that the French king is a partisan of the dispossessed claimant. In response to his mother's recognition that war is now inevitable, John cites "our strong possession and our right for us" (1.1.39). Elinor cautions him, however, to trust

> Your strong possession much more than your right,
> Or else it must go wrong with you and me.
>
> (1.1.40–41)

John Elliott, William Matchett, and J. D. Wilson (pp. xliv, lix) argue on the basis of the just-quoted lines that Shakespeare stresses John's illegitimacy in this scene.[8] To support their contention they cite Chatillon's emphasis on John's "borrowed Majesty" (1.1.4) and his assertion that John rules "usurpingly" (1.1.13), to which John only replies, "What follows if we disallow of this?" (1.1.16) They also cite Elinor's insisting upon John's possession much more than his right as proof that Shakespeare is stressing

John's illegitimacy. I disagree. I find that the tenor of the opening scene's confrontation between John and Chatillon is to emphasize the foreign challenge to English integrity. John's choosing not to engage in debate over his title with an ambassador is no concession about the weakness of his title such as Henry VI makes when confronted by York in Parliament ("I know not what to say. My title's weak" [*3H6*, 1.1.138]). When directly confronting King Philip before Angiers, John specifically claims "Our just and lineal entrance to our own" (2.1.85). Elinor's emphasis on possession is no more than practical advice, for in case of conflicting claims, the one who has the crown does have an edge on the other, as Glanvill admits. Sidney Painter cites Glanvill to show that the law of succession established no clear decision in the case of a conflict between nephew and brother, but that Glanvill personally favored the claim of the former. However, Glanvill's concluding remark on the topic was that "the party in possession will prevail."[9]

To further substantiate his contention that Shakespeare emphasizes John's illegitimacy, Elliot cites Chatillon's description of the lawlessness and impetuosity of John's followers to France in act 2, scene 1, lines 65-71 ("Shakespeare and the Double Image of *King John*," p. 75). But Chatillon's assessment is hardly impartial. Why should one accept unchallenged his interpretation of John's rule, especially when it becomes apparent through the remainder of the play that both Philip and the Dauphin are not genuinely interested in Arthur's right but in their own self-seeking. The fact that in Shakespeare's play it is foreigners, not Englishmen, who oppose John's title is significant. Since John does claim his "just and lineal" right to the throne (2.1.85) when he meets King Philip, a claim that both Elliot and Matchett ignore, it would seem that John's not answering to Chatillon's charges was a matter of maintaining his royal dignity with an ambassador and that Elinor was not denying John's right but emphasizing the practical aspect of his advantage over Arthur: while both John and Arthur had plausible claims to the throne, John enjoyed the added advantage of possession, of which he should make the most. John does, of course, say at Angiers, "Doth not the crown of England prove the king?" (2.1.273), but the citizens persist in requiring proof of arms to decide between the claims of John and Arthur:

> Till you compound whose right is worthiest,
> We for the worthiest hold the right from both.
>
> (2.1.281–82)

Similarly, Elinor's reference to John's "unsur'd assurance to the crown" (2.1.471) need not be interpreted to mean any more than her practical acknowledgment that a strong counterclaim does exist.

The lords' opposition to John develops from his disregarding their counsel and from their suspecting his complicity in Arthur's death, not because he rules in Arthur's place. And the lords' defense is of Arthur's person, not of his claim to the throne. The lords support John until they are convinced that his disregarding their counsel has left him free to order a lawless act against Arthur. Since this is the point at which John loses most of his native support in Shakespeare's play, I feel that these two aspects of John's interpretation of the Crown are the ones Shakespeare intends that one accept as denying his right to the throne. In short, what makes John an illegitimate ruler in the eyes of his own nobility so that they are justified in renouncing their fealty to him is not his possessing the throne after his brother in place of his nephew but his ruling without consistent regard to law or the counsel of his lords. Arthur himself is incidental to the claim made in his behalf—Philip never says that he will rule better than does John. Arthur does not think he merits the effort made to win the crown for him: "I am not worth this coil that's made for me" (2.1.165). This fact marks a contrast with the first tetralogy, where Henry's model as king and York's alternative are critical factors for the lords and commons who must choose between them. The choice in *John* is fairly abstract.

The issue around which I am circling here, as in the other eight plays, is the definition of *de jure* rule. Possession, *de facto* rule, is certainly not synonymous with *de jure* rule in the plays. Henry VI, Edward IV, Richard III, and Richard II are all temporarily or permanently deposed, while John, Henry IV, and Henry V are all challenged by rebels who would depose them if they could. In *John* several answers are proposed to the question of royal legitimacy. None of the answers proves satisfactory until the final moments of the play, when lineality reinforced by baronial support makes John's son king. Philip acting for Arthur finds that assertion of lineality is not sufficient. John finds that possession is not sufficient. Philip and John both learn that Angiers citizens will not choose between lineality and possession and that combat between the two kings will not resolve the issue. John learns that even being crowned will not "prove the king," in that his second coronation is shortly followed by his losing baronial support.

Pandulph, the papal legate, provides one other definition of the Crown, that it is conferred by the pope.

> KING JOHN.   Thus have I yielded up into your hand
> The circle of my glory.
> PANDULPH.   Take again
> From this my hand, as holding of the pope,
> Your sovereign greatness and authority.
>   (5.1.1–4)

First John and then Lewis defy Pandulph and the pope, after which they each suffer significant loss of support. When John is deserted by his nobility he thinks that the only way he can save his people from foreign invasion is to be reconciled with the Church, whose anger at his defiance "blew this tempest up" (5.1.17). As the audience learns, however, John did not need to humble himself to Pandulph. Pandulph will not be able to halt the invasion, and the English nobility will be reconciled with John because of Melun's warning, not for any reason connected with the Church (unless one

thinks Melun's warning has heavenly inspiration). Thus
John's submission to the Church, which was required by
historical fact, is treated in *John* with irony. But after
Lewis refuses Pandulph's order to end the conquest of
England ("Am I Rome's slave?" [5.2.97]), he finds him-
self doing less well militarily.

> Ah, foul shrewd news! beshrew thy very heart!
> I did not think to be so sad to-night
> As this hath made me.
>
> (5.5.14–16)

In the rush to conclude the play with England at peace,
nothing more is done with the idea that church support
either does or does not contribute to national strength.
John's and Lewis's experiences annul rather than reinforce
each other. Perhaps this cancellation is intended by Shakespeare to show that the church has a diminished political
role to play. But then the difficult question is whether the
discrediting applies only to the Church of Rome or to the
English Church as well.

Pandulph's moral leadership is of a doubtful nature. He
plays at *Realpolitik* with borrowed troops, egging Lewis on
at the thought of "what better matter breeds for you / Than
I have nam'd!" (3.3.170-71) when what he has just named
is "revolt and wrath" (3.3.167). He leads Lewis into
claiming England as his own once Arthur is dead. The other
religious figure mentioned in this play is a monk who (it is
reported) poisons John, despite the fact that John has been
reconciled with the Church. Pandulph's discreditable example and the conflicting evidence of John's and Lewis's
experiences would seem to discount the role of the Church
in governmental affairs, which might reflect a constitutional
reality in England after 1534, when positive law was declared superior to canon law.[10]. Thereafter the Church as
such was no longer a contender for constitutional power.
Though religion played an important part in parliamentary
opposition to the Crown, Parliament had to be the vehicle

for expressing that opposition, not the Church as a fourth constitutional branch.

If *John* is an early play, and if it shows a discrediting of the Church as a political influence, that may explain the minimal role which the Church plays in the first tetralogy. When angered at Humphrey in *1 Henry VI,* Winchester says, "Rome shall remedy this" (3.1.51), but Humphrey dismisses the threat: "Roam thither then" (3.1.51). Once he is bishop, Winchester is no moral inspiration, a fact that is emphasized by his tormented death with no sign of grace (*2H6,* 3.3.29). The only other prelates appear in *Richard III*, where they are all shown to be easily manipulated: Cardinal Bourchier is persuaded to break sanctuary (3.1.57), the Bishop of Ely leaves an important council meeting to fetch strawberries to please the protector (3.4.34), and two bishops join Gloucester in staging a scene to show his piety (3.7.94).

To return to the question of title to the Crown, in *John* neither church blessing, nor possession, nor lineality, nor military might prove adequate until Prince Henry is granted homage by Faulconbridge and the lords at the end of the play. Whether this conclusion is intended to signify the triumph of lineality or election is difficult to interpret, however, because of the lack of corroborating evidence in the play.

D.   The Law

Several facets of law are alluded to in the play; among them are a basic premise of civil law, God's law of retribution, the Church as arbiter in international legal disputes, and, above all, the relationship of the individual to higher law. This last is the principal aspect of law that is treated in this play, both in the quarrel and second rupture between King Philip and King John and in the relationship between King John and Hubert on the question of Arthur's death.

The relationship between English positive law and "natural" or "higher" law, also labeled "law of reason," received considerable attention during the sixteenth century. The papal excommunication of Elizabeth further intensified the issue for Catholics who had to face the practical question "of whether the subject should obey man rather than God if the ruler was in opposition to God."[11] Legal historians have not yet been able to agree on the precise relationship between positive and higher law in the sixteenth century; perhaps it will never be possible to reach agreement because of a lack of sixteenth-century consensus. Rather than risk further confusing an already confused area by attempting an analysis, in order to convey some sense of the context within which Shakespeare approached the problem, I shall quote excerpts from sixteenth-century writers who deal with the particular aspects of the problem that Shakespeare treated. I have chosen Saint German, who wrote before the Henrician Reformation, and Hooker, who wrote toward the end of Elizabeth's reign, in the hope that those matters on which they seem to be in agreement may represent generally accepted views.

Saint German wrote in 1518:

> The law of reason is written in the heart of every man, teaching him what is to be done, and what is to be fled: and because it is written in the heart, therefore it may not be put away, nor is it never changeable by no diversity of place nor time: and therefore against this law, prescription, statute nor custom may not prevail: and if any be brought in against it, they be not prescriptions, statutes nor customs, but things void and against justice. And all other laws, as well the laws of God as to the acts of men, as other, be grounded thereupon.[12]

Hooker wrote in the first book of his *Laws of Ecclesiastical Polity*:

> Laws of Reason . . . the general principles thereof are such, as it is not easy to find men ignorant of them, law rational therefore, which men commonly use to call the Law of Nature, meaning thereby the law which human nature knows itself in reason universally bound unto, which also for that cause may be termed most fitly the Law of Reason; this law, I say, comprehends all those

things which men by the light of their natural understanding evidently know, or at leastwise may know, to be beseeming or unbeseeming, virtuous or vicious, good or evil, for them to do.[13]

Disagreements, however, can easily arise when it comes to applying a law "written in the heart of every man," a law that men "evidently know." The difficulty is illustrated in the first confrontation between John and Philip, when John asks Philip,

> From whom hast thou this great commission, France,
> To draw my answer from thy articles?

and Philip replies,

> From that Supernal Judge that stirs good thoughts
> In any beast of strong authority
> To look into the blots and stains of right.
> That judge hath made me guardian to this boy:
> Under whose warrant I impeach thy wrong
> And by whose help I mean to chastise it.
>
> (2.1.110–17)

But John rejects this explanation—"Alack, thou dost usurp authority" (2.1.118).

What external, objective principles is each individual to follow in reconciling the inevitable differences among men following the dictates of their individual consciences, particularly when all too often their consciences serve "commodity"? In her rage at Arthur's not being king, Constance declares that principles of God's law as revealed in the Old Testament are at work in the universe:

> this is thy eldest son's son,
> Infortunate in nothing but in thee:
> Thy sins are visited in this poor child;
> The canon of the law is laid on him,
> Being but the second generation
> Removed from thy sin-conceiving womb.
>
> (2.1.177–82)

This is a reference, as Lily Bess Campbell points out, to *Numbers* 14:18, to "visiting the wickedness of the fathers upon the children, in the third and fourth generation" (*"Histories,"* p. 122). If God's law of retribution is working in the universe, perhaps Philip and John should stop trying to arrange matters to suit themselves. An implication of Constance's reference would be that they should all accept the workings of Providence. But the response in *John* to the idea of a moral universe is as follows: John tells Constance to "have done" (2.1.183); Elinor calls her ill advised (2.1.191); King Philip warns

> Peace, lady! pause, or be more temperate;
> It ill beseems this presence to cry aim
> To these ill-tuned repetitions.
>
> (2.1.195–97)

Philip proposes that they seek the opinion of the people to resolve the dispute:

> Some trumpet summon hither to the walls
> These men of Angiers: let us hear them speak
> Whose title they admit, Arthur's or John's.
>
> (2.1.198–200)

But as seen above, the people did not provide a solution to the dilemma; rather, as Faulconbridge observed, the fine moral issue raised by the controversy is resolved according to "commodity." Philip renounces Arthur's cause in order to increase the fortunes of Lewis, the Dauphin, while John agrees to giving up the city of Angiers in order to gain greater security for his other territories.

When Pandulph has excommunicated John and threatened Philip with the same if he does not make John his enemy, Philip asks Pandulph's guidance. "May we"

> so jest with heaven,
> Make such unconstant children of ourselves,
> As now again to snatch our palm from palm,
> Unswear faith sworn . . . ?
>
> (3.1.168–71)

Pandulph tells him "yes" in a reply that clearly depends upon sophistry:

> that which thou hast sworn to do amiss
> Is not amiss when it is truly done,
> And being not done, where doing tends to ill,
> The truth is then most done not doing it:
> The better act of purposes mistook
> Is to mistake again; though indirect,
> Yet indirection thereby grows direct,
> And falsehood falsehood cures. . . .
>
> (3.1.196–203)

He tells Philip that his first obligation is to heaven, to be champion of the church (3.1.191-93) and that as his oath to John is against religion, his later vow to John is "in rebellion to thyself" (3.1.215) because of his primary vow to heaven. Yet Philip's pledge of peace to John was made before he was excommunicated, so that if Pandulph is arguing the supremacy of an earlier over a later vow, Philip's question is still unanswered. Reluctantly, it seems, fearing Austria's warning of rebellion that would follow excommunication, Philip tells John, "England, I will fall from thee" (3.1.246). Though Pandulph succeeds in persuading Philip, his moral guidance in the play is consistently of a dubious nature (see above), so that neither the Church nor the Bible is portrayed as a workable standard for guiding the individual when both are so easily misused by commodity-minded spokesmen.

For those peoples living under a system of Roman or civil law, the possibility of disagreement in interpreting law was provided for by the precept that what pleases the sovereign has the force of law, so that there was a single, ultimate reference. Law and sovereign's will were considered to be identical.[14] Arthur's mother Constance, speaking in the French king's pavilion in France, makes this identification between John and the law:

> Law cannot give my child his kingdom here,
> For he that holds his kingdom holds the law. . . .
>
> (3.1.113–15)

John's peers make a similar identification (see above) between John and the law but reject such a system of government when in their perception it permits the continued imprisonment and death of Arthur. John himself denounces the same equation of law and king when he seeks to blame Hubert for Arthur's death, though his dissatisfaction is after the fact; when he wanted Arthur dead, he used the association between his will and law.

> It is the curse of kings to be attended
> By slaves that take their humours for a warrant
> To break within the bloody house of life,
> And on the winking of authority
> To understand a law. . . .
>
> (4.2.208–12)

But Hubert assures John that he is mistaken, that despite the signed warrant from John, he did not transgress against nature by resorting to murder. Thus Hubert seems to illustrate both Saint German and Hooker's insistence that the law of reason is "always good and righteous, stirring and inclining a man to good, and abhorring evil" (St. German, *Doctor and Student*, p. 5), for "no man can reject it as unreasonable and unjust" (Hooker, *Ecclesiastical Polity*, I.8.9 in *Works*, 1:233).

John, however, unlike Hubert, has been moved less by reason than by "commodity." The danger to himself and the realm of his peers' displeasure at his mishandling of Arthur leads him to reject the identification between his will and the law by regrettng Arthur's alleged death. John sends the Bastard (4.2.166–69) and then Hubert (4.2.261–69) to win the English peers back to his side. He tells the Bastard, "I have a way to win their loves again" (4.2.168); in the context of their anger at thinking that John had disregarded their counsel in abusing Arthur, I suggest that this line implies that he will pledge to heed their advice in the future. But there is no time for a reconciliation. The lords renounce their fealty, whereupon they find Arthur's body; the horror of his death reinforces the rupture with John.

Neither John nor the Dauphin nor Pandulph nor the English lords have a happy time of it in this play. One explanation for their sorrows is that they have all acted according to self-seeking motives even if to do so they had to manipulate the law, like Suffolk in *1 Henry VI* who "framed the law unto his will" (2.4.9). It appears in *John* that disaster is a likely reward for self-seeking motives. This is also the main thrust of the exploration of the relationship between the individual, higher law, and law in general in the first tetralogy, especially in the scene (*R3*, 1.4) between Clarence and the murderers (see section 2D above).

The only protection against the disasters incurred in *John* and in the first tetralogy when individuals decide for themselves what they will do lies in the consultative process. This solution is not consistently suggested as an alternative until the second tetralogy, first at Coventry, then when Bolingbroke seeks York's support in prosecuting Richard's advisers. *John* at times seems to come close to presenting this idea but never does so explicitly, so that it is difficult to say from a thematic point of view whether in terms of the law *John* is closer to the second or the first tetralogy.

Elliott contends that the unfavorable aspects of Shakespeare's portrait of John reflect the survival in Holinshed of the medieval view of John as a villainous failure alongside the newer Tudor version of John as a national hero ("Shakespeare and the Double Image of *King John*," pp. 65-72). John's defiance of the pope was bound to find a hostile reception among medieval chroniclers, as Barry Adams points out in his introduction to *King Johan*, because medieval chroniclers were almost exclusively ecclesiastics who "naturally sided with the Pope in his long and bitter struggle with the recalcitrant English king. [The medieval chroniclers] were therefore inclined to see and emphasize the worst in John's behavior."[15] Citing Ruth Wallerstein's survey of the treatment of John, Adams concludes that "there seems to be no example of a medieval historian who actually championed John's cause or defended his character" (*John Bale's "King Johan*," p. 30).[16] Medieval criticisms of John were primarily couched in moral terms, as Adams illustrates with the following reference to Giraldus Cambrensis:

> John, he says, unable to equal his brothers and parents in good qualities, strove to outdo them in depravity, and so applied himself that his tyranny surpassed that of all other tyrants, past and present. [*John Bale's "King Johan*," p. 28]

But Holinshed was skeptical of the medieval moral condemnations of John:

> (to say what I think) he was not so void of devotion towards the church, as diverse of his enemies have reported, who of mere malice conceal all his virtues, and hide none of his vices; but are plentiful enough in setting forth the same to the uttermost, and interpret all his doings and sayings to the worst, as may appear to those that advisedly read the works of them that write the order of his life, which may seem rather an invective than a true history; nevertheless, since we cannot come by the truth of things through the malice of writers, we must content ourselves with the unfriendly description of his time. Certainly it would seem the man had a princely heart in him, and wanted nothing but faithful subjects to have assisted him in revenging such wrongs as were done and offered by the French king and others.[17]

If the unfavorable aspects of Shakespeare's portrait of John center around only John's doubtful morality, then I would agree with Elliott that Shakespeare is closer to the medieval interpretation of John ("Shakespeare and the Double Image of *King John*," p. 69). But criticism per se of John is not necessarily medieval. From the perspective of the sixteenth-century constitution there were aspects of John's reign that merited censure in terms that were not solely moral but reflected positivistic law as well. There is, in fact, a crucial division between medieval and modern legal and constitutional thought.

It is extremely difficult to determine precisely when one

concept replaces another in legal history, while in constitutional history the problems are even more complex. The
same evidence will often support more than one interpretation.[18] One difference between medieval and modern law
is the relative emphasis on moral and positive law under
each system, with moral law being the essence of medieval
law and increased reliance on positive law marking off modern law from its past. According to medieval law, there were
moral concepts in effect whether or not Parliament had enacted statutes embodying those concepts. For a long time,
in fact, Parliament's legislative role was understood to be
that of declaring existing moral law rather than making new
law by statute.[19] William Harrison's statement quoted in
chapter 1B, that without a parliamentary law there can be
no forfeiture of "life, member, or lands of any Englishman,"[20] marks a significant step in the development of a
"modern" perception of law. Georges Edelen suggests in
his introduction that Harrison "thinks and speaks as an
ordinary Elizabethan" so that "in Harrison we come exceptionally close to . . . what the common people thought
about common things" (*Description of England*, p. xxxv).
Harrison's emphasis on statutory law is a good indication,
therefore, that by mid- to late sixteenth century the newer
concept of law was gaining over the old.

Salisbury reproaches John in terms of his not heeding
the barons' counsel and in departing from the "antique and
well-noted face / Of plain old form" by staging a second
coronation (4.2.21-22). Salisbury's outrage at Arthur's
death leads him to abandon John because of his immoral
behavior in that Salisbury blames John for Arthur's death.
I find in this two-staged rupture between John and his nobility elements of both a moralistic evaluation of John's rule
and a legalistic evaluation. John is renounced because his
nobles feel that he committed an immoral act against Arthur.
But they were already well prepared for such a renunciation
because of John's not following their advice in terms of
obeying custom or releasing Arthur. I therefore find a suggestion of both "modern" and "medieval" criticism of John

in the lords' renunciation, not in terms of a specific reference to statute-making but in terms of a different perception of the roles of lords and king in governing, of which statute-making is simply one indication that the Crown's prerogative is bounded by consent of the earls.

Medieval custom also provided for a king or chief lord's consulting with his men and following customary traditions. The extent to which a king was bound to heed the counsel of his lords depended on whether or not he could keep their support despite his not following their advice. This was also true in Elizabethan times, as witnessed by Elizabeth's relationship to her Commons; she felt that she would go against their wishes on the succession but not on the matter of monopolies or royal purveyors (see chapter 1). Whether or not "consult" meant "heed" at any given instance cannot be determined with certainty. While it is possible to discuss the constitution in terms of general movements over centuries and to see general directions in which the constitution develops, a specific incident is part of a continuum and so reflects the past and anticipates the future at the same time. Therefore, one could argue from the same evidence that I cite that the break between John and his lords finds its basis in the medieval constitution.

For myself, I frankly am undecided about *John*. Were I certain that the play was written between the two tetralogies, I would probably argue that the lords' abandoning John when they do and for the reasons they cite is the fulcrum of this play. While I do stress this incident to indicate the possibility of this interpretation, I recognize a predominance of medieval assumptions in this play that counters the lords' decision. For instance, though the Bastard could not be more forceful in supporting John, he says that he holds "all England" when he holds Arthur's body (4.3.142). There is also a great deal of attention to nationalism in this play, making it equally possible to regard Melun's warning to the English lords as the pivotal point of the play at which the denouement begins.

The citizens are first asked to choose their king, then are

threatened with utter destruction in *John*; in the first tetralogy the support of the commons is consistently linked to a contender's gaining and retaining the Crown. The role of the Church is given fairly extensive treatment in *John* but minimal attention in the first tetralogy, yet the role of the Church in the four plays is consistent with the conclusions apparently reached about the Church in *John*. Nationalism plays a major role in *John,* as Ruth Wallerstein also points out in her discussion of Shakespeare's play where she sees an emphasis on the virtues of any English king, however bad (*King John in Fact and Fiction*, p. 43); this stress on England is also prevalent in *1 Henry VI* but does not reappear in the history plays until *Henry V*. Emphasis on the consultative process is minor in both *John* and the first tetralogy but major in the second tetralogy. For all of these reasons and for the lack of commitment I sense on Shakespeare's part in *John* (see my comments on Matchett's interpretation above), I am inclined to see *John* as contemporaneous in composition with *1 Henry VI*. The legal aspects of the lords' rejection of John would then be Shakespeare's first, brief exploration of an idea with contemporary implications that would not receive full attention until the second tetralogy.

NOTES TO CHAPTER 3

1. J. D. Wilson, ed., *King John* (Cambridge: At the University Press, 1936), pp. lv–lvi; E. A. J. Honigmann, ed., *King John* (London: Methuen, and Cambridge, Mass.: Harvard University Press, 1954), p. lviii; D. F. Ash, "Anglo-French Relations in *King John*," *Etudes Anglaises* 3 (1939): 355; G. B. Harrison, ed., *Shakespeare, The Complete Works* (New York: Harcourt, Brace, and World, 1952), p. 541.

2. S. C. Sen Gupta, *Shakespeare's Historical Plays* (Oxford: Oxford University Press, 1964), p. 102.

3. Theodore F. T. Plucknett, *A Concise History of the Common Law,* 4th ed. (London: Butterworth and Company, 1948), p. 25.

4. Owen Hood Phillips, *Shakespeare and the Lawyers* (London: Methuen, 1972). p. 70.

5. William H. Matchett, "Richard's Divided Heritage in *King John,*" *Essays in Criticism* 12 (July 1962):253.

6. George W. Keeton, *Shakespeare and His Legal Problems* (London: A. and C. Black, 1930), pp. 118–31.

7. *Taswell-Langmead's English Constitutional History,* 11th ed., ed. Theodore F. T. Plucknett (London: Sweet and Maxwell, 1960), p. 453.

8. John R. Elliott, "Shakespeare and the Double Image of *King John,*" *Shakespeare Studies* 1(1965):72–76; Matchett, "Richard's Divided Heritage," pp. 232–34.

9. Sidney Painter, *The Reign of King John* (Baltimore, Md.: Johns Hopkins Press, 1949), p. 3; the quotation from Glanvill is from Ranulf de Glanvill, *The Treatise on the Laws and Customs of the Realm of England Commonly Called Glanvill,* ed. G. D. G. Hall (London: Nelson for the Selden Society, 1965), p. 78. Glanvill was discussing the general question of a brother versus a nephew as inheritor, not specifically John and Arthur.

10. G. R. Elton, ed., *The Tudor Constitution, Documents and Commentary* (Cambridge: At the University Press, 1960), pp. 346–56.

11. Lily Bess Campbell, *Shakespeare's "Histories"—Mirrors of Elizabethan Policy* (San Marino, Calif.: The Huntington Library, 1947), p. 156.

12. Christopher Saint German or Germain, *Doctor and Student: Or, Dialogues Between a Doctor of Divinity and a Student in the Laws of England* [1518], reprint, ed. William Muchall, 17th ed. (London: A. Strahen and W. Woodfall, 1787), p. 5.

13. Richard Hooker, *Of the Laws of Ecclesiastical Polity,* I, viii, 9, in *The Works,* 7th ed. ed. J. Keble, rev. R. W. Church and F. Paget (Oxford: Clarendon Press, 1888), 1:233–34.

14. W. S. Holdsworth, *A History of English Law* (Boston: Little, Brown and Company, 1924) 4:106.

15. Barry B. Adams, ed., *John Bale's "King Johan,"* (San Marino, Calif.: The Huntington Library, 1969), p. 30.

16. Ruth Wallerstein, *King John in Fact and Fiction* (Philadelphia: E. Stern and Company, 1917), pp. 3–22.

17. Raphael Holinshed, *Chronicles of England, Scotland, and Ireland* (London: J. Johnson et al, 1807), 2:339.

18. S. F. C. Milsom, professor of legal history in the London School of Economics and literary director of the Selden Society, made these observations in a lecture given March 21, 1974, on "Law and Morals and Elementary Concepts" at Indiana University.

19. S. B. Chrimes, *English Constitutional Ideas in the Fifteenth Century* (Cambridge: At the University Press, 1936), p. 25.

20. William Harrison, *Description of England,* ed. Georges Edelen (Ithaca, N.Y.: Cornell University Press, 1968), p. 154.

4

The Second Tetralogy

Comparisons between Shakespeare's second and first tetralogies are inevitable. In his entire canon of plays Shakespeare wrote a sequence of four plays in only one genre, the English history play, and he wrote such a sequence twice. Furthermore, many of the same people appear in the two sequences either as characters (Gloucester, Exeter, Bedford, Salisbury) or in references (Duke of York, Earl of Cambridge, Henry V). However, there are only a few general comparisons that can be made easily. Where the first group of plays spans a period of sixty and some odd years encompassing well over a hundred principal characters, the second group comprehends only about a twenty-year span and well under a hundred important roles. More significant than these statistical differences is the fact that the earlier plays move from incident to incident with only glancing references back, usually in the form of brief reproaches:

> Hadst thou been kill'd when first thou didst presume,
> Thou hadst not liv'd to kill a son of mine.
>
> (*3H6*, 5.6.35–36)

149

So says Henry VI to Richard, Duke of Gloucester, when Richard comes to assassinate Henry. The later plays, on the other hand, circle back again and again to the circumstances surrounding one incident, the deposition of Richard II, which the audience is first allowed to see and then to hear of in conflicting versions. Unlike the experience provided in Luigi Pirandello's plays where "one is right if one thinks one is right," the perceptive viewer or reader of Shakespeare's second tetralogy is able to judge later versions of the deposition by comparison with what he himself has seen or read.[1] Instead of exploring a variety of circumstances in which the question arises of a subject's right to rebel against a king, the second group of plays centers on a variety of perceptions of one incident when subjects *did* participate in the deposing of a king.

Another general difference between the two tetralogies is that the fewer characters and incidents of the second tetralogy allow for greater attention to personality; where in the first tetralogy characters are often typed representatives of a social role (Talbot, the loyal soldier; Winchester, the ambitious churchman; Gloucester, the righteous counselor; Henry, the childlike king), in the second tetralogy characters are more highly individuated. Societal position is still important in the second tetralogy: one always knows that Hotspur is a rebelling noble, for instance, but "rebelling noble" is not an adequate summary of his role. Therefore, one is less preoccupied in the second tetralogy with the abstract question of a subject's right of rebellion than with the personal differences between a Richard II and a Bolingbroke, a Hotspur and a Hal, a Worcester and a Henry IV. But the concentration by Henry IV on ruling and by Hal on preparing to rule politicizes the personal rivalries between the Lancastrians and all others.

A.   The Commons

Popularity is a critical factor in Shakespeare's version of the deposition of Richard II. It is first introduced by Richard himself, when, for the first time, he is alone on stage with his loyal followers and they discuss Henry Boling-broke's departure.

> Ourself and Bushy
> Observ'd his courtship to the common people,
> How he did seem to dive into their hearts
> With humble and familiar courtesy;
> What reverence he did throw away on slaves,
> Wooing poor craftsmen with the craft of smiles
> And patient underbearing of his fortune,
> As 'twere to banish their affects with him.
>
> (1.4.23–30)

As is so often the case in personal comments, Richard's description reveals more about the observer than the observed. He and his supporters see the people as "poor craftsmen" and "slaves" on whom attention is "thrown away," so that in their view respectful treatment *must* be inspired by "craft."[2] They betray a patrician contempt for the common people that makes them suspect any who have direct dealings with them.

> Off goes his bonnet to an oyster-wench;
> A brace of draymen bid God speed him well,
> And had the tribute of his supple knee,
> With "Thanks, my countrymen, my loving friends"—
> As were our England in reversion his,
> And he our subjects' next degree in hope.
>
> (1.4.31–36)

That Richard was truly speaking for the others as well as for himself is confirmed when Bagot reveals his contempt of the commons by calling them "wavering," adding that their love

> Lies in their purses, and whoso empties them,
> By so much fills their hearts with deadly hate.
>
> (2.2.129–30)

Bushy calls the commons "hateful" and warns that he expects them to tear him to pieces "like curs" (2.2.136–38).

In the first tetralogy, when leaders did not treat them with respect, the commons of Kent who joined in Cade's rebellion rejected them. Here in the second tetralogy the commons' reaction is similar. While there are many factors other than Richard's attitude toward the people that enter into his deposition, I think that one can safely compare York's reporting that the commons are cold toward Richard (2.2.88) with the commons' rejection of the disrespectful emissaries from Henry VI in the first tetralogy.

Richard is consistently unpopular. Scroop reports that

> White-beards have arm'd their thin and hairless scalps
> Against thy majesty; boys, with women's voices,
> Strive to speak big, and clap their female joints
> In stiff unwieldy arms against thy crown;
> Thy very beadsmen learn to bend their bows
> Of double-fatal yew against thy state;
> Yea, distaff-women manage rusty bills
> Against thy seat: both young and old rebel,
> And all goes worse than I have power to tell.
>
> (3.2.112–20)

York describes Richard and Bolingbroke's entrance into London as follows:

> Whilst all tongues cried "God save thee, Bolingbroke!"
> .   .   .   .
>   men's eyes
> Did scowl on Richard. No man cried "God save him!"
> No joyful tongue gave him his welcome home,
> But dust was thrown upon his sacred head. . . .
>
> (5.2.11–30)

Between the two events reported by Scroop and York is the actual transfer of the crown from Richard to Bolingbroke, which Northumberland says is at the "commons' suit." York enters Westminster Hall, where the lords are assembled, bringing Richard's offer to yield the throne to Bolingbroke.

After arresting the Bishop of Carlisle, Northumberland asks, "May it please you, lords, to grant the commons' suit?" (4.1.154), with the implication that the change in kings is instigated at the commons' request. Northumberland's reference to the commons sounds like manipulation of rhetoric to suit his own purposes; this suspicion is reinforced when, in trying to get Richard to read aloud a list of his crimes, Northumberland warns that "the commons will not then be satisfi'd" (4.1.272); but there are sufficient other confirmations of the relative popularity of Richard and Bolingbroke to allow this reference to the commons to be accepted by those present, whatever Northumberland's personal motives may be. Richard's army disperses without waiting for him (2.4); the gardener reports that Richard is totally unsupported against Bolingbroke (3.4.85); the two reports by Scroop and York confirm Richard's prior and subsequent lack of support, and Richard himself admits that "all"

> Have torn their souls by turning them from us,
> And we are barren and bereft of friends,
>
> (3.3.82–84)

except for the support he expects from God in the form of pestilence and "unbegot" children who will threaten Bolingbroke.

Bolingbroke knows that "opinion" helped him to the crown (*1H4*, 3.2.42), so that he sees in the attitude of the people the key to retaining power. He describes his courtship of the people quite differently from the way Richard did.

> By being seldom seen, I could not stir
> But like a comet I was wondered at,
> That men would tell their children, "This is he!"
>
> . . . .
>
> And then I stole all courtesy from heaven,
> And dress'd myself in such humility
> That I did pluck allegiance from men's hearts.
>
> (*1H4*, 3.2.46–52)

Henry calls the people "men" not slaves; his terms of contempt are reserved for Richard, his followers, and their attitudes. They were "capering fools" who laughed at boys and "beardless vain comparatives" until the people grew sick of them (3.2.60–84). There is craft revealed in Henry's lesson to his son; craft is particularly implied by the choice of the word "stole," so that Richard was therefore correct in fearing Bolingbroke. There is, however, no strong confirmation here of the hypocrisy Richard imputed to him. Bolingbroke is showing that extra effort is necessary to secure the people's support: fearing that his own courtesy was not adequate, he "stole" courtesy from heaven, to cite his own example, and he kept the people's interest and respect by avoiding overexposure, so that, like a bishop, his appearances would always evoke interest.

> Thus did I keep my person fresh and new,
> My presence, like a robe pontifical,
> Ne'er seen but wonder'd at. . . .

(3.2.55–57)

Richard, on the contrary in Henry's view, gave no thought to his public image as king but sought his amusement wherever he wished with no concern for the consequences. Henry says that Richard

> carded his state,
> Mingled his royalty with cap'ring fools,
> Had his great name profaned with their scorns,
> And gave his countenance against his name
> To laugh at gibing boys, and stand the push
> Of every beardless vain comparative,
> Grew a companion to the common streets,
> Enfeoff'd himself to popularity,

(3.2.62–69)

with the result that he lost the respect of the people who became surfeited with him (3.2.71).[3]

Given the consistent theme developed thus far through

Shakespeare's English history plays, in which the people have an uncanny instinct for identifying the effective leader, I believe that Shakespeare intends us to regard Bolingbroke's popularity with the people as genuine, even if cultivated, and not the result of the skill with which he masks his hypocrisy, as Richard would have it. Henry sincerely fears for his son's chances as future king because he thinks that Hal's pleasure in "slumming" will result in loss of popular respect, which will then endanger his rule as Richard's was endangered. Drawing upon his personal experience as practical politician, Henry gives Hal his best advice about how to keep the people's respect and support. His concern that Hal learn this lesson reveals Henry's acknowledgment of and respect for the power of common consent as a sine qua non of rule.

The relationship between popular support and a leader's attitude toward the people is further illustrated by the Archbishop of York. In order to spur Northumberland on to continue his son's battle against Henry IV, Morton reports that "more and less do flock to follow" the Archbishop (2H4, 1.1.209). The Archbishop, however, reveals to his co-conspirators that he thinks the people are the "fond many" (1.3.91) who first rejected Richard, then desire him again and reject their new love Bolingbroke. The image with which he conveys this idea betrays his contempt for his followers.

> Thou, beastly feeder, art so full of [Bolingbroke]
> That thou provok'st thyself to cast him up.
> So, so, thou common dog, didst thou disgorge
> Thy glutton bosom of the royal Richard;
> And now thou wouldst eat thy dead vomit up,
> And howl'st to find it.
>
> (2H4, 1.3.95–100)

It is, I think, no coincidence that his army disperses instantly once the soldiers have received their pay. From the order that they be paid and allowed to leave to the report that they are gone, less than thirty lines are spoken; Prince John of Lancaster can then arrest the Archbishop of York with impunity.

Misjudging the basis of Bolingbroke's popularity is not confined to Richard and his party but recurs among the rebels when he is Henry IV. In Hotspur's account of the deposition, it was Northumberland's popularity that assured Bolingbroke's success once Northumberland made his support of Bolingbroke public knowledge. Though Hotspur is speaking of the nobility, I include the passage here because I shall not be surveying Bolingbroke's popularity in discussing the lords.

> HOT.   . . . when he was not six and twenty strong,
> Sick in the world's regard, wretched and low,
> A poor unminded outlaw sneaking home,
>
> . . . .
> Now when the lords and barons of the realm
> Perceiv'd Northumberland did lean to him,
> The more and less came in with cap and knee.
>
> (*1H4*, 4.3.56–68)

And the mistake is further perpetuated by Mowbray, son of the man who was first challenged by Bolingbroke as the tetralogy opened. Young Mowbray thinks that his father could have stopped the danger to Richard's reign but that Richard committed a fatal error in interrupting the Bolingbroke-Mowbray lists. He is probably correct about Richard's error.

> O, when the King did throw his warder down,
> His own life hung upon the staff he threw;
> Then threw he down himself and all their lives
> That by indictment and by dint of sword
> Have since miscarried under Bolingbroke.
>
> (*2H4*, 4.1.125–29)

But, as Westmoreland quickly points out, he was not correct in thinking his father would have ended the danger:

The Earl of Hereford was reputed then
In England the most valiant gentleman.
Who knows on whom Fortune would then have smil'd?
But if your father had been victor there,
He ne'er had borne it out of Coventry;
For all the country, in a general voice,
Cried hate upon him; and all their prayers and love
Were set on Hereford, whom they doted on,
And bless'd, and grac'd, indeed more than the King.

                                                 (4.1.13–39)

And Westmoreland's account of Bolingbroke's popularity
at that time coincides with the reports of Scroop, the gardener, York, the Duchess of Gloucester, and even Richard,
while Hotspur's and Mowbray's accounts remain their own
partisan views.

    Finally, Henry IV's ultrapolitic son has studied well the
role of popular opinion in sustaining the Crown. To better
assure his future success, he takes care that "Tom, Dick,
and Francis" know that he is "no proud Jack" (*1H4*, 2.4.8–
11) and puts in the time necessary to know well the mind
of Poins:

> It would be every man's thought, and thou art a blessed fellow to
> think as every man thinks. Never a man's thought in the world
> keeps the roadway better than thine. [*2H4*, 2.2.52–55]

Though Henry IV misunderstands Hal's motives, Warwick
insists that

> The Prince but studies his companions
> Like a strange tongue, wherein, to gain the language,
> 'Tis needful that the most immodest word
> Be look'd upon and learnt:
>
>   (4.4.68–71)

and that once king, he will banish his lowly followers. Warwick proves correct. True to legend, Shakespeare's Henry V
does banish his former companions. As king he has other

means than tavern-hopping to keep in touch with his people. He announces in his first scene on stage after his father's death:

> Now call we our high court of parliament,
>
> . . . .
>
> Our coronation done, we will accite,
> As I before remember'd, all our state.
>
> (5.2.134–42)

For greater emphasis he twice repeats his intention—to call a meeting of Parliament, of all his state, a phrase that I agree with G. B. Harrison in glossing as "the three estates of the realm . . . which made up the Parliament."[4] I think that Humphreys is incorrect in glossing *state* as "men of rank"[5] because *state* is coupled with *all*, a combination traditionally associated with the estates in parliament (see chap. 1). Thus Henry acknowledges the two aspects of the Parliament in its capacity to advise him as king's high court and in its capacity to accord or withhold consent as representative assembly. That the man whose every gesture was carefully premeditated (Palmer includes an excellent discussion on Henry's compulsion to satisfy himself that he is "doing only what is right and proper" [*Political and Comic Characters*, p. 185]) should think it necessary to twice promise in his first appearance as king to meet formally with his people, I believe records a commitment to the constitutional structure of England as it existed in the later years of Elizabeth's reign.[6]

In the first tetralogy the people, particularly the commons, have little formal apparatus through which to make their views known yet have great power in helping determine through their support who will be king; in the second tetralogy, the people and the support they offer a leader progress from being a recurring theme to being accorded formal recognition. In short, in terms of the position of the people in the governing structure of the realm, Shakespeare through the eight plays of the two tetralogies has recorded

a movement away from Henry VI's assumption that the
people owe him support to Henry V's recognition that he
must seek their support by regularly consulting with them.
Shakespeare embellished upon the sources in his presentation
of both Henry VI and Henry V to underscore just this
difference between the two kings. For instance, when Winchester and Gloucester's servants skirmish in Henry VI's
Parliament (see section 2A) in what is called the "pebble
stone" incident, *Fabyan*, the sole source of this incident,
reports only that "the people took great bats and staves in
their necks, and so followed their lords and masters, unto
the Parliament." Henry's appeal to feudal obligations and
the servants' denial are Shakespeare's addition to this report. Both Hall and Holinshed report that Parliament, not
Henry VI, settled the dispute between Gloucester and Winchester. And among the several illustrations of Henry V's
"shape of a new man" once king, Holinshed includes the
fact that shortly after Henry's being crowned he called a
Parliament "in which diverse good statutes, and wholesome
ordinances, for the preservation and advancement of the
commonwealth were devised and established."[7] Shakespeare
places particular emphasis on this detail by having Henry
twice repeat his intention and then by having the Lord Chief
Justice and Lancaster affirm that he has kept his word.

LANC.   The King hath call'd his parliament, my lord.
CH.JUST.   He hath.

                                                (5.5.103–4)

Henry's attending to Parliament is further emphasized when
Henry V begins; the Archbishop of Canterbury and the
Bishop of Ely are worried about the "bill / Urg'd by the
commons" (1.1.70–71) that would deprive the Church of
more than half its possessions. They are anxious because
they believe that Henry listens to the commons. Canterbury
reveals that to protect the Church he has had to offer a huge
amount of money to strengthen Henry's interest in fighting
in France; foreign wars would postpone consideration of the

bill against the Church. The audience will soon see, however, that the Archbishop has been "had," since Henry intended to go to France even without the backing of Church money. But this does not undercut Henry's attentiveness to the commons even if in this, as in everything else, he uses his action to serve his own purposes as well.

There are only a few commoners who appear in this group of plays. In *Richard II* the gardeners, who moralize about the state as they oversee their miniature kingdom, and the young groom who visits Richard in prison reveal more about Richard than about the common people and so will be considered in the discussion of the deposed king. In the two parts of *Henry IV*, there are the gang and Falstaff, who as a knight should be considered among the lords but who chooses to spend his time in baser company in Eastcheap. Through Falstaff and the gang, Shakespeare is able to provide, in addition to just plain fun, considerable information about general conditions in the kingdom and a close examination of the relationship between a king and his people, an examination that is then transferred from the relationship between Hal and the gang to Henry V and the army in the last play.

One learns from the scene in which Gadshill prepares for the robbery that the country is experiencing inflation to such a degree that carriers gossip over the rising price of oats as having destroyed a hostel keeper (*1H4*, 2.1.11–12).[8] One learns from Francis something about the conditions of apprentices, since he would gladly desert his position (2.4.50), and from Falstaff's actions one hears of and sees the abominable practices of the recruiting sergeants (*1H4*, 4.2. and *2H4*, 3.2). His confessing that he has abused his powers as recruiter to assemble "the cankers of a calm world and a long peace" (*1H4*, 4.2.29–30) provides a significant qualification of the army with which Henry IV battles the rebels. Unlike the confrontation between Richmond and

Richard III, where spirits had blessed the one and condemned the other, the battle between the forces of Hotspur
and Henry IV will be fought primarily on a worldly plane.
Minute attention to detail, in Henry's having decoys dressed
as kings in the field (notice the contrast with the undefended
Edward IV in *3 Henry VI*), and unrelenting effort, in Hal's
refusing though wounded to retire from battle, will secure
the victory. Henry IV and his son win through plain hard
work, not supernatural blessing.

There is one aspect of the complex relationship between
Falstaff and Hal that is particularly relevant to the exploration of constitutional structure in these plays. Through the
consistent difference in *Weltanschauung* that the two men
reveal in almost their every conversation, the relationship
between the two men contributes to a consistent theme, developed in this tetralogy, of the barrier a crown interposes
in any association between man and man-as-king. Other
times when one is most aware of this barrier are when
Henry IV cannot sleep (*2H4*, 3.2.4–31) and when Henry V
rails against ceremony (*H5*, 4.1.246–290). In Hal and
Falstaff's first appearance on stage, when Falstaff talks of
stealing, Hal refers to the gallows (*1H4*, 1.2.38); when
Falstaff calls the Hostess a sweet wench, Hal talks of sheriff's men (1.2.42). When they call each other to account for
this difference, they each deny the relevance of the other's
references to themselves.

FAL.   What a plague have I to do with a buff jerkin?
HAL.   Why, what a pox have I to do with my hostess of the tavern?
                                          (1.2.45–46)

This contrast persists. When the Sheriff comes to Eastcheap
in pursuit of the Gadshill robbers, Hal prepares himself by
saying, "Now, my masters, for a true face and good conscience" (2.4.495); then he promises the Sheriff that Falstaff "shall be answerable" (2.4.515), while Falstaff uncon-
cernedly falls fast asleep (2.4.521). In *2 Henry IV*, where
Falstaff would be content to rest forever dining with the

Hostess and Doll Tearsheet, Hal is quickly sated with their company saying,

> . . . I feel me much to blame,
> So idly to profane the precious time,
> When tempest of commotion . . .
> > doth begin to melt
> And drop upon our bare unarmed heads.
> Give me my sword and cloak. Falstaff, good night.
>
> (2.4.358–63)

This continuing contrast between the "riot" of Falstaff and Prince Hal's self-conscious preoccupation with the state is, I think, intended to keep the audience aware of the dramatic irony in Henry's fear for his son, an idea to which I shall return in discussing the kings.

Though Hal is always aware of his position as heir to the throne, I do not think he recognizes the fact that everyone with whom he associates is equally aware of his position. While Hal boasts of winning the respect of drawers and tinkers, it is clear from his own words that their courtesy to him owes a great deal to his position.

> They take it already upon their salvation, that though I be but Prince of Wales, yet I am the king of courtesy, . . . and when I am king of England I shall command all the good lads in Eastcheap. [1H4, 2.4.8–14]

Where Hal is very self-assured in trapping Falstaff in enormous exaggerations, Falstaff manages to retain his dignity by deferring to the magic of royalty and the instinct of a loyal subordinate, thus specifying that the respect Hal receives is for his position not his person. Nor is this excuse the only occasion in which Falstaff refers to Hal as prince. Here are a few other examples from their first scene together (1H4, 1.2.):

> I prithee sweet wag, when thou art king
>
> (1.2.16)

were it not here apparent
that thou art heir apparent

(1.2.55–56)

I'll be damned for
never a king's son in Christendom

(1.2.94–95)

nor thou cam'st not of the blood
royal, if thou darest not stand

(1.2.136–37)

the true Prince may (for recreation sake) prove
a false thief. . . .

(1.2.150–51)

The frequency of Falstaff's references to Hal's position remains constant throughout the rest of this play and into the next. In fact, some mention is made of Hal as heir or prince in Falstaff's almost every utterance. To judge from the sheer multitude of references, this emphasis is calculated, I think, to keep attention focused on the court through the seemingly unrelated tavern scenes. Falstaff's references are a constant reminder of what should be important amidst the frivolous.

But despite these references given to Falstaff, and despite Shakespeare's taking great care to portray Falstaff's flaws, the character gets away from him. The very number of Falstaff's references to Hal as heir to the throne become hyperbolic, tending to ridicule as much as to convey respect for his young friend. Since the gusto and spontaneity of the Falstaff scenes are always what one recalls from these plays, these scenes diminish the impact of the court scenes. Indeed, as A. R. Humphreys points out, Falstaff "provides amidst all his vices a vast salutary criticism of the world of war and policy,"[9] which marks an important stage in the development that Una Ellis-Fermor sees in Shakespeare's political plays. By the time he came to write *Antony and Cleopatra*, Ellis-Fermor suggests, Shakespeare rejected not Falstaff but

Henry V. In her view, Shakespeare attained "the mature realization that upon the individual life of the spirit the world of affairs could have no final claim."[10] That mature realization is not yet present in *2 Henry IV*, where Shakespeare takes fewer risks in the balance between court and tavern by thoroughly discrediting the gang and Falstaff; to do so Shakespeare draws attention to disease and physical grossness, and in constitutional terms he stresses Falstaff's, Doll's, and the Hostess's abuses of the law. But even so Shakespeare evidently feared that he had not sufficiently discredited Falstaff, for in order to allow the new king, Henry V, to shine in his own right, Shakespeare first banished Falstaff to at least ten miles distance from the new court, then in *Henry V* decided that he must die.

Since for most of *Henry V* England is shown to be at war, the role of the people is largely represented by the army. It forms a microcosmic society that can reflect on English society as a whole in that it encompasses a range from Pistol and Bardolph as thieves through the captains right up to the king as commander in chief. Fluellen, the Welsh captain, and Pistol, the survivor from Eastcheap days, receive the greatest attention. Through Fluellen's relationship to the other officers, particularly Gower, Macmorris, and Jamy, Shakespeare draws attention to the subordination of individual differences that is achieved by Henry's army (see 3.2). What particularly impresses Fluellen is Henry's knowledge and application of discipline according to the law of arms in enforcing the death penalty for stealing (3.6.57) and in ordering the execution of prisoners after the French killed the boys left behind in the English camp (4.7.1–11), a decision that inspires Fluellen to compare Henry with Alexander the Great. The respect he feels for Henry is mutual; after overhearing Gower and Fluellen in one of their continuing discussions of the laws of war, Henry acknowledges that "there is much care and valor in this Welshman" (4.1.84).

Falstaff's role of reminder that Hal is first and foremost the prince is given in *Henry V* to a less overwhelming figure,

Williams, whose encounters with the king serve to remind Henry how different he is from other men. When, despite all his public gestures aimed at satisfying popular opinion, particularly his adamant denials of ransom, Henry in disguise learns that soldier Williams remains skeptical, Henry is frustrated to the point of anger.

WILL.   That's a perilous shot out
           of an elder-gun, that a poor and a private displeasure
           can do against a monarch. You may as well go about
           to turn the sun to ice with fanning in his face with
           a peacock's feather. You'll never trust his word
           after! come, 'tis a foolish saying.
K. HEN.   Your reproof is something too round: I should be
           angry with you if the time were convenient. [4.1.203–
           10]

Marilyn Williamson points out that Henry's impulse to fight with Williams shows "that he is still learning to be a king" and "should be taken to modify the official view of his reformation . . . as an absolute change of the sort that the Archbishop describes."[11] Henry and Williams exchange gages until the battle is over.

    Henry involves Fluellen in the impending confrontation with Williams.

K. HEN.   What think you, Captain Fluellen? is it fit this sol-
           dier keep his oath?
FLU.   He is a craven and a villain else, an't please your
           majesty, in my conscience.
K. HEN.   It may be his enemy is a gentleman of great sort,
           quite from the answer of his degree.
FLU.   Though he be as good a gentleman as the devil is,
           . . . it is necessary, look your grace, that he keep his
           vow and his oath. If he be perjured, see you now,
           his reputation is as arrant a villain and a Jack-sauce
           as ever his black shoe trod upon God's ground and
           his earth, in my conscience, la! [4.7.135–47]

If Henry is to retain Fluellen's high regard, he must respect

Williams's integrity in keeping his oath. So that even if Henry wished to ignore the lessons he had learned as his father's son about the Crown, Fluellen's presence in the confrontation with Williams will be a reminder of the limits to his command as king, even in the flush of victory. He cannot ask that a subordinate perjure himself out of respect for rank, a lesson not learned or even acknowledged by Richard II in his treatment of the unfortunate Mowbray who is asked to and does sacrifice himself so that the crimes of his superior in ordering Woodstock, the Duke of Gloucester, killed will not be revealed at the public inquiry brought about by Bolingbroke's challenge.

Henry arranges for Fluellen to wear Williams's glove in his hat, not only on the strength of "his Eastcheap habits," which leads him to "compound the trick" of his disguise, as Williamson suggests ("The Episode with Williams in *Henry V*," p. 279), but to protect Williams. All of these common soldiers, as Harold Goddard states, "are plainly men of sincerity and worth. Somehow Shakespeare convinces us that it is of this stuff that England is made. The three men evoke a respective sincerity from Henry."[12] I agree with Williamson that Henry is "deeply shaken at feelings his men reveal as they wait for the morning's battle" ("The Episode with Williams in *Henry V*," p. 276). Henry's disguising himself "to become a man" among men and not a king (Goddard, *Meaning of Shakespeare*, p. 240), has resulted in an unfortunate quarrel. When Fluellen confirms that Williams, if he is an honest man, which Henry knows him to be, must call Henry to account, Henry sees to it that Williams does not innocently place himself and the king in a compromising situation; Henry has Fluellen not the king receive Williams's blow (4.7.157). Henry also makes certain that Warwick and Gloucester prevent any serious quarrel from erupting (4.7.176–87).

When Henry reveals to Williams that it was the king whom he challenged, Williams is not then moved to unsay what before he had said. Instead he distinguishes Henry the person from Henry the king and specifies that his respect is for the office.

WILL.   All offences, my lord, come from the heart: never came any from mine that might offend your majesty.

K. HEN.   It was ourself thou didst abuse.

WILL.   Your majesty came not like yourself: you appeared to me but as a common man; witness the night, your garments, your lowliness; and what your highness suffered under that shape, I beseech you, take it for your own fault and not mine. . . . [4.8.47–56]

Henry's response is to offer him money, a glove filled with crowns, for this distinction between the person and the office of the king was and would remain an ultimately unassailable element in the complex notion of the Crown. Richard II was the only king in all these plays who did not recognize the distinction; Henry V as son of his successor would not long forget the lesson of Richard's deposition; therefore he makes no serious attempt at answering Williams, the common soldier.

Pistol persists from *2 Henry IV* through the end of the war in France when he vows to "turn bawd" and steal in England. I see in Pistol's survival after the great unity achieved by Henry and his men in victory over the French, particularly in his apearance immediately following Fluellen's and Henry's attempted peacemaking with Williams, part of a continuing theme through both tetralogies. Shakespeare uses Pistol to indicate the limits of Henry's success. The chorus in the epilogue will mention the most serious limit to the successes of "This star of England" (1.5):

> Fortune made his sword,
> By which the world's best garden he achieved.
> And of it left his son imperial lord.
> Henry the Sixth, in infant bands crowned king,
> Of France and England, did this king succeed,
> Whose state so many had the managing
> That they lost France and made his England bleed.
>
> (Epil. 6–12)

These lines follow Henry's joyous wooing of Katharine of France. The realities of the historical situation were that

Henry's achievement was only temporary and carried within it the seeds of destruction. Henry's personal rule made no provision for a government without a strong leader like himself. What made Henry's government work was the ability with which he united the views of the commons and lords through his leadership. If his leadership can inspire Pistol to nothing better than being a bawd and thief, followers less powerful than himself will not be able to keep united commons and lords who had become accustomed to making their views known—with the resulting chaos seen in the first tetralogy.

B.   The Lords

Consultation between lords and king in the first tetralogy and in *John* was largely carried out on an ad hoc basis. Henry VI gave greater attention to the advice of Suffolk in marrying Margaret than to the advice of Gloucester and the council; despite Edward IV's private arrangement to consult with Warwick, he did not keep his agreement; John consulted with his lords but ignored their advice. In the second tetralogy, however, the council receives increasing mention and plays a greater and greater role in the government of the realm.

The council is first mentioned during the Bolingbroke/Mowbray lists that Richard suddenly stops.

> Let them lay by their helmets and their spears,
> And both return back to their chairs again.
> Withdraw with us, and let the trumpets sound,
> While we return these Dukes what we decree.
>   [A long flourish.]
> Draw near,
> And list what with our council we have done.
>   (*R2*, 1.3.119–24)

The critical decisions to banish the two are thus presented as having been made jointly by King and council, which probably explains why the decisions are accepted by the combatants (as Henry VI's decision with commons' support to banish Suffolk is accepted in *2 Henry VI*).

One next hears of a council when, as *1 Henry IV* opens, Henry meets with some of his lords to hear a report of the most recent council session (1.1.30–33). The scene closes with Henry's preparing for the subsequent council meeting (1.1.102). The respect that Henry accords to his lords by providing for their regular meeting as a council to the king has an effect that extends well beyond the confines of the court. Falstaff, despite his notorious irreverence, betrays his respect for the council when he confesses to Hal that

> an old lord of the Council rated me the other day in the street about you, sir, but I marked him not, and yet he talked very wisely, but I regarded him not, and yet he talked wisely, and in the street too. [*1H4*, 1.2.81–85]

This provides an occasion for Hal to joke about a passage in *Proverbs* (1.2.20–24), but, more significantly, it shows the contrast between Henry IV's government and the functioning of all other governments thus far presented in Shakespeare's English history plays. No Holland or Bevis can complain of Henry IV's council as they did of Henry VI's that members were not good workmen (*2H6*, 4.2.10–20). If a council member can impress Falstaff with his concern by seizing the occasion of a chance meeting in the street to reproach him for his relationship with the Prince, that is a remarkable demonstration of the awareness of Henry IV's council and of its dedication to the king in going beyond the confines of administrative duty to serve him well.

In his private meeting with his son to chastise him for his misbehavior, Henry specifically mentions the council.[13] Henry stresses the council because it has been so important in supporting his own government and because (as I have suggested, Shakespeare has made Henry's perception of the relationship between Crown and people (of which the council in the plays is one form of representation) a legitimating factor in his successfully replacing Richard, who disdained the people.

> Yet let me wonder, Harry,
> At thy affections, which do hold a wing
> Quite from the flight of all thy ancestors.
> Thy place in Council thou hast rudely lost,
> Which by thy younger brother is supply'd,
> And art almost an alien to the hearts
> Of all the court and princes of my blood. . . .
>
> (3.2.29–35)

But Hal's disregard of the council is part of his base image calculated to increase the wonder at his transformation. He has sometimes, in fact, used Falstaff and company as a comic anticouncil to prepare him, after a fashion, for dealing with a royal council—such as when he allows Poins to persuade him that there is an acceptable way to join in a robbery (*1H4*, 1.2.), or when Falstaff rehearses him for meeting with his father (2.4.), or when Hal regulates his demonstration of grief at his father's illness to match what is expected of him according to Poins (*2H4*, 2.2).

In his first appearance as King, Henry V tells all present,

> let us choose such limbs of noble counsel
> That the great body of our state may go
> In equal rank with the best-govern'd nation. . . .
>
> (*2H4*, 5.2.135–37)

His reformation will not only impress those in his court but will be carried as far as France when in *Henry V* the Constable reports

> How well supplied with noble counsellors,
> How modest in exception, and withal
> How terrible in constant resolution
>
> (2.4.33–35)

the new king is. Then, as *Henry V* draws to a close, after having named a council to negotiate the terms of the treaty with France (5.2.83–90), Henry reveals to Kate that he would credit a council at least as much as if not more than a king, depending on whether one understands the italicized "they" in the following passage as referring to Kate's lips or to the tongues of the council (my italics).

> You have witchcraft in your lips, Kate: there is more eloquence in a sugar touch of them than in the tongues of the French council; and *they* should sooner persuade Harry of England than a general petition of monarchs. [5.2.292–96]

That Henry V would place such confidence in a council, whether French or English, stems from the experiences of his ancestors that his father cited in reproaching him. His grandfather, John of Gaunt, as council member took his position so seriously that he unwillingly consented to the lengthy banishment of his son, thereby subordinating his obligation as father to that of adviser (*R2*, 1.3.237–46). He risked the disfavor of the king in his last moments of life in seeking to dissuade Richard from his disastrous governmental policies. The fact that during Richard II's reign such dedication to the common good had been more present in the council than in the king is further illustrated by York's reproach to Richard after he seizes Gaunt's wealth.

I would like to pause here to examine a line spoken by Gaunt in his final meeting with Richard—"Since thou dost seek to kill my name in me" (*R2*, 2.1.86). This line possibly indicates that someone at court has warned Gaunt of Richard's intentions against his house once Gaunt is dead, and if so, this line would clear Bolingbroke of the suspicion that he returned to England before he had cause. If his father knew of Richard's intentions before Richard acted, there would be no reason why Bolingbroke could not also have known.

The most common interpretation of this line is that Gaunt means "by banishing his heir."[14] However, Bolingbroke was not banished forever, as was Mowbray, but for a period of six years, so that *kill* seems to be too strong a word unless Gaunt has heard differently. In private conversation Richard had told Aumerle, Bagot, and Green:

He is our cousin's cousin, but 'tis doubt,
When time shall call him home from banishment,
Whether our kinsman come to see his friends.

(1.4.20–22)

The lining of [Gaunt's] coffers shall make coats
To deck our soldiers for these Irish wars.

(1.4.61–62)

The second statement is clear—Richard intends to seize
Gaunt's wealth, and since without wealth a noble name
would represent little power, Gaunt could, if he in fact had
been warned of Richard's plan, be interpreting this as seeking to kill his name by not allowing the wealth to remain in
his family. The first statement is less clear. Is Richard referring to his supporters as Bolingbroke's "friends," implying with sarcasm that he doubts whether Bolingbroke will
come to see Richard and his followers at the end of his
period of banishment? Or is there, as Peter Ure suggests
from a hint in A. W. Pollard's notes to the 1916 edition
of the play, to be found in Richard's words a threatening
sneer that Ure paraphrases as follows: "It's doubtful, when
the period of his banishment ends, whether this kinsman of
ours will be permitted to come and see his dear cousins"
(*King Richard II*, p. 41n), meaning, I take it, that Richard
will extend his banishment indefinitely. Richard's desire for
Gaunt's wealth and his desire to prolong Bolingbroke's
banishment would leave Gaunt without wealth and without
an heir, two threats that would certainly justify the strength
of his statement: "thou dost seek to kill my name in me."
James Winny says in *The Player King* that

[Richard] seizes Lancaster's estates, denies Bolingbroke access to
his inheritance, and allows his favourites to erase all marks of
ancestral right from the banished man's properties. The sober
truth behind Gaunt's remark . . . is now revealed. Richard is
trying to put a stop to the house of Lancaster. . . . Banishment,
dispossession, and outlawry are intended to reduce Bolingbroke
to a penniless nobody. . . .[15]

I find it more likely that Gaunt had been warned by someone at court than that he is only referring to his son's six-year banishment. For then Bolingbroke could also have had prior information, which is suggested by York's revealing that Bolingbroke has already offered homage to Richard:

> If you do wrongfully seize Herford's rights,
> Call in the letters patent that he hath
> By his attorneys-general to sue
> His livery, and deny his off'red homage,
> You pluck a thousand dangers on your head,
> You lose a thousand well-disposed hearts. . . .
>
> (2.1.201–6)

One might even wonder from his words whether York knows that Bolingbroke is coming and chooses to utter a cryptic warning and depart rather than inform the king of whom he so heartily disapproved.

> I'll not be by the while. My liege, farewell.
> What will ensue hereof, there's none can tell;
> But by bad courses may be understood
> That their events can never fall out good.
>
> (2.1.211–14)

When at their first meeting together Bolingbroke's complaint to York echoes York's very reproach to Richard,

> I am denied to sue my livery here,
> And yet my letters patent give me leave.
>
> . . . .
>
> attorneys are denied me,
> (2.3.128–33)

one might further wonder at York's role in this whole affair. Once he meets with Bolingbroke, York makes one reproach, states that he will be neutral, then not only invites Bolingbroke to spend the night in the castle with him but goes with him to seize and execute Richard's supporters (2.3.155–67); York, similarly in act 3, scene 3 and act 4, scene 1, first warns Bolingbroke against seizing the Crown, then acts as the go-between negotiating Richard's transfer of the Crown to Bolingbroke. I also suspect that without fore-warning, an action as shocking as Richard's is shown to be in seizing Gaunt's wealth would not find a York ready with detailed reproach and a Ross, a Northumberland, and a Willoby ready with an instant catalogue of Richard's fail-ings. Such an act as Richard's would more likely provoke a stunned silence that in a following scene could result in plots. The immediacy of the lords' reactions, I think, further confirms the suggestion in Gaunt's line and in York's reveal-ing that Bolingbroke has offered homage that Richard's intentions were known earlier. Also, as I will show later in this section and in the Crown section, Shakespeare was so careful to keep Bolingbroke free of aggression against Richard that it is unlikely that in the question of his return Shakespeare would do the contrary by making Bolingbroke look wrong.

If a lord at court had warned Gaunt, the descendants of John of Gaunt had been well taught by experience that lords' support is important. In either case, Gaunt's son and grand-son cultivate the lords' favor largely through the vehicle of the council. This cultivation is amply rewarded by a harvest of loyalty from the majority of the lords; most of the lords support Henry IV and Henry V, to whom they also provide accurate information that contrasts with the information provided to their rivals. For example, Westmoreland's re-port from the council about the fighting in Wales is brought up to date by Henry's more recent and accurate report from Sir Walter Blunt, who stands in his presence still stained from his rapid journey to bring Henry current news (*1H4*, 1.1.64). Henry knows that Hotspur has won and that he refuses to send any more than one of his prisoners. Though Hotspur may have been justified in this refusal according to the rules of arms, the council supports Henry's view that Hotspur is wrong, for Westmoreland says that his defiance is a result of Worcester's teaching, an opinion that will be confirmed by what is subsequently revealed of the relationship between Hotspur and his uncle. After Henry claims that Mortimer is a traitor and, therefore, should not be ransomed, confirmation of Henry's assertion is provided when Worcester says that a conspiracy does exist involving Douglas and the Archbishop of York, who will join with Mortimer and Glendower against Henry (1.3.186–293). A further confirmation of the loyalty of most lords to Henry IV is provided when Hotspur learns from a letter that a lord whom he expected to join in the rebellion not only will not join but evidently intends to inform the king. After reading the letter, Hotspur says, "Let him tell the King, we are prepared" (2.3.34–35).

Shakespeare's introduction of Rumor to present *2 Henry IV* emphasizes the accuracy of the information brought to Henry IV. Northumberland is first told that his forces have won, that the king is near death from wounds, and that Hal is slain by Hotspur. He does receive the less favorable but more accurate news quickly thereafter, but Henry in contrast is *never* shown receiving such false reports. Warwick says that Hal is using Falstaff to learn about the people but that he will abandon him later and so tells the king. Warwick also immediately reports to Henry that his son, though he has taken the crown, is beweeping his death, thus correcting the error before it can mushroom (4.5.87). On another occasion Warwick counters Henry's depression at Northumberland's defection, which Richard had foretold, by showing that the prediction revealed no extraordinary insight on Richard's part but only the obvious projection to later circumstances of Northumberland's demonstrated breach of faith (3.1.80–92). Warwick also discounts the effects of rumor and teaches Henry to do the same in estimating his adversaries (3.1.96–98), a lesson that no one teaches Northumberland.

Finally, Bedford, Exeter, and Westmoreland's meeting in the council chamber reveals that Henry V knows of the treason plotted against him in ample time to take action before he leaves England's shores for foreign war (*H5*, 2.2.1–11). The only other king who similarly left England was Richard II, whom no one warned of the impending threat; he was thus unprovided and England was undefended as York demonstrates, with the result that Richard lost the throne. This steady stream of accurate information is as strong an indication of the lords' support of Henry IV and Henry V as one could wish.

Thus, the respect for the lords that both Henry IV and Henry V demonstrate through the ways in which they use their councils is intimately related to the respect that the lords demonstrate for them in their loyal service. Though each king is threatened by some of his lords, far more remain loyal and provide to the two kings the information and means necessary to secure their thrones. Richard, on the contrary, is actively defended at the time of the deposition by only Aumerle and Carlisle, who with Bagot were with him on the Irish expedition; Bushy and Green take refuge in Bristol Castle (*R2*, 2.2.134–47). Richard, before he has any proof, suspects that Bushy and Green have made peace with Bolingbroke and rails against them (3.2.127–34), when in fact they had been executed before Richard could have learned of their preferring the security of Bristol Castle over the perils of actively defending their king. The interrelationship of support and respect between leaders and commons is paralleled by that existing between lords and kings and illustrated both in the positive examples of Henry IV and Henry V and in the negative example of Richard II. A considerable amount of the strength that Henry IV and Henry V enjoy stems from their formal recognition of the need to consult with the lords as with their commons; Henry IV's recognition of this need is illustrated by his actions, Henry V's recognition by his declaring once king that he will choose noble counsel in order to make his country a well-governed one.

Shakespeare's dramatization of the relationship between Bolingbroke and the lords who support him in becoming king seems to be designed to keep Bolingbroke as free as possible from the guilt of the wrongs done to Richard, given the unavoidable fact of his becoming Richard's successor. As Shakespeare presents the deposition, all the aggressions against Richard are the actions of others, while whatever respect is accorded to Richard stems from Bolingbroke. Even York's denunciation of Bolingbroke for returning to England with troops (*R2*, 2.3.) is short-lived because York agrees that Richard has done great wrong to Bolingbroke. York concludes:

> if I could, by Him that gave me life,
> I would attach you all, and make you stoop
> Unto the sovereign mercy of the king;
> But since I cannot, be it known unto you,
> I do remain as neuter.
>
> (*R2*, 2.3.154–58)

Since even York's neutrality is not of long duration, this denunciation may be nothing more than face-saving ceremony on his part and not a genuine reproach of Bolingbroke.

In the second tetralogy there is a shift in emphasis away from the challenger to his supporters that marks a sharp contrast with the first tetralogy, where the impetus to challenge the title of the king on the throne arose directly from the persons who would profit from such a challenge, the Duke of York and his sons. Shakespeare's version of the challenge to Richard seems to take into account the description in Hall's *Chronicle* that

> the grave persons of the nobility, the sage prelates of the clergy, the sad magistrates and rulers of the cities, towns, and comminaltie perceiving daily more and more the realm to fall into ruin and desolation (in manner irrecuperable as long as king Richard either lived or reigned,) after long deliberation, wrote into France to duke Henry . . . soliciting and requiring him with all diligent celerity to convey himself into England, promising him all their aid, power, and assistance if he . . . would take upon him the scepter rule . . . of his native country. [P. 6]

J. A. R. Marriott similarly describes the impetus to replace Richard as stemming not from Bolingbroke but from the lords; Marriott says that the revolution of 1399 was the triumph of an oligarchical movement; "in the deposition of Richard of Bordeaux, [we have] the accession of a baronial nominee, Henry of Lancaster . . . [who] came to the throne on the top of a wave of a great conservative reaction."[16] Shakespeare focuses on two nobles in Bolingbroke's party, Worcester and Northumberland.

As soon as Northumberland and the others are proclaimed traitors, Green reports to the Queen that the Earl of Worcester

> Hath broken his staff, resign'd his stewardship,
> And all the household servants fled with him
> To Bolingbroke,
>
> (*R2*, 2.2.58–60)

a report that is repeated by Hotspur to Northumberland in the next scene.

> . . . he hath forsook the court,
> Broken his staff of office and dispers'd
> The household of the king.
>
> . . . .
>
> But he, my lord, is gone . . .
> To offer service to the Duke of Herford.
>
> (2.3.26–32)

Shakespeare, by having the same information repeated twice within a short interval of time, places great emphasis on Worcester's actions. In that Worcester acts not only for himself but as steward of Richard's household, when he turns from Richard to Bolingbroke he precipitates a rebellion for deposition rather than for simple redress of grievances. Worcester himself does not appear in this play. But in *1 Henry IV* he makes clear that he knew full well what he was doing. He reminds Henry IV that he helped make him king:

. . . that same greatness too which our own hands
Have holp to make so portly.

(*1H4*, 1.3.12–13)

And though one could not see him in action in *Richard II*
or hear his motives directly from him, one can see him
manipulating Hotspur in *1 Henry IV* to serve his own purposes, actions that reflect retrospectively on his support of
Bolingbroke in *Richard II*. Worcester chooses an opportune
moment when Hotspur is blazing with anger to mention
that Mortimer was named heir to the throne by Richard
(1.3.143–44); he supports Hotspur in his desire to change
the course of the river Trent so that his portion of the
realm will be improved lest a conflict over dividing the
realm keep him from fighting (3.1.108–10); yet he knows
that the enterprise into which he is leading Hotspur is not
free from reproach:

. . . well you know we of the off'ring side
Must keep aloof from strict arbitrement,
And stop all sight-holes, every loop from whence
The eye of reason may pry in upon us. . . .

(*1H4*, 4.1.69–72)

The explanation Worcester offers of Bolingbroke's succession is masterful in its manipulation of language:

You took occasion to be quickly woo'd
To gripe the general sway into your hand. . . .

(5.1.56–57)

He thus describes Bolingbroke as both passive and active,
in "taking" the occasion but in "being woo'd" to seize the
throne. What Worcester does not say is who did the wooing nor who supported Bolingbroke in his passive-action. If
one remembers Shakespeare's attention to Worcester's pre-
cipitous actions in deserting Richard, Worcester must,
though he refuses to do so now in public, accept much of the
responsibility for what has happened. But Worcester pre-

fers to put the blame entirely on Bolingbroke in this scene.
A clear picture of the kind of duplicity practised by Worcester emerges from his not properly relaying the offer of
single combat to Hotspur and from his admitting only to
Verner that "we did train him on" (5.2.21). Thus Westmoreland's assessment that Hotspur's defiance of Henry IV
stems from Worcester (1.1.95) proves correct.

It might be well to pause here to compare Worcester's
accusation that Henry broke an oath sworn at Doncaster
that he "did nothing purpose 'gainst the state" (*1H4*,
5.1.43) with the breaking of fealty oaths in the first tetralogy. Henry VI had been accused, in effect, of not fulfilling
his coronation oath so that he thereby released his subjects
from their obligation to serve him. Worcester is accusing
Henry IV of breaking a private agreement that does, therefore, not directly bear on the subsequent relationship between king and people. In that there is only Worcester's
word about Henry's oath, and since Worcester's own actions
belie his stated role in the affair, Shakespeare's handling of
the situation leaves Bolingbroke relatively free of the specific charge. I say "relatively" because, despite the care
with which Shakespeare handles Bolingbroke's role in Richard's deposition, I doubt if there is anyone who in reading
or watching this play even for the first time is surprised
when Bolingbroke becomes king.

Northumberland is the other lord who plays a critical
role in arranging the transition from Richard to Bolingbroke. While Shakespeare keeps Bolingbroke offstage and
silent about his intentions of returning to England, he has
Northumberland say,

> If then we shall shake off our slavish yoke,
>
> .   .   .   .
>
> And make high majesty look like itself,
> Away with me in post to Ravenspurgh.
>
> (*R2*, 2.1.291–96)

Then at their first appearance together, to Bolingbroke's
three lines, Northumberland speaks seventeen, all praising

Bolingbroke's "fair discourse" (2.3.6). This disproportion in lines may suggest not that Bolingbroke was garrulous offstage and taciturn onstage but that Northumberland has done all the talking, which is why he found the discourse "fair."

It is Northumberland who tells York that Bolingbroke has sworn "his coming is / But for his own," meaning his inheritance of Lancaster (2.3.147–48), yet it is Northumberland who does not call Richard "king" (3.3.6), an omission to which Shakespeare has York draw attention.

> It would beseem the Lord Northumberland
> To say "King Richard."
>
> (*R2*, 3.3.7–8)

And it is Northumberland who does not bow to Richard, a fact that Shakespeare underscores through Richard's reaction:

> We are amaz'd, and thus long have we stood
> To watch the fearful bending of thy knee,
> Because we thought ourself thy lawful king;
> And if we be, how dare thy joints forget
> To pay their awful duty to our presence?
>
> (3.3.72–76)

Bolingbroke, in contrast, had specifically instructed Northumberland to convey his respects to Richard in terms of bowing:[17]

> Noble lord,
>
> .   .   .   .
>
>   thus deliver:
> Henry Bolingbroke
> On both his knees doth kiss King Richard's hand. . . .
>
> (3.3.31–36)

Upon seeing Richard in person, Bolingbroke evidently does as he said he would—

> Stand all apart,
> And show fair duty to his Majesty
>
> (3.3.187–88)

—because Richard immediately tells him to get up from his knee (3.3.190–95). In the deposition scene it is Northumberland who harasses Richard until Bolingbroke intervenes by telling him, "Urge it no more, my Lord Northumberland" (4.1.271). There is no evidence to confirm that Bolingbroke has delegated Northumberland to do whatever is necessary so that he may look good in contrast, as Leonard Dean and John Palmer suggest.[18]

Just as for Worcester, one learns more about Northumberland in the two parts of *Henry IV* than one does in *Richard II*. The impression of him that is conveyed by his being too sick to help his son in the first part ("crafty-sick" in Induction, *2H4*, l. 37), by his raging "Let order die," when he learns of his son's defeat and death (*2H4*, 1.1.154), by his waiting in Scotland while his confederates go to battle the king (2.3.67) is not a favorable one. What was it that such a man hoped to gain by deposing Richard? If he would not support his own son and his closest associates but would support Bolingbroke, is there the picture of a man who was daring in his prime but cowardly in age? The effect of time is certainly a factor. But I think a stronger factor contributing to Northumberland's vigor in deposing Richard, then his paralysis against Bolingbroke, is his continuing cowardice and desire for self-preservation. In aiding Bolingbroke, he joined the bandwagon of inevitable success. Like Fitzwater who joined in the chorus accusing Aumerle of lying, Northumberland hoped to "thrive in this new world" (*R2*, 4.1.78) of Bolingbroke. In supporting Bolingbroke against Richard, then in not actively opposing Henry IV, Northumberland testifies to Henry's security on the throne, though ironically, his actions and inaction were possibly decisive in Bolingbroke's gaining and retaining the throne in Shakespeare's version.

The portraits of Worcester and Northumberland, two key

supporters in Bolingbroke's successful opposition to Richard, do not suggest a group of conspirators led and manipulated by Bolingbroke to serve his own purposes, an assumption that underlies any acceptance of Hotspur's view of Bolingbroke as a "vile politician." In the case of Worcester, it looks as though he tried, to his own peril, to manipulate a Bolingbroke who was too perceptive for Worcester's wiles to succeed. In the case of Northumberland, it looks as though there is an example of an essentially weak man who sought to protect his own interest. One must suspect the intentions of a man who when called upon to act in his own right, does nothing yet is aggressive when acting in another's behalf, a pattern of behavior that Northumberland also shows in the deposition scene when he claims to be pressing the commons' suit, thus using rhetoric to disguise his own self-interested intentions.

Shakespeare's minimal focus on Bolingbroke and the attention he gives to diminishing his key supporters reflect the anomaly of Bolingbroke's situation as a conservative usurper (Marriott, *English History in Shakespeare,* pp. 101–2), who takes possession of the Crown then defends the institution of the monarchy against the very men who helped him to be king. In Shakespeare's portrait of Henry IV's reign, the opposition is divided among itself, for the opposition arises from particular needs in the rebels rather than as a response to a national crisis. In Shakespeare's version, the rebellions against Henry IV provide a proving ground for the future Henry V more than a reflection on Henry's inadequate rule; all other rebellions in Shakespeare's English history plays arise, on the contrary, in response to specific mistakes or failings in the kings. It is Hotspur who is willful (see particularly *1H4*, 1.3.129–35) in language that echoes Edward IV at his worst. It is not the king and his party but the rebels who are profoundly divided among themselves and who intend to divide the kingdom, when it was a truism dating from at least the days of Geoffrey of Monmouth and the legend of Lear that to divide the kingdom was to bring ruin to the land (remember what hap-

pened when Gloucester divided the council in *Richard III*).
Although, to heighten the dramatic contrast, Shakespeare
makes it seem as if king and son are as divided as the
rebels, this is not the case. Where Worcester and Mortimer
together chastise Hotspur (3.1.141–83), Henry IV makes
certain that he and Hal are alone when he reproaches his
son (3.2.2), a contrast that is made the more strong by the
two scenes' being juxtaposed. And even more significantly,
where Henry shows support of his son's offer of single combat despite his continuing misgivings, Northumberland lets
his son go unsupported to battle where he inevitably dies.
Since one of the themes of the first tetralogy was that unity
within the contending party strengthens its right to occupy
the throne with popular support, this contrast in the second
tetralogy between the disunified rebels and the unified royal
family is an example of Henry IV's stronger claim than
Mortimer's (whom the rebels support) to the throne.
Moody Prior points out that "though critics have judged
the king in many ways and often with a savage lack of
sympathy, no one has ever suggested that the play leaves
us with the impression that the country would have been
better off if Hotspur and his fellow rebels had won the
day at Shrewsbury."[19]

Only the Archbishop of York among the rebels claims to
have grievances against Henry that result from concern
with the commonwealth, though the particular lines in which
he explains his cause are unfortunately unintelligible.[20]

> My brother general, the commonwealth,
> To brother born an household cruelty,
> I make my quarrel in particular.
>
> (*2H4*, 4.1.94–96)

Westmoreland denies his right as a single individual to
undertake such an enterprise—"such redress . . . , it not
belongs to you" (4.1.97–98). Among the Archbishop's co-
conspirators meanwhile, his motivation is understood to
stem from private grievances:

WOR.   . . . that same noble prelate, well-belov'd,
       The Archbishop.
HOT.   Of York, is it not?
WOR.   True, who bears hard
       His brother's death at Bristow, the Lord Scroop.
                            (*1H4*, 1.3.263–65)

His opposition to Henry IV is, like Clifford's opposition to any Yorkist, in part because a York killed his father (*3H6*, 1.1.163–66), but the Archbishop is not Clifford, and so he bolsters his opposition by references to general concerns. As Humphreys says, "the Archbishop's motives are noble. But his speech is florid and fulsome, the rhetoric of illusion, and its graphic quality is the quality not of realization but of prejudiced assumption" (*2H4*, p. lxv). His evident discomfort as Archbishop at being in the position of warrior ("these ill-beseeming arms," [*2H4*, 4.1.83]) makes him eager to accept the promise of redress despite the others' misgivings (4.2.66–86).

Thus Shakespeare shows that Northumberland chose better than he knew in wanting Bolingbroke to make "high majesty to look like itself" (*R2*, 2.1.295), for Bolingbroke would see to it that his own version of the Crown, true to the constitutional balance respecting commons, lords, and law, would prevail and not Northumberland's or Worcester's or the Archbishop's who, Skakespeare suggests, wanted the Crown to serve their individual interests. Shakespeare does not show Henry to be wasteful, as was Richard II, nor a poor defender of the realm, as was Henry VI, who allowed English conquests to be lost and negotiated away. In that Henry IV in his struggle to retain the Crown is defending it against men who would divide the kingdom, Henry's interests and England's are at one in this conflict.

C.   The Crown

Unlike the first tetralogy, the second contains only a few brief generalizations about the position of king. Richard II

states that a king must be impartial (*R2*, 1.1.115); Gaunt
says that a king should have foreign, not domestic enemies,
should win what he spends, and should not kill his kindred
(2.1.178–83). The Bishop of Carlisle says that subjects
cannot judge a king (4.1.121). The Queen says that a king
should be like a lion (5.1.29), and the Duchess of York
says that a king should speak pardon (5.3.116). By and
large there is less talk in this group of plays about the office
of king than action in supporting or not supporting a particular monarch. One must therefore infer from Richard and
Bolingbroke themselves what expectations and assumptions
about kingship the one fails to meet and the other does meet
since the one loses the Crown and the other retains it. I
shall introduce comparisons with the handling of the same
material in *Woodstock* as a means of highlighting Shakespeare's intentions. Henry V is of far less significance in
constitutional terms than Richard II or Henry IV, for he
only furthers the initial steps taken by his father. He is not
an originator but a "completor" who attains perfections in
the areas indicated by his father to be essential to ruling
well. Therefore Henry V will be accorded much less attention than his two predecessors. I agree with Moody Prior's
statement that *2 Henry IV* "may be regarded as the last
serious study of kingship in the cycle" (*The Drama of
Power*, p. 340).

As I understand Shakespeare's presentation of the deposition of Richard II, Richard himself causes his rejection
by the people through abuse of his public trust—in squandering wealth, in angering the lords and commons by imposing
taxes of dubious legality, in allowing the murder of his
uncle, and so on. Richard Jones writes that it was the
historical Richard who forced the decision to depose him;
"the action of his opponents was always in reaction to his
designs"; the English community rejected his attempt to
establish a more unfettered and more powerful dynastic
monarchy than England had known.[21] Just as he had done
in dramatizing the conflict between Humphrey, the Duke
of Gloucester, and the council in *1* and *2 Henry VI* as a

personal one rather than as a disagreement over the definition of a protector's constitutional role, Shakespeare translates the ideological differences between Richard and the forces backing Bolingbroke into personal differences. One therefore is less aware of constitutional problems for Richard's successor than of personal ones, although what seem to be personal difficulties for Richard's successor are largely constitutional problems as well. Whoever would replace Richard would face the difficult tasks of reestablishing public trust in the monarchy, of reasserting order, and of winning the support of the people so that the country would not remain divided along the lines caused by what are presented as his predecessor's ineptitudes. Yet the new ruler would always bear a double burden. He, like his predecessor, and according to standards he set for his predecessor, would rule under close scrutiny by the populace as a whole and in particular by the coalition that aided him in gaining power. His motives would likewise be subject to scrutiny because, regardless of gestures of concern for public weal, he did profit from the demise of his predecessor.

In the play one finds personal criticism of both Richard and Henry. Shakespeare has long been respected for his balanced judgment, which enabled him to let many points of view receive their due attention. In his portraits of Richard and Henry he examines the virtues and failings of two different interpretations of the Crown. I will suggest, however, in the following pages that Shakespeare has emphasized Richard's faults and minimized Bolingbroke's. In particular, he makes Richard a willful king who acts with little regard for public opinion while he makes Bolingbroke preoccupied with public opinion (for the very reasons indicated above). Within the context of the growing strength of Parliament in Elizabeth's waning years, I think that Shakespeare's emphasis on Bolingbroke's regard for public opinion has an additional significance beyond the bare Machiavellianism that many critics have imputed to Bolingbroke.

According to the analysis in *Taswell-Langmead* of the

historical record of depositions, the procedure for deposing an English king consists of three steps: (1) a "voluntary" abdication; (2) acceptance of the abdication; and finally, (3) a formal deposition in which the legal bonds of king and subject are declared to be dissolved.

> No English king has been deposed until after he had abdicated; the "deposition," therefore, is not an aggressive act by subjects against the monarch, but the final and formal ratification of the monarch's own resignation.[22]

The deposition, in effect, becomes a ceremony to confirm a transference of power that actually takes place elsewhere, usually on a battlefield. The ceremony has more dramatic and symbolic value than constitutional significance. The "aggressive act by subjects" takes place considerably before the deposition.

Peter Ure has observed of *Richard II*,

> this is not a play about how power is gained by *expertise,* nor even about how cunning overcomes stupidity—Richard is simply not there, either to provide the one, or counter the other. [P. lxvii]

I would counter that Bolingbroke is not there any more than Richard; in fact, if one totals the scenes in which they each are present, Richard appears in one more scene than Bolingbroke (nine to eight). Both Richard and Bolingbroke are on stage long enough to demonstrate the unfitness of the one and the fitness of the other to rule. But the real transfer of power actually takes place without very much attention to either of them. Given Richard's loss of popular support, which Shakespeare dramatizes with great economy in comparison with the first tetralogy, Bolingbroke as an individual is almost incidental to the deposition.[23] His personal motives matter very little because if he did not step into the power vacuum, someone else would.

Of the four sanctions for kingship shown to be necessary at the end of the first tetralogy, Richard gives evidence of having only two and part of a third: lineality, possession, and some support from the people. He gives almost no evidence of active concern for the common good. Systematically, beginning in the first scene, Shakespeare develops a contrast between Richard and Bolingbroke showing that the weaknesses of Richard are countered by the strengths of Bolingbroke; Richard undermines those sanctions that he has for being king while Bolingbroke's sanctions are strengthened until he, not Richard, is king.

In the first scene, whether he is attempting to downgrade the issue and maintain a pose of impartiality or is recognizing that the conflict is too heated for discussion, Richard says that Bolingbroke and Mowbray are "in rage, deaf as the sea" (*R2*, 1.1.19). Richard then makes a public appeal for reconciliation between the two lords that results, when they refuse, in his demonstrating, as Palmer has observed, that Richard "is plainly not master in his own house" (*Political and Comic Characters of Shakespeare*, p. 122). The damage to the public image of the monarchy is not lost upon Richard, who immediately states, in an effort to say at least what he has not been able to show, "we were not born to sue, but to command" (1.1.196). Bolingbroke in a similar situation will order that "These differences shall all rest under gage" (4.1.85), knowing better than to invite inevitable refusal to a public appeal for reconciliation. Both at Coventry and in Parliament Bolingbroke is seeking to have exposed the circumstances of the death of Richard's uncle Gloucester. This fact does not destroy the evidence of his better handling of conflict than Richard; once Bolingbroke sees how unreconcilable the adversaries are in act 4, scene 1, he quickly postpones consideration of the issue. Richard's ignoring Gloucester's death, meanwhile, reflects unfavorably on him as king, a fact that is emphasized in act 1, scene 2.

The dialogue between Gaunt and the Duchess of Gloucester in scene 2 makes clear that Richard was responsible for his uncle's death:

> God's substitute,
> His deputy anointed in His sight,
> Hath caus'd his death. . . .
>
> (1.2.37–39)

The Duchess prays for Hereford's success against Mowbray so that the perpetrator of the crime will be punished, thus strengthening Bolingbroke's case; no reinforcement is provided for Mowbray's contentions about Bolingbroke. In comparison with the handling of the death of Gloucester in *Woodstock*, Shakespeare's keeping the crime in the background curiously emphasizes Richard's guilt. In *Woodstock*, the king's responsibility for what happens is made clear when he orders his uncle "attached, condemned, and close imprisoned" (4.1.120); but then he is shown to be lamenting his decision and sending too late the order to reprieve his uncle (4.3.173–74). Shakespeare's Richard is given no such opportunity. The Duchess and Gaunt agree that he is responsible, and there it ends except for Bolingbroke's abortive inquiry in act 4, scene 1, which results in infinitely conflicting accusations but no defense of Richard. In addition to detracting from Richard's image as king, this scene between Gaunt and the Duchess serves another function. Since it will be this same Duchess whom York regards as his only source of funds to defend England for Richard against Bolingbroke (*R2*, 2.2.90–91), this scene anticipates Richard's later lack of support. For though the Duchess inconveniently, in York's view, dies before she can be of help, it is not simply an unfortunate sequence of events that leaves Richard friendless in his hour of need. From the information provided in scene 2 about the Duchess's attitude toward Richard, it is highly unlikely that she would have helped him had she been alive.

From the way in which Shakespeare has Richard stop the lists in scene 3 at the height of expectation, most critics have concluded with Palmer that Shakespeare intends to bring out flaws in his character and in his character as ruler. Palmer calls him a "boy-king who would never grow up;

the whole scene is in the nature of a practical joke" (*Political and Comic Characters of Shakespeare*, p. 131). Knowing full well the seriousness of the danger the powerful lords' quarrel imports for the realm and the consequent severity of the sentences that will be imposed on them, Richard nonetheless cannot resist the temptation to make them look foolish. At the height of their tension, when they are poised to begin combat, he orders them to stop and hear what he has to say. That Richard understands how thoroughly he has angered them as well as he recognizes that politics makes strange bedfellows is revealed by his making Bolingbroke and Mowbray swear that they will never become reconciled while abroad at the same time as he releases them from any further obligations of fealty to himself.[24] The perversity with which Richard knowingly does precisely what he should not do, perhaps from an irrepressible need to always be at center stage, is already emerging as one of his major characteristics by act 1, scene 3. Bolingbroke, meanwhile, despite the stresses that are placed upon him in this scene, shows such control that his father asks, "O, to what purpose dost thou hoard thy words. . . ?" (1.3.253). Where Mowbray is astounded and exclaims that the sentence is "all unlook'd for" (1.3.155), Bolingbroke urges Mowbray to confess (1.3.198), using a momentary lull in the activities to reinforce his accusation. To his father's advice that he pretend he is merely traveling, Bolingbroke states his rejection as a realist of the imagination:

> O, who can hold a fire in his hand
> By thinking on the frosty Caucasus?
>
> (1.3.294–95)

He makes his final words to the court a rousingly patriotic assertion:

> Where'er I wander boast of this I can,
> Though banish'd, yet a true-born Englishman.
>
> (1.3.308–9)

So that to Richard's self-destructiveness, which since he is king has national as well as personal implications, is contrasted Bolingbroke's self-preservation.

When Shakespeare has Richard tell his followers that he has "farmed" the realm and that he will resort to blank charters to obtain enough money from the rich to cover the expenses of his Irish campaign, Shakespeare thus makes Richard directly responsible for abuses that the author of *Woodstock* blames on others. In the anonymous play, Tresilian devises the blank charters to which Richard consents out of "love" for his "flatterers" after one of them threatens to join the uncles in opposing the king (4.1. 139ff.). The lawlessness with which the charters are used is shown to be entirely the responsibility of Tresilian and his servants. By making Richard and not his followers speak of the charters and farming the realm, Shakespeare denies Richard the possible excuse that he has been misled by poor advice. When Shakespeare has Richard pray for Gaunt's rapid death, he demonstrates his moral unfitness to be the Lord's elected deputy (1.4.60). It is also in this scene that Richard reveals his contempt both for the people and for Bolingbroke's popularity (see section 4A).

Gaunt's discussion of the value of a dying man's words prepares not Richard but the audience to heed his evaluation. His suggestion that Richard is seeking his own destruction well fits Richard's behavior to this point: Gaunt's accuracy makes his deathbed assessment a sweeping condemnation of Richard as king.

> O, had thy grandsire with a prophet's eye
> Seen how his son's son should destroy his sons,
> From forth thy reach he would have laid thy shame,
> Deposing thee before thou wert possess'd,
> Which art possess'd now to depose thyself.
>
> (2.1.104–8)

It is significant that Gaunt should refer to Richard's having been designated king by his grandfather. Speaking as son of Edward III, Gaunt can presume to gauge what Edward intended; thus, when he suggests that Edward would never have named Richard king had he foreseen his destructiveness, Gaunt denies Richard's primary sanction for possession as his grandfather's designated heir. After Richard seizes Gaunt's wealth (Gaunt then was, not incidentally, the richest man in England),[25] York's response further emphasizes the self-willed destructiveness with which Richard is undermining traditional patterns of inheritance.

> Take Herford's rights away, and take from time
> His charters, and his customary rights;
> Let not to-morrow then ensue to-day:
> Be not thyself. For how art thou a king
> But by fair sequence and succession?
>
> (2.1.195–99)

Gaunt's reference to Richard's having been designated heir by his grandfather and Northumberland's revealing in the same scene that he, in going to join Bolingbroke, is thinking about the "crown" and "majesty" (2.1.293–95) suggest that Shakespeare was aware of the peculiarities of the succession from Edward III through Richard II to Henry IV. According to *Taswell-Langmead*, the accession of Richard II had been "the first instance, in the succession to the Crown of England, where the claim of representative primogeniture [meaning the selection of the most competent descendant of the first-born] was preferred to that of proximity of blood [choosing the closest blood relative of the deceased ruler]" (p. 493). Thus the "lineality" of Richard's claim was neither as direct nor above challenge as many literary students have assumed. Had Henry IV chosen to argue for a rule of male primogeniture from the time of Edward II onwards, then Henry IV would have been the lawful successor of Richard II (*Taswell-Langmead,* p. 497). Robert Parsons indicates that Elizabethans were aware that the pattern of succession was interrupted by Richard II's following his grandfather to the throne. He cites arguments by those who favored the House of Lancaster, which state that John of Gaunt ought to have succeeded his father King Edward III before King Richard. On this assumption Lancastrian supporters, according to Parsons, further argued that the logical successor when Richard proved inadequate was Gaunt's son Bolingbroke, since he was "two degrees nearer to the king deposed than was Edmond Mortimer, descendant of Lionel Duke of Clarence."[26] This is why Richard fears Bolingbroke as much as he does, since the crown, according to one interpretation, *was* "in reversion his" (*R2*, 1.4.35), and this is why the logical choice for Richard's successor, according to the same interpretation, was Bolingbroke. However, Bolingbroke greatly complicated constitutional history by not making this claim. The only plausible claim that a commission found for Henry was that Richard could be deposed "by authority of the clergy and people called together for the purpose," but Henry had to spend the rest of his reign defending the Crown against the implications of a parliamentary title (*Taswell-Langmead*, p. 491). Both of these problems seem to be incorporated into Shakespeare's treatment of Richard, whom he shows to be abandoned by his people, and Henry, whom he shows to be defending the Crown against the very lords who supported him.

In ignoring Gaunt's and York's criticisms, Richard strips himself of not one but two sanctions for rule, respect for designated succession and popular support. One learns in act 2, scene 1 that many lords have deserted him and in the next scene, which introduces the Queen, that the commons as well are cold toward Richard (2.2.88). In Shakespeare's play, the Queen is quite different from the Queen in *Woodstock*, who expresses grave concern for the realm; the *Woodstock* Queen gives whatever help she can to the poor and seeks to mediate between Richard and his uncles (see particularly act 2, scene 3 and act 3, scene 1). Richard's Queen in Shakespeare's play, however, is shown to be almost entirely ignorant of the situation in England. She is melancholy but can divine no cause for her condition (2.2.36). When she learns of Richard's danger, she reacts only in terms of herself, not of the country: "I will despair" (2.2.68). She similarly reacts to overhearing the gardener's account of Richard's fall, revealing her contempt for the lowly gardener:

> Dar'st thou, thou little better thing than earth,
> Divine his downfall?
>
> (3.4.78–79)
>
> Gard'ner, for telling me these news of woe,
> Pray God the plants thou graft'st may never grow.
>
> (3.4.100–101)

Her anger is immediately contrasted with the gardener's graciousness:

> Poor queen, so that thy state might be no worse,
> I would my skill were subject to thy curse.
>
> (3.4.102–3)

He then plants rue for remembrance of the weeping queen. The picture of the queen that emerges from these two scenes does not make her love for Richard a mitigating factor in one's assessment of him, as Palmer would have it (*Political and Comic Characters of Shakespeare*, p. 168). If Shakespeare had intended that her esteem for Richard should increase his stature, he would have portrayed her more nobly as did the author of *Woodstock*. When, in her only meeting with Richard onstage in this play, the Queen challenges the weakness with which he is meeting his fate, she implants a suggestion that in part explains Richard's warlike death. Richard, like the Queen's image of a lion who

> dying thrusteth forth his paw
> And wounds the earth, if nothing else, with rage
> To be o'erpow'r'd,
>
> (5.1.29–31)

beats his keeper and kills two servants before Exton succeeds in killing him. The Queen's conception of the role of

king, like Suffolk's of the role of the nobility in *2 Henry VI*
(4.1.124–29, see section 2A), apparently consists of little
more than a sort of public performance. Her advice to
Richard reflects little on the realities of his reign and serves
only to inspire a brief martial moment.

Richard concerns himself neither with his succession as
his grandfather's heir, nor with his popularity among the
people, but with exceptional powers that he alone in this
play associates with his royalty. For example, on returning
from Ireland, Richard implies that his hands have a unique
quality of which the earth will be sensible:

> weeping, smiling, greet I thee, my earth,
> And do thee favours with my royal hands. . . .
>
> (3.2.10–11)

He further seems to expect that angels literally will fight
for him:

> God for His Richard hath in heavenly pay
> A glorious angel: then, if angels fight,
> Weak men must fall, for heaven still guards the right.
>
> (3.2.60–62)

Wilbur Sanders points out that "even the Son of God . . .
did not use his legions of angels."[27] Yet even within Richard's own terms, all had deserted him, for by some preternatural association between the person of the king and the
cosmos, Richard's fall had been already determined, as a
Welsh captain makes clear in explaining that he could no
longer hold the army together awaiting Richard's return:

> The bay-trees in our country are all wither'd,
> And meteors fright the fixed stars of heaven,
> And pale-fac'd moon looks bloody on the earth,
> And lean-look'd prophets whisper fearful change,
>
> .   .   .   .
>
> These signs forerun the death or fall of kings.
> Farewell: our countrymen are gone and fled,
> As well assured Richard their king is dead.
>
> (2.4.8–17)

Later, preternatural confirmation of the transference from Richard to Bolingbroke is innocently provided by the groom's account of the coronation.

GROOM.　. . . Bolingbroke rode on roan Barbary—
　　　　　That horse that thou so often hast bestrid,

. . . .

K. RICH.　Rode he on Barbary? Tell me, gentle friend,
　　　　　How went he under him?
GROOM.　So proudly as if he disdain'd the ground.
K. RICH.　So proud that Bolingbroke was on his back!
　　　　　That jade hath eat bread from my royal hand;
　　　　　This hand hath made him proud with clapping him.
　　　　　Would he not stumble?

(5.5.78–87)

Gaunt in the banishment scene had specifically warned Richard against any expectation that a king could command forces other than those of men:

K. RICH.　Why, uncle, thou hast many years to live.
GAUNT.　But not a minute, king, that thou canst give. . . .

(1.3.225–26)

Gaunt had also emphasized that in choosing between his personal well-being and the well-being of the realm, he put the latter before the former in agreeing to his son's banishment. The implication of the first warning is that the person of the king possesses no extraordinary powers, that he cannot control the mysteries of nature; the implication of the second lesson is that distinctions can be made among the various roles or positions that one fills. A sum of these two ideas produces a total that implies deposition of a king who does not manage his kingdom well. But since, as York observes, Richard is beyond advice:

　　　all too late comes counsel to be heard,
　　Where will doth mutiny with wit's regard.
　　Direct not him whose way himself will choose,

(2.1.27–29)

Richard *never* learns these lessons offered by Gaunt.

Thus, when he learns of the army's departure, Richard says, "arm, arm, my name!" (3.2.86). After Scroop's detailed description of the revolt in progress and after learning that his followers have been executed, Richard goes to the opposite extreme:

> I live with bread like you, feel want,
> Taste grief, need friends—subjected thus,
> How can you say to me, I am a king?
>
> (3.2.175–77)

He states that if he cannot command the universe, he'll "pine away—/A king, woe's slave, shall kingly woe obey" (3.2.209–10). Richard's all-or-nothing stance may explain why no compromises are later proposed by either party to the deposition. The inappropriateness of Richard's reactions is not lost upon even his closest advisers, who do not hide their sentiments from him. Richard pauses in his greeting of English soil to ask that his lords "mock not my senseless conjuration" (3.2.23). Later, as he begins to wallow in his grief as deposed king, Richard pauses to tell the company, which includes his own as well as Bolingbroke's followers, "Well, well, I see / I talk but idly, and you laugh at me" (3.3.170–71). Yet he persists in allowing himself to dwell on reactions that worsen his situation, as Aumerle and the Bishop observe in act 3, scene 2. Bolingbroke, meanwhile, shows himself quick to respond to good counsel even from unexpected quarters. In the deposition scene when the Bishop of Carlisle objects: "What subject can give sentence on his king . . . and he himself not present?" (4.1.121, 129), the first lines Bolingbroke speaks after Northumberland arrests Carlisle are to order that Richard be brought forth:

> Fetch hither Richard, that in common view
> He may surrender; so we shall proceed
> Without suspicion.
>
> (4.1.155–57)

While giving advice to Bolingbroke and company was the furthest thought from Carlisle's mind, as he denounced their unthinkably presumptuous judgment of their king, Bolingbroke did not fail to recognize in the specific terms of Carlisle's reproach a suggestion for prudent procedure, and so Bolingbroke immediately sent for Richard. A public abdication could not later be denied.

In the deposition scene Richard acknowledges his mistakes in one brief reference: "must I ravel out / My weav'd-up follies?" (4.1.228–29) but dwells instead on his participation in the deposing of a king, not on the faults that lead to that act. In his final moments Richard mentions his failure as head of state:

> here have I the daintiness of ear
> To check time broke in a disordered string;
> But for the concord of my state and time,
> Had not an ear to hear my true time broke:
> I wasted time, and now doth time waste me. . . .
>
> (5.5.45–49)

Nonetheless, instead of exploring the lesson in statecraft, Richard pursues the image of time, constructing an elaborate metaphor of himself as a clock.[28] Despite the severity of his instruction, Richard therefore does not seem from a constitutional point of view to have learned very much, since in his final moments he is as volatile as he was before, and the behavior he shows to the groom would as quickly alienate lords and commons as anything he did before. Richard rants about the actions of his horse in carrying Bolingbroke, then recognizing the futility of his anger, he not only stops but exclaims, "Forgiveness, horse!" (5.5.90) Finally, in his dying moments, Richard again refers to the extraordinary powers he had earlier claimed:

> That hand shall burn in never-quenching fire
> That staggers thus my person. Exton, thy fierce hand
> Hath with the king's blood stain'd the king's own land.
>
> (5.5.108–10)

The pathos of Richard's human dilemma does not warrant his retention as ruler, however.

The possession of the Crown is transferred to Bolingbroke who is soon crowned:

> On Wednesday next we solemnly set down
> Our coronation. Lords, prepare yourselves.
>
> (4.1.319–20)

Hugh Richmond finds that in the early scenes Richard shows "if anything, too great a spirit of conciliation and spontaneous good nature" and that the early scenes of the play are stately because of "the dignified rhetoric of the High Middle Ages." Richmond explains Richard's using blank charters and "farming" the realm as "hasty administrative judgments" that result from "Richard's casualness." He says that in wishing for Gaunt's speedy death Richard is guilty of "flippancy and even of bad taste." The murder of Gloucester Richmond explains as a desperate gesture of self-defense on Richard's part, basing his conclusion on information not provided in the play. Then Richmond describes England under Bolingbroke's rule as a "degenerate new society" that "can never hope to recover the finer temper that had characterized Richard's court." In the opinion of Hugh Richmond, therefore, *Richard II* is

intended to present a largely historical account of the political decline from the primal innocence of the ideal medieval society to a Machiavellian pragmatism in the modern vein. Shakespeare systematically identifies in Bolingbroke that new type of amoral personality to whom success and title will necessarily go in the modern life that has been cut off from medieval cosmic values.[29]

But if one is to speak of a decline, must one not say that it has begun already with Richard? I think that Richmond minimizes the flaws of Richard's rule too much when he considers them to be the result of Richard's "casualness," "flippancy," and "bad taste." While Bolingbroke is a pragmatist, and perhaps even a Machiavellian pragmatist, I hope to show in this chapter that, even though the transition from Richard to Bolingbroke does not result in immediate joy for England, the transition is not necessarily a decline. Bolingbroke represents other, positive values that replace the medieval cosmic ones that Richard has betrayed.

I would guess that a survey of the historical record of coronations would result in an analysis correlative to the analysis of depositions in *Taswell-Langmead*—that coronations confirm the possession of power attained elsewhere. The coronations of Edward II and Richard II, for example, which both tended to minimize the role of people's consent by emphasizing heredity and royal designation, notably did not guarantee the longevity of those two kings on the throne. When the people's approval centered elsewhere than on the reigning kings, new kings were duly crowned. Those new kings had then to take great care to win popular support for their reigns by ruling well, as Shakespeare shows in his treatment of Henry IV. But even Marlowe, though he was much less concerned with political than with personal conflicts in *Edward II*, shows the young king pledging impartial enforcement of the law (see chapter 1D) and asking the lords to join him in mourning (5.4.98) with the implication that he will ask their assistance in other matters as well.

There are many readers of *Richard II* who would agree with M. M. Reese that

> if Richard's futility in the everyday business of kingship could not in the end deprive him of his essential royalty, it may be that Bolingbroke's competence in these matters cannot suffice to make him truly a king,[30]

and with Peter Ure, who sees in the rebellions that Bolingbroke will face and in his uneasy spirit, largely caused by his "unthrifty son" (5.3.1.), Shakespeare's demonstration that the

[Name of "King" is not] only a shadow, disarmed before the untitled holder of power and of no force in politics. [*King Richard II*, p. lxxx]

I disagree. Bolingbroke, once he possesses the Crown, has all the sanctions that Richard possessed: royal blood (3.3.107, 113), overwhelming popular support by all the peers (3.4.88) and the commons, and possession. The subsequent challenges to his rule arise not so much from his failings as king but from the particular natures of the men who helped him to become king. To the sanctions of royal blood, possession, and popularity, Bolingbroke will add an active concern for preserving "high majesty" and with it the integrity of the realm. If, as York exclaims on seeing Richard, "Yet looks he like a king" (3.3.68), so will Bolingbroke when he is wearing the crown; the Earl of Douglas will tell Henry IV, "yet, in faith, thou bearest thee like a king" (*1H4*, 5.4.35). Those such as Hotspur who call him a "vile politician" (*1H4*, 1.3.238) are too partial in their judgment for their opinions to be accepted without qualification. And there will be as many omens foretelling Henry's demise as king as there were for Richard's:

GLO.   The people fear me, for they do observe
         Unfather'd heirs and loathly births of nature.
         The seasons change their manners, as the year
         Hath found some months asleep and leap'd them over.
CLAR.   The river hath thrice flow'd, no ebb between, [etc.].
                                         (*2H4*, 4.4.121ff.)

If there are rebellions both under a king who supposedly enjoys all the traditional sanctions of rule *and* under the rule of a king who supposedly possesses only some sanctions, then the fact of rebellion cannot be cited as evidence of the second king's lesser legitimacy. Rebellion factors out of the Bolingbroke/Richard equation, though rebellion under Bolingbroke, of course, indicates that he is not a panacea for England's problems.[31] Bolingbroke's uneasiness about the conduct of his son does not in any way undermine his authority, because every Elizabethan would recognize dramatic irony at work here, since Bolingbroke's son was to become one of England's most famous and well-regarded kings.

When Northumberland, Ross, and Willoby discuss among themselves Richard's outrages against both England in general and Hereford in particular, and when Northumberland reveals that Bolingbroke is returning from banishment with many lords, prelates, and Breton troops *R2*, 2.1.279–88), he does not say, as is specified in Hall, that Bolingbroke has been sent for to take over the rule of England. This is a significant omission, for Shakespeare thereby keeps Bolingbroke free of direct aggression against Richard. In fact, Bolingbroke specifically says that he will be "the yielding water" to Richard's fire (3.3.58). John Bromley's suggestion that Bolingbroke's image in the next few lines is of urinating on the earth[32] reveals the kind of hostile treatment Bolingbroke has received at the hands of so many literary critics who are inclined by disposition to prefer the "poetic" Richard to the practical Henry.

There is nowhere in the play a statement that Bolingbroke is coming for the Crown, though it is sometimes possible to read this implication into his words, as when, in learning of his banishment he says,

> That sun that warms you here, shall shine on me,
> And those his golden beams to you here lent
> Shall point on me and gild my banishment.
>
> (*R2*, 1.3.145–47)

Shakespeare avoids, however, any explicit statement. For instance, when in act 3, scene 3 York directly reproaches Bolingbroke, Shakespeare makes Bolingbroke's response suggest a passive stance on his part:

YORK. Take not, good cousin, further than you should,

> Lest you mistake: the heavens are o'er our heads.
> BOL.   I know it, uncle; and oppose not myself
> Against their will.

(3.3.16–19)

Shakespeare has Bolingbroke admit to an active role only in terms of his inheritance of Lancaster (2.3.70):

> What would you have me do? I am a subject,
> And I challenge law; attorneys are denied me,
> And therefore personally I lay my claim
> To my inheritance of free descent.

(2.3.132–35)

And finally, Shakespeare will make Richard offer to be deposed so that Bolingbroke need not ask (3.3.143ff.). Within the context of the transfer of power, as Shakespeare handles it, it would be perfectly plausible for Richard to propose redress of injustice, as Roy Battenhouse suggests, and not offer to resign.[33] This would, however, be too great a departure from historical fact. But Battenhouse's suggestion indicates how much of Richard's deposition results from his own doing, not Bolingbroke's. Shakespeare makes Richard *anticipate* yielding to force rather than *actually* yielding to force.

When Bolingbroke himself appears again in England, he is fully aware of his weak position and acts accordingly, unlike Richard, who did not modify his behavior in the face of the strong opposition expressed by York and Gaunt or in the face of the danger posed by Bolingbroke's popularity.

> BOL.   as my fortune ripens with thy love,
> It shall be still thy true love's recompense.

(2.3.48–49)

> Evermore thanks the exchequer of the poor,
>
> .   .   .   .
>
> Stands for my bounty.

(2.3.65–67)

Bolingbroke notably makes no specific promise here to
which Northumberland or Hotspur can later hold him.
After stating that he has come for his inheritance, however, Bolingbroke asks York to accompany him in pursuing
Richard's followers. In saying that he will go after Bushy,
Bagot, and company, Bolingbroke shrewdly implies that,
as in *Woodstock*, the faults are theirs and not Richard's,
an implication that York is eager to accept. Though York
claims that he does not want to break the law, he indicates
that he might go along with Bolingbroke in this pursuit.
This is the only aggressive act that Shakespeare permits
his Bolingbroke. In that it shows him assuming an authority
to which he has no legal right, this action against Richard's
followers lessens the credibility of his limited claims. But
in that Bolingbroke's going after Bushy, Bagot, and Green
goes far toward winning York to his cause, the effect of
the aggression is mitigated by Shakespeare's showing that
it is welcomed by those who recognize Richard's poor
governance. Bolingbroke's assumption of martial powers
by which he can summarily execute offenders takes place
before he is king. But even in this illegal act Bolingbroke
makes certain that he has the support of the lords before
proceeding. Had Shakespeare's Richard tried to secure
support for seizing Gaunt's property, his reign might have
fared better, because, according to Bracton, a man lawfully
outlawed, as Bolingbroke's banishment indicated he was,
"cannot retain the inheritance unless his chief lord so
wishes."[34] As Jones points out, the historical Richard in
fact "took pains . . . to have Henry of Lancaster declared
to be ineligible legally to inherit as a consequence of the
sentence at Coventry," a judgment subscribed to by both
York and Northumberland (*The Royal Policy of Richard II*, pp. 184–85). What seems to matter is not the
specific law involved but what one can, in practical terms,
get away with, since an illegal act once carried out with
public support then becomes a precedent. Thus, here is a
return to the notion of common consent. King-in-Parlia-

ment is sovereign and can change common law, but not the king alone.

York will be so thoroughly won over to Bolingbroke that he will, as did Gaunt before him, put the welfare of the state before his family in rushing to the new king with news of his son's treason. The exaggeration with which the pleading for Aumerle's life is handled is probably intended to introduce a comic note into Bolingbroke's accession.

> BOL.   Our scene is alter'd from a serious thing,
>   And now chang'd to "The Beggar and the King."
>   (5.3.77–78)

Despite Bolingbroke's being called "king of smiles" (*1H4*, 1.3.243),[35] this is the only time in all three plays when he actually might smile. Goddard's interpretation of the tragicomedy in this scene is that behind each action is a sense of guilt for which the character is compensating. He says that Aumerle is concerned for his part in Gloucester's death, that the Duchess is concerned because her husband thinks her unfaithful, that York feels guilt for his treachery to Richard when regent, and that Henry pardons Aumerle in an attempt to purchase "indulgence in advance for the murder of Richard, against whose life he is conspiring" (*The Meaning of Shakespeare*, 1:158). I think rather of Henry that he pardons Aumerle to keep York's long-range support, fearing that if he executed York's son, York would eventually resent him for it. Henry's saying, "I pardon him, as God shall pardon me" (*R2*, 5.3.129) will not bear the imputation that he is conspiring Richard's murder, for there is only the word of a doubtful moralist, Exton, and his servant, that Henry was directly involved. Henry in saying "God pardon me" is uttering a pious, commonplace phrase. Prior's interpretation that York betrays his son not from fear of Henry IV but from fear of "further disruption at this point of a fragile political order" (*The Drama of Power*, p. 238) is the most satisfactory reading thus far offered.

The contrasts both great and small between Bolingbroke and Richard are made apparent at every turn. When his fortunes were not "ripe," Bolingbroke did little to encourage flattery. For instance, his reply to Northumberland's seventeen lines of flattery is a brief:

> Of much less value is my company
> Than your good words. But who comes here?
> (2.3.19–20)

Later, knowing that he is about to become king, Bolingbroke dismisses the lords who fall over each other in their eagerness to demonstrate that they support him. He tells the lords who joined in the Aumerle-Bagot accusations:

> Little are we beholding to your love,
> And little look'd for at your helping hands.
> (4.1.160–61)

Richard's definition of a subject's relationship to a lord, meanwhile, centers around the very flattery that Bolingbroke was careful to discourage just a moment before:

> RICH.   I hardly yet have learn'd
> To insinuate, flatter, bow, and bend my knee.
> (4.1.164–65)

Though Richard probably does not intend to imply that this was the sort of relationship that he accepted from his subordinates while Bolingbroke does his best to deter such an attitude, I find that the juxtaposition of Richard's words with Bolingbroke's cutting short the accusations emphasizes Richard's inadequate perception of the relationship between subject and king. Where Richard is described and is shown to be frivolously courting disaster, Bolingbroke is shown to be careworn to the point of illness from the burdens of ruling, particularly in *2 Henry IV* as his death approaches (see 3.1.5ff. on his not sleeping and 4.4.114ff. on his illness). Where Shakespeare seems to emphasize Richard's faults, his handling of Bolingbroke's responsibility for Richard's death seems designed to keep him as blameless as possible under the circumstances. If one contrasts Richard's death with the death of the princes in *Richard III*, for instance, one finds only the word of an ambitious lord and his servant that Bolingbroke suggested the murder, and even at that it was an allusion, not a command (5.5.4), whereas in *Richard III*, Richard directly orders the executions. Henry's remorse, regret, and guilt are immediate upon his learning of Richard's death 5.6.35ff.), unlike Richard II's conduct towards Gaunt, Gloucester, and the realm in his financial abuses for which he shows no remorse.

It might be argued that Bolingbroke's suffering is proof that he has committed a great crime and should not be king. I see in his suffering proof of his worthiness to be king in his effort at restoring the monarchy from the wretched state in which he found it so that his son will be free to go on to other concerns. In his final meeting with his son, I do not see Bolingbroke's guilt predominant but simply a sense that the interregnum he provided for his son is coming to an end. Henry IV tells Prince Hal:

> Pluck down my officers; break my decrees;
> For now a time is come to mock at form—
> Harry the fifth is crown'd! Up, vanity!
> Down, royal state! All you sage counsellors, hence!
>
> (*2H4*, 4.5.117–20)

But, as I have already observed, once king, Henry V will immediately disprove his father's fears by appointing noble counsel to help him rule well. Henry's telling the prince,

> God knows, my son,
> By what by-paths and indirect crook'd ways
> I met this crown, and I myself know well
> How troublesome it sat upon my head,
>
> (4.5.183–86)

is the only instance where Shakespeare has Henry explicitly

indicate his responsibility for what has happened. I do not think, however, that one should read into this general feeling of regret in a dying man as he looks back over the events of a turbulent life proof that Shakespeare intends the reader to place solidly on Bolingbroke's shoulders any more than part of the blame for what has happened. For from his handling of the events of Richard's deposition and death, Shakespeare has made Henry as innocent as possible so that his sense of guilt now comes from his sensitive conscience, as did his suffering after the deposition. If one recalls that it was only Bolingbroke whose conscience would not permit him to let Gloucester's murder go unrevenged at a time when he had little more than royal disfavor to gain from his bringing up the matter, one can see that Shakespeare has provided other evidence of Bolingbroke's sensitive conscience. Prior has observed, however, that "critics sometimes write about Henry as though his moral awareness makes him the more despicable" (*The Drama of Power*, p. 241). Bolingbroke is depressed at the revolts against him, because they made his succession seem "but as an honour snatch'd with boist'rous hand" (*2H4*, 4.5.191) rather than his having allowed himself to be used by heaven, as he told York.

Those who share John Bromley's belief that "this is not remorse; it is . . . a series of factual recognitions" (*The Shakespearean Kings*, pp. 72–73) are being unduly hard on Bolingbroke in allowing themselves to have their judgment of him be determined by the testimony of hostile or ambitious witnesses and by circumstantial rather than by concrete evidence against him. Bromley reveals his prejudice against Henry IV when he says, "precisely because Henry IV is Shakespeare's most complete political portrait, we undervalue him when we regard him as only a symptom of that disease which afflicts the body politic" (p. 60). He is "Machiavelli's king": "utterly without illusion, his remorse nothing but rhetorical posture, cold, cynical, willing not only to have done what must be done but also to mask his instrument behind exile and to obscure his judicial murders in a haze of a false crusade" (p. 66). What Bromley has concluded, therefore, is that Bolingbroke represents nothing positive: popular support means nothing; judicial reforms (see section D below) mean nothing; prudence in securing general support by consulting with the lords and seeing to the effective functioning of the judiciary have no value. If Bromley's interpretation was what Shakespeare intended, I think he would have emphasized rather than minimized any sense of Bolingbroke's hypocrisy and his misuse of exile, then stressed that Bolingbroke, once in power, abused the realm; this would show that Bolingbroke's ultimate goals were self-serving and not the benefit of the realm. Furthermore, those who point to Henry's illness as the result of Henry's own policies do not acknowledge the possibility that Henry has willingly sacrificed himself for the good of England. A Richard who foolishly ignored advice was not worn down, but a Henry was reduced to melancholy. Bromley's and others' interpretations greatly reduce "the complexity of Shakespeare's dramatic design. A proper appreciation of Henry's frustrated career depends on understanding that Henry and his supporters . . . were inspired by honorable motives" (Prior, *The Drama of Power*, p. 235). Even Irving Ribner, who felt that Bolingbroke was personally responsible for Richard's murder and that his title was illegal, concluded that

> his reign is not therefore condemned. It has manifestly succeeded where Richard's had failed, and Henry's success in maintaining order goes far to compensate for the illegality of his title. . . . [36]

A. R. Humphreys suggests that "Henry IV's career, then, proclaims less that God punishes deposition than that the king must rule" (*1H4*, p. lii).

Henry IV's remembrance of the "bypaths and indirect crooked ways" in which he came to the throne is passed on to his son:

> Not to-day, O Lord!
> O not to-day, think not upon the fault

My father made in compassing the crown!
(*H5*, 4.1.298–300)

This sense of accountability serves to spur both kings to greater efforts of leadership (see the previous section for a discussion of Henry IV and his lords). Henry V does not wallow in self-pity when outnumbered as did Richard but would please even Norman Vincent Peale with the power of his positive thinking (see *H5*, 4.1.1–33 and his St. Crispian speech, 4.3.18ff.). He does not leave the country's defense unprovided for as did Richard, whose naming York regent was not sufficient provision. Henry need not resort to extralegal means of taxation, because he has the support of lords, commons, and church (even though the motives of the church leaders in supporting Henry may not be spotless). Above all, he knows the limits of a king's power—what marks him off as king is not supernatural power but ceremony and responsibility (4.1.244ff.)

At the beginning of this section I suggested that one would have to infer from Shakespeare's treatment of Richard and Bolingbroke whatever conclusions the playwright intended to convey about the nature of the Crown. One must look to Bolingbroke and Richard because of the absence of many direct speeches about the Crown and because Henry V, in constitutional terms, acts upon principles set out by his father, not on any innovative ideas of his own. Hal's hobnobbing with commoners is his means of keeping in touch with the people, whereas his father (except for taking off his bonnet to wenches) limited himself to the company of lords. Hal's staged reformation is not a constitutionally innovative act in that his change stresses traditional values, and in particular, those values emphasized by his father. I have tried to show that without producing an angel/devil, white/black opposition, Shakespeare has emphasized Richard's flaws as ruler and minimized Bolingbroke's guilt in becoming his successor. Once Richard undermines his right to the throne as designated heir of his grandfather by trying to deny Bolingbroke his inheritance (and thereby frightening the propertied lords), he quickly finds that he must resign the throne. Richard's contempt for the people and his financial abuses of the realm leave him friendless, as the Gardener observed:

> King Richard he is in the mighty hold
> Of Bolingbroke. Their fortunes both are weigh'd.
> In your lord's scale is nothing but himself,
> And some few vanities that make him light.
> But in the balance of great Bolingbroke,
> Besides himself, are all the English peers,
> And with that odds he weighs King Richard down.
>
> (*R2*, 3.4.83–89)

Henry IV is not frivolous or extravagant as was Richard; he pays particular attention to legal reform, as even Hotspur attests (see below), and to consulting with his lords; he is aware at all times of conditions throughout the realm and is prepared for any eventuality (such as his drawing together "the special head of all the land" in *1H4*, 4.4.28 to oppose the rebels). As Una Ellis-Fermor says in *The Frontiers of Drama*:

> Henry IV is an exceedingly able, hard-working statesman whose career reveals gradually but clearly the main qualification for kingship, the king's sense of responsibility to his people, that sense of service which, while making him no more than the state's greatest servant, makes all his privileges and exemptions, even a measure of autocracy itself, no more than necessary means for that service. [Pp. 42–43]

But for all his effort, Henry can achieve little more than keeping on the lid. Bromley suggests that this is because "we may regard the wounds of England as running sores; none of the cures, from John to Henry Bolingbroke, heals the wounds" (*The Shakespearean Kings*, p. 62). Henry's son in going to war achieves a brief moment of glory, but even there one is constantly aware of the horrible price that is paid in terms of human sacrifice. Though Henry V prefers to pass over his responsibility for the suffering in his conversation with Williams, Shakespeare has so handled this scene that sensitive readers and viewers do not miss the valid criticism of the king (Goddard, *The Meaning of Shakespeare*, p. 242 and Palmer, *Political and Comic Characters of Shakespeare*, p. 238). The criticism becomes the stronger if one considers this *Henry V* as a sequel to *2 Henry IV*, where Bolingbroke advised his son to "busy giddy minds / With foreign quarrels" (4.5.213–14).

It does not require prolonged contemplation of men in society or genius, of which Shakespeare had more than his share, to realize how complex are the factors that contribute to creating or destroying a decent society. Replacing a Richard with a Henry can go only part way toward correcting the problems of England. Perhaps, as Ellis-Fermor suggests, what is necessary is a composite figure uniting the virtues of all the kings of these plays (*The Frontiers of Drama*, pp. 36–37). Or, perhaps, the problem is not one of politics alone but ethics as well and includes every citizen of every estate of the realm—from king to lowest commoners.

Shakespeare's version of the transfer of the Crown from Richard II through Henry IV to his son Henry V emphasizes the sanction of popular support, which is intimately related to dedication to the well-being of the realm in Richard's successors. Only a portion of Henry's army will be at Gaultree, according to Hastings, because Henry must defend England against the French and Glendower as well as against the Archbishop (*2H4*, 1.3. 70–73); yet his troops at Gaultree number a good 25,000 (1.3.11) or 30,000 (4.1.22), the same as or a greater number than all the men the Archbishop commands (1.3.67). When Northumberland does not come, the rebel army lacks supplies because they were dependent upon him (1.3.12–14). One may therefore infer that rebellion against Henry in *2 Henry IV* represents only a small portion of the population and nothing like the almost total rejection of Richard II. As I tried to show in the section on the people, both Henry IV and Henry V take great care to keep open the lines of communication with the people by using Parliament and the council. In the next section I will show that they also take particular care to see that the law is impartially enforced, so that "dedication to the well-being of the realm" in the second tetralogy is shown to mean acting within the framework of the English constitution as it existed toward the end of the sixteenth century when the opinions of the people and the traditions of the law established more-precisely-defined limits on the Crown than previously existed.

D. The Law

Shakespeare's Henry VI does not know the law; Edward IV feels that his will should stand for law on occasion; Richard II's record is not much better. Richard commits errors by intervening in the lists, by "farming" the realm, and by his poor handling of Bolingbroke's situation. In beginning the lists the Marshall says:

> On pain of death, no person be so bold
> Or daring-hardy as to touch the lists,
> Except the marshall and such officers
> Appointed to direct these fair designs.
>
> (R2, 1.3.42–45)

Richard was not one of those officers. As Kantorowicz has pointed out, drawing on Blackstone's *Commentaries,*

> Though the king may never judge despite being the "Fountain of Justice," he yet has legal ubiquity: "His Majesty in the eye of the law is always present in all his courts, though he cannot personally distribute justice."[37]

Yet Richard intervenes. He allows the lists to progress to a climactic moment, then stops them to announce a verdict that he and the council had already determined. But Richard should not have allowed the ceremony of judgment by battle to begin if he were not going to abide by its decision. In "farming" out the kingdom, meaning leasing to others the revenue due the Crown in return for a fixed payment, Richard becomes, in Gaunt's words,

> Landlord of England . . . not king,
> Thy state of law is bondslave to the law. . . .
>   (2.1.113–14)

Richard has, as Wilson suggests in his gloss of this line, diminished his royal prerogative by making his legal status as king subject to the common law governing mortgages (*King Richard II*, p. 160). As far as Bolingbroke's situation goes, both York and Bolingbroke feel that he has been refused due legal process because Richard revoked his letters-patent to institute suits for obtaining his father's lands (see Ure's explanation, *R2*, pp. 62–63n, of 2.1.202–4 based on Holinshed). Bolingbroke says specifically, "I challenge law; attorneys are denied me" (2.3.133).

Shakespeare, without whitewashing Bolingbroke's abuses of law, shows Bolingbroke to be more circumspect in his proceedings than Richard. Both Gaunt and York think that Richard's advisers contributed a large share to the unfortunate character of his reign. York says that Richard's ear "is stopp'd with . . . flattering sounds" (2.1.17), while Gaunt directly tells Richard that "a thousand flatterers sit within thy crown" (2.1.100). Even his stated respect for England's laws does not restrain York from joining Bolingbroke in the pursuit of Richard's followers. Though this action on Bolingbroke's part was not legal, and his declared intention of washing their blood from off his hands by citing their crimes was unrealizable (3.1.5–7), Bolingbroke handles the matter expeditiously, naming their abuses before sending them to be executed. In that Bolingbroke acts with the approval of many lords, in that the procedure is handled in public view, and in that the reasons for the sentencing are made public, the net balance of the scene is to exculpate Bolingbroke to a significant degree. He emerges as a forceful, effective administrator who proceeds with consistent regard for public opinion. In act 5 Bolingbroke pardons

Aumerle to win his "after-love" (5.3.34) and God's pardon (5.3.129). The emphasis in this scene on the Crown's power to grant pardon was perhaps intended by Shakespeare to illustrate the working of an important royal prerogative. Bolingbroke at the end of this play will allow the Bishop of Carlisle to live out his life, citing the "high sparks of honour" (5.6.29) he has seen in him; in the next play, Prince Hal will similarly allow the Earl of Douglas to go "ransomless and free" as a means of "cherish[ing] such high deeds" of valor (1H4, 5.5.26–31). It was one of the powers of the monarch, according to Thomas Smith, to "dispense with the laws and pardon an offense *modo stet rectus in curia*, that no man object against the offendor."[38] Richard would have been well advised to have exercised this prerogative, perhaps in the Bolingbroke-Mowbray resolution.

That Shakespeare intended to portray Henry IV as a significantly better head of the judiciary than Richard II is confirmed in *1 Henry IV* by testimony from an unexpected source. In enumerating his grievances to Sir Walter Blunt, Hotspur includes the following description of Bolingbroke:

> He presently, as greatness knows itself,
> Steps me a little higher than his vow
> Made to my father while his blood was poor
> Upon the naked shore at Ravenspurgh;
> And now forsooth takes on him to reform
> Some certain edicts and some straight decrees
> That lie too heavy on the commonwealth;
> Cries out upon abuses, seems to weep
> Over his country's wrongs; and by his face,
> This seeming brow of justice, did he win
> The hearts of all that he did angle for. . . .
>   (4.3.74–84)

Since it was Northumberland who saw to the execution of Bushy and Green (R2, 3.1.35), Hotspur's trying to put the blame entirely on Bolingbroke's shoulders is disingenuous. It is significant that Hotspur considers Bolingbroke's legal

reforms to have been the decisive action that won Bolingbroke all the support he needed, for this confirms the critical
nature of the administrative change from Richard's rule to
Bolingbroke's. Hotspur thus contradicts in part his assertion
(*1H4*, 4.3.58) that his father, not Bolingbroke, was the
popular one (see section 4A).

The effective functioning of the legal system under
Henry IV receives mention on several occasions in both
plays named for him. The Sheriff locates the robbers at the
tavern (*1H4*, 2.4.480ff.). The Lord Chief Justice is so
confident in *2 Henry IV* of the working of the legal system
that he knows Falstaff, whatever his intentions may be, has
no real "power to do wrong" (2.1.128). Falstaff would be
arrested if he could not persuade the Hostess to drop the
charges she has brought against him (2.1.136–60). The
Hostess, meanwhile, is uneasy in act 2, scene 4 because she
has been warned by "Master Tisick, the debuty [*sic*]"
(2.4.83) about the reputation of her tavern; in the same
scene Falstaff mentions an "indictment" against her for
allowing meat to be served on fish days (2.4.339–42).
The Hostess and Doll are arrested for the death of one or
two people whom they had beaten (5.4.6, 17–18).

The Lord Chief Justice contributes a good deal to
Henry's effective judiciary, but he is not the only legal
officer present in *2 Henry IV*. Justice Shallow, aided by his
cousin Silence, who has a "commission" as deputy (3.2.89),
plays a role in applying the law. Shallow, for all his fool-
ishness, is not a fool, as even Falstaff reluctantly admits
("now he has land and beefs" [3.2.322]). Shallow can in
the space of a minute go from discussing mortality to ques-
tioning the price of bulls (3.2.36–42) and successfully oversee the management of his affairs. He wants Falstaff to
pick the best of the recruits for the king's service—"I
would have you served with the best" (3.2.250); and for
all Falstaff's charm, Shallow is not deceived by the pathetic
selection of soldiers: "He is not his craft's master, he doth
not do it right" (3.2.273), Shallow observes of the drill
through which Bardolph and Falstaff put Wart. When

Shallow's servant Davy asks Shallow to go easy on his friend, Shallow indicates his awareness that "Visor is an arrant knave, on my knowledge" (5.1.37); he only promises that "he shall have no wrong" (5.1.49), which is a safely evasive answer that leaves Shallow free to impose an equitable judgment and not be unduly lenient, as Davy wishes.[39] Shallow's authority comes from his position as king's justice, as he tells Pistol: "I am, sir, under the King, in some authority" (5.3.109). It requires hard work indeed to govern the realm when the instruments of local government are such as Shallow; yet, Bolingbroke's government does work, and the credit for its effectiveness must rest largely with the king and, in terms of the law, with his Lord Chief Justice. The one less-than-honorable action of Bolingbroke's reign that is given detailed attention by Shakespeare is Prince John of Lancaster's arresting the Archbishop after misleading him into a false sense of security by promising redress of grievances but making no mention of amnesty. Falstaff's subsequent comparison between John and Hal serves to strengthen the anticipation of the rule of Henry V and to make one rejoice with Falstaff that Hal, not his brother, will be king. I think this contrast between the two sons is the more significant aspect of the Gaultree incident than the unfavorable reflection on the distant Henry IV.[40]

First with Falstaff and then with the princes, the Lord Chief Justice prides himself on his impartiality.

To Falstaff:

> It is not a confident brow, nor the throng of words that come with such more than impudent sauciness from you, can thrust me from a level consideration. [*2H4*, 2.1.109–12]

To Hal's brothers:

> Sweet Princes, what I did, I did in honour,
> Led by th'impartial conduct of my soul.
>
> (5.2.35–36)

When the new king himself enters and challenges the Lord

Chief Justice to justify the "indignities" he laid upon him when a prince (5.2.69), the Lord Chief Justice replies with a twenty-nine line encomium to the commonwealth, to authority, to law, and to the Crown that begins thus:

> The image of [your father's] power lay then in me;
> And in th'administration of his law. . . .
>
> (5.2.74-75)

In the *Famous Victories of Henry the Fifth*, an earlier play that uses much of the same historical material, the reconciliation between Henry V and the Chief Justice takes place well after Henry is king, in fact not until Henry prepares to leave for France after having been challenged by the Dauphin with a gift of tennis balls.

HEN. 5   Oh, my lord, you remember
you sent me to the Fleete, did you not?

JUST.   I trust your Grace have forgotten that.

HEN. 5   I, truly, my lord; and for revengement I
have chosen you to be my Protector over
my realme, until it shall please God
to give me speedy return out of France.

JUST.   And if it please your Majesty, I am far
unworthy of so high a dignity.

HEN. 5   Tut, my lord! You are not unworthy,
because I think you worthy; for you that
would not spare me, I think, will not
spare another. It must needs be so. And therefore,
come, let us be gone, and get our men in a
readiness.[41]

As Richard II in Shakespeare's play names York governor in his absence when he departs for Ireland but makes no acknowledgment of York's advice, just so the king in *Famous Victories* names the Lord Chief Justice governor in his absence without giving any indication that the justice's advice will influence his own behavior. Shakespeare invests the reconciliation with much greater significance.

In Shakespeare's play the Lord Chief Justice directly challenges Henry as king:

> as you are a king, speak in your state
> What I have done that misbecame my place,
> My person, or my liege's sovereignty.
>
> (5.2.99–101)

And Henry replies directly: "You are right, Justice, and you weigh this well" (5.2.102). After saying that he would support the Lord Chief Justice as did Henry IV even against his own son, Henry pledges:

> You shall be as a father to my youth.
> My voice shall sound as you do prompt mine ear,
> And I will stoop and humble my intents
> To your well-practis'd wise directions.
>
> (5.2.118–21)

In that the Lord Chief Justice specifically acted as officer of the law in restraining the prince and in calling the new king to account, this pledge by Henry that he will "stoop" to his "wise directions" has, in addition to the moral significance of Henry's seeking advice from a figure who is old and wise, constitutional significance when Henry speaks of the relationship between king and head of the judiciary. For greater emphasis, he repeats the pledge: "you, father, shall have foremost hand" (5.2.140). In his first public appearance as king, Henry twice pledges to make the law foremost in governing his state just as he twice states his intention to consult with Parliament to the end that

> . . . God consigning to my good intents,
> No Prince nor peer shall have just cause to say,
> God shorten Harry's happy life one day!
>
> (5.2.143–45)

The first action of the new regime is the banishment of Falstaff, which Henry asks the Lord Chief Justice to arrange. Humphreys suggests that John and Westmoreland represent one extreme of justice, "the justice which metes without mercy what each deserves; such justice is needed in statecraft but only in emergencies." Falstaff represents the other extreme, of "anarchy (the defect of justice). . . . adumbrated in Falstaff's prospects, trumpeted in his cry 'the laws of England are at my commandment'. . . ." Hal, in choosing the Lord Chief Justice, is choosing the embodiment of "those qualities which Hal requires, good government in the microcosm of man and the macrocosm of the state" (*2H4*, p. xlviii). The second action of the new regime, as John of Lancaster reports, is the King's calling of "his Parliament" (5.5.103), which the Lord Chief Justice confirms (see section 4A for a discussion of the stress Shakespeare places upon this fact).

In *Henry V* Henry shows himself to be abiding by his pledged respect for the law though the Lord Chief Justice himself is absent from this play. Before going to war against France, Henry demands a "justly and religiously" (1.2.10) presented account from the Archbishop of Canterbury of the Salic Law upon which his claim of French territory is based. It is difficult to tell from Shakespeare's handling of this information whether one is to understand that the Archbishop is manipulating Henry's decision, or whether Henry is manipulating the Archbishop, whether both or neither of them is being honest: in the previous scene the Archbishop had revealed his strong desire for foreign wars to divert the Commons' attention from the Church, while the Ambassador reveals (1.2.246) that Henry has already informed the French of his claim. But from a constitutional point of view it matters little whether Henry's public ceremony to show legal justification arose from his genuine respect for law or because he felt it necessary. In fact, the latter reason would suggest even more forcefully the strength of the law as a restraint on the monarchy if, despite any personal feeling to the contrary, Henry knew his procedure had to appear lawful, though this would also show that international law can be made pliable. The other major incident in this play involving Henry V directly in the administration of the law centers around the conspiracy against him. Though his disappoint-

ment at the treason is profound, particularly in the case of
Lord Scroop, to whom he attributes most human perfec-
tion (2.2.94ff.), Henry does not intervene personally.

> Their faults are open:
> Arrest them to the answer of the law;
> And God acquit them of their practices!
>
> (2.2.142–44)

Since for the rest of this play England is at war, the law
is the law of arms. Fluellen testifies that Henry's knowledge and application of "the disciplines of war" are excellent. Shakespeare shows Fluellen to be preoccupied with
the disciplines of war; Fluellen seizes every opportunity to
debate "Roman disciplines" with Gower and the others
(see, for instance, 3.2.61ff.); thus his assessment of Henry
is given some credibility. But Henry's decisions as martial
commander are handled with some ambiguity by Shakespeare. For instance, in act 4, scene 6 Shakespeare introduces an incident that greatly distressed Holinshed, Henry
V's ordering the French prisoners killed.

> But, hark! what new alarum is this same?
> The French have reinforc'd their scatter'd men:
> Then every soldier kill his prisoners!
> Give the word through.
>
> (4.6.35–38)

Holinshed called this a "dolorous decree, and pitiful proclamation" that caused a "lamentable slaughter" (*Chronicles*, 3:81–82) but judged that it was "contrary to Henry
V's accustomed gentleness" and was only undertaken because of "the outcry of the lackies and boys" when the
English camp was robbed; this made Henry fear that the
prisoners would attack their captors (p. 81). But Shakespeare does not introduce the information that would mitigate the horror of Henry's order until the following scene:

FLU.   Kill the poys and the luggage! 'tis expressly against the

law of arms: 'tis as arrant a piece of knavery, mark you
now, as can be offer't; in your conscience now, is it not?

GOW. 'Tis certain there's not a boy left alive; and the cowardly rascals that ran from the battle ha' done this
slaughter: besides, they have burned and carried away
all that was in the king's tent; wherefore the king most
worthily hath caused every soldier to cut his prisoner's
throat. O, 'tis a gallant king! [4.7.1–11]

As Gower puts it, the prisoners are killed in retaliation for
the robbery of the king's tent, not only because the French
killed unarmed boys or because the prisoners posed a threat
to the English. Gower's concluding praise might have an
ironic edge.

Palmer has written of *Henry V* that there is "no play
in which Shakespeare's peculiar blend of moral detachment
and imaginative sympathy is seen to better advantage, with
the result that *Henry V* is at once the glorification of a
patriot king and an exposure of the wicked futility of his
enterprise" (*Political and Comic Characters of Shakespeare*, p. 228). Citing the mixed critical reception that the
play has received, ranging from Hazlitt's hatred of Henry
V to other critics who have fervently extolled him as an
embodiment of heroic kingship, Palmer concludes that

the answer must be that Shakespeare as little intended to present
as to demolish a hero. He found this man in the chronicles and,
bringing him on to the stage, gives him precisely the qualities
proper to his fame. There is neither censure nor commendation.
. . . Shakespeare knew what sort of man succeeds in public life
and in Henry he presents us with just that sort of man. [p. 247]

I concur. Henry V has learned what efforts of leadership are required in a king, what vigilance, what commitment to the public weal. What he continues to learn is, as
Ronald Berman puts it, "the problem of putting ideas into
action."[42] With the best intentions in the world, a king,
because of the power he wields, must inevitably make
decisions that will be ambiguous in their application, harm-

ing some for the benefit of others. What has to be evaluated is the total record. Unfortunately, Henry V's record is too brief for one to do much more than gauge his intentions. Because Shakespeare gives no hint of any personal extravagance or willfulness on Henry's part or places any emphasis on personal preferences at the expense of the common good as he did for Henry VI, Edward IV, and Richard II, I think Shakespeare intends that one accept Henry's intentions as being for the best.

NOTES TO CHAPTER 4

1. This is true whether or not Shakespeare planned the plays as a tetralogy, of which there is no certain proof. There are indications in *Richard II* that he was planning a sequel, particularly when Henry IV speaks of his "unthrifty son," and there is an unfulfilled promise in the epilogue to *2 Henry IV* of another play with Falstaff in it and a fulfilled promise of one with Katharine.

2. As John Palmer points out in his *Political and Comic Characters of Shakespeare* (London: Macmillan, 1965), Richard's sensing danger from Bolingbroke's popularity does not cause him to modify his behavior (p. 138). To appreciate the complexity of Shakespeare's portrait of Bolingbroke, one should not reinforce Richard's lines with one's memory of subsequent references to Bolingbroke as a performer but should take the accusations against him one at a time and in context.

3. These lines could also be read as Henry's assessment of Richard as a popularity seeker who went about it the wrong way.

4. G. B. Harrison, ed., *Shakespeare, The Complete Works* (New York: Harcourt, Brace and World, 1952), p. 692.

5. *2 King Henry IV,* ed. A. R. Humphreys (London: Methuen; Cambridge, Mass.: Harvard University Press, 1966), p. 168n.

6. These lines can make sense perfectly well without any reference to the constitution of Shakespeare's time if one understands Henry's pledge to the people as a ploy to gain popular support to bolster his kingship against challenge. The sixteenth-century constitutional structure serves to add another dimension to those already understood.

7. Edward Hall, *Chronicle Containing the Histories of England,* 1548–1550 (London: J. Johnson et al, 1809), pp. 130ff.; Raphael Holinshed, *Chronicles of England, Scotland, and Ireland,* vol. 3 (London: J. Johnson et al, 1808):61–62, 147f.; Geoffrey Bullough, *Narrative and Dramatic Sources of Shakespeare,* vol. 3 (London: Routledge and Kegan Paul; New York: Columbia University Press, 1960):48–49,n3.

8. The great difficulty that anyone must overcome in discussing the plays of this tetralogy, because everyone who has read them has fixed an interpretation in his mind, was recently illustrated to me in separate conversations about this scene with two knowledgeable readers. One of them insists that Robin Ostler was simply a groom, the other that this scene is an allegory of the kingdom: inflation being the cheapened kingship, Robin Ostler being Richard.

9. From the New Arden edition of *1 Henry IV* (Cambridge, Mass.: Harvard University Press, 1960), p. xliii. Roy Battenhouse, "Falstaff as Parodist and Perhaps Holy Fool," *PMLA* 90 (January 1975):32, even suggests that "while . . . Falstaff is shamming vices and enacting parodies, his inner intent is a charitable almsgiving of brotherly self-humiliation and fatherly truth-telling."

10. Una Ellis-Fermor, *The Frontiers of Drama*, 2d ed. (London: Methuen, 1964), pp. 54, 53.

11. Marilyn Williamson, "The Episode with Williams in *Henry V*," *Studies in English Literature 1500-1900* 9 (1969):280-81.

12. Harold C. Goddard, *The Meaning of Shakespeare*, 1951, 2 vols., reprint, (Chicago and London: University of Chicago Press, Phoenix Books, 1960), 1:240-41.

13. Henry lost his council seat according to Holinshed because of his conflict with the Lord Chief Justice (*Chronicles*, 3:61). Holinshed's *Chronicles* is a sixteenth-century work and as such also is to a large extent a product of its time. See, for instance, his skeptical attitude toward the denigrators of King John quoted in the previous chapter. It is beyond the scope of this study to consider Holinshed's use of his sources, but I suspect that he, too, gives more attention to council, law, and Parliament than did his sources.

14. John Dover Wilson, ed., *King Richard II*, 1939, reprint (Cambridge: At the University Press, 1961), p. 159; Peter Ure, ed., *King Richard II* (London: Methuen; Cambridge, Mass.: Harvard University Press, 1956), p. 55.

15. James Winny, *The Player King* (New York: Barnes and Noble, 1968), p.60.

16. J. A. R. Marriott, *English History in Shakespeare* (London: Chapman and Hall, 1918), p. 17.

17. Some critics such as John Bromley see "hypocritical obsequiousness" in Bolingbroke at this point, but such an interpretation would require that one accept all the hostile assessments of Bolingbroke and none of his own declarations as true, a practice that I personally prefer not to follow. Bolingbroke does not indicate his hypocrisy (as does Richard III, for instance). Perhaps there is partial truth in both interpretations.

18. Leonard F. Dean, "From *Richard II* to *Henry V*, A Closer View," in *Twentieth Century Interpretations of "Richard II,"* ed. Paul M. Cubeta (Englewood Cliffs, N.J.: Prentice-Hall, 1971), p. 63; Palmer, *Political and Comic Characters of Shakespeare*, p. 163.

19. Moody Prior, *The Drama of Power* (Evanston, Ill.: Northwestern University Press, 1973), p. 194.

20. Humphreys, in the New Arden edition of *2 Henry IV* (London: Methuen; Cambridge, Mass.: Harvard University Press, 1966), p. 120 n, suggests several readings, none of them wholly satisfactory, of these lines, which he describes as "possibly corrupt—'brother general' and 'household cruelty' sound dubious."

21. Richard Jones, *The Royal Policy of Richard II: Absolutism in the Later Middle Ages* (Oxford: Basil Blackwell, 1968), pp. 1, 5.

22. *Taswell-Langmead's English Constitutional History*, 11th ed., ed. Theodore F. T. Plucknett (London: Sweet and Maxwell, 1960), p. 493.

23. One could also argue that Bolingbroke always intended to seize the Crown, that he provoked the Mowbray quarrel to make Richard look bad and to draw attention to himself, that in leaving England he already was planning to return with troops. But to do so one would have to read aggression into Bolingbroke's silences and rely heavily upon the fact that the play does not contradict such an interpretation (as Matchett does in his reading of *John* [see 3A]). Bolingbroke would then be guilty of omitting to propose compromises and guilty of accepting the Crown. Either way, however, the essential differences remain between Richard's and Bolingbroke's interpretations of the Crown.

24. Whereas in the first tetralogy there were several feudal pledges given and renounced, in the second tetralogy this is the only dramatization of the feudal obligations of lord to king; I find it significant that this one feudal ceremony should be a release of obligation: "Swear by the duty that you owe to God— / Our part therein we banish with yourselves—" (1.3.180–81).

25. T. B. Pugh, "The Magnates, Knights and Gentry," in *Fifteenth-century England 1399–1509, Studies in Politics and Society*, ed. S. B. Chrimes et al. (Manchester: Manchester University Press, 1972), p. 107.

26. Robert Parsons, *A Conference About the Next Succession to the Crowne of Ingland* [1594], in *English Books Before 1640*, University Microfilms, Reel 387, S.T.C. no. 19398, Huntington Library, San Marino, Calif., pt. 2, p. 94.

27. Wilbur Sanders, *The Dramatist and the Received Idea* (Cambridge: At the University Press, 1968), p. 188.

28. While there are some students of the play who see Richard as a poet-playwright who has had kingship thrust upon him though his poet's temperament was ill-suited to the position, Peter Ure has countered this interpretation of Richard by saying, "the poetry is there because Richard is a character in a poetic drama, not because Shakespeare thought that Richard lost his kingdom through a preference for blank verse over battles" (*King Richard II, p. lxix*). Ure says that Richard's poetry is Shakespeare's medium, which he uses to show "what is going on in Richard's mind and heart" (p. lxxi).

29. H. S. Richmond, *Shakespeare's Political Plays* (New York: Random House, 1967), pp. 127, 139, 128, 129, 137, 139–40.

30. M. M. Reese, *The Cease of Majesty, A Study of Shakespeare's History Plays* (New York: St. Martin's Press, 1961), p. 253.

31. See Michael Manheim, *The Weak King Dilemma in the Shakespearean History Play* (Syracuse, N.Y.: Syracuse University Press, 1973), p. 55.

32. John C. Bromley, *The Shakespearean Kings* (Boulder, Col.: Colorado Associated University Press, 1971), p. 66.

33. Roy Battenhouse, "Tudor Doctrine and the Tragedy of *Richard II*," *Rice University Studies* 60 (Spring 1974): 39.

34. *Bracton on the Laws and Customs of England*, ed. George E. Woodbine, trans. and rev. Samuel E. Thorne, 2 vols. (Cambridge, Mass.: Harvard University Press, Belknap Press, 1968), 2:376.

35. Hotspur, of course, was implying duplicity. But even false smiles are missing from Bolingbroke's face—he is serious in the Mowbray scenes, brusque on returning to England, earnest with York, careful in the scenes with Richard, anxious over his son, and so on; he is never smiling on stage.

36. Irving Ribner, "The Political Problem in Shakespeare's Lancastrian Tetralogy," *Studies in Philology* 49 (1952) ·183. If the opinion of a modern historian may be cited in addition, A. L. Brown has written that his "impression is that [the historical Henry IV] came to the throne an honourable, chivalrous man with old-fashioned ideas and ideals . . . but that these were not enough for the problems he met." From "The Reign of Henry IV: The Establishment of the Lancastrian Regime," in *Fifteenth-Century England 1399–1509*, ed. Chrimes et al., p. 24.

37. Ernst H. Kantorowicz, *The King's Two Bodies, A Study in Mediaeval Political Theology*, (Princeton, N.J.: Princeton University Press, 1957), pp. 4–5.

38. Thomas Smith, *De Republica Anglorum*, 1583, ed. L. Alston (Cambridge: At the University Press, 1906), pp. 58–63.

39. These lines are usually interpreted to mean that Davy has succeeded in influencing his master and that Shallow is not an equitable judge. But such an interpretation attributes to Shallow a committed error that Shakespeare had been careful to leave unspecified.

40. Paul A. Jorgensen, "A Formative Shakespearean Legacy: Elizabethan Views of God, Fortune, and War," *PMLA* 90 (March 1975):231, sees in Lancaster's actions, "a logical extreme, begun by Bolingbroke, of Shakespeare's assigning victory to human resourcefulness." As Prior points out, however, the incident remains "distasteful" (*The Drama of Power*, p. 240).

41. This play is most easily found in *Chief Pre-Shakespearean Dramas*, ed. Joseph Quincy Adams (Cambridge, Mass.: Houghton Mifflin Company, 1924), pp. 667–90. The lines quoted here are 1191–1207.

42. Ronald Berman, Introduction to *Twentieth Century Interpretations of "Henry V"* (Englewood Cliffs, N.J.: Prentice-Hall, 1968), p. 9.

5

Conclusion

It was almost immediately apparent after Elizabeth's death that a change in monarch portended challenge to the delicate constitutional equilibrium that had been maintained during her reign. James, on his journey to London, ordered the execution of a thief. In the words of Catharine Drinker Bowen, biographer of Sir Edward Coke,

> news of it went quickly through the counties. At Newark-on-Trent a thief was caught and confessed he had followed the King all the way from Berwick, cutting purses. Without trial, without a hearing, James had him hanged. Was this, then, the law in Scotland, and did James look to bring it across the border? . . . "I hear," wrote Elizabeth's goodnatured godson, Sir John Harrington, "our new king hath hanged one man before he was tried; 'tis strangely done: now if the wind blows thus, why may not a man be tried before he hath offended?" [1]

When it came time for James's first Parliament, from the very opening ceremonies there were difficulties when someone committed the serious error of not summoning the Commons to the Lords' House to hear the king's speech. A yeoman of the guard, adding insult to injury, offended those Commoners who went to the Lords' House on their own initiative by not promptly admitting them. Though the king three days later repeated his speech to the Commons, the damage had been done. Some of the Commons remained irritated, drawing up at the end of the sessions a *Form of Apology and Satisfaction* in such strong language that the majority recommitted it. James, meanwhile, by the time he prorogued the Parliament, was himself so irritated that his speech to the Commons was filled with reproaches.[2]

One question that I have repeatedly asked myself in contemplating the constitutional relationships portrayed in Shakespeare's plays is whether the relationships reveal a consciously structured pattern or an unconscious mirroring of contemporary realities. I have decided that it is not possible to reach a definitive conclusion for all nine plays in the absence of external evidence confirming Shakespeare's intentions. Since such evidence almost definitely will not be found, one will never know for certain. In only one scene are the references so complete and so consistent that they must be deliberate—in Henry V's first appearance as king when he tells the lords, princes, and Lord Chief Justice of his intention to govern the land well by consulting with counsel and Parliament and by submitting to the law. This play, *2 Henry IV*, was written sometime in 1598, though it is not possible to pinpoint precisely when in that year; it was first printed in a Quarto edition in 1600.[3] Elizabeth's advancing age may have spurred Shakespeare to suggest the specific constitutional equilibrium described by Henry's intentions; there is also a possibility that James VI of Scotland's views on the monarchy, which he made known with the publication of *The Trew Law of Free Monarchies* in September of 1598, had reached Shakespeare and inspired him to specify the importance of law, Parliament, and council to a king in the proper government of England.[4] James made clear in *Trew Law* that the assumptions upon which he would operate as king were not those that had developed through English common law. He claimed that kings are makers of law, not laws of kings (McIlwain, ed.,

Political Works of James I, p. 62), that the king has power of life and death over the whole land, that the king is above the law (p. 63), that the king may make law without "any advice of Parliament or estates," and that this last specifically is true for England as well as Scotland (p. 62). Though James did acknowledge a king's responsibility for his people when he said that a king "to procure the weal and flourishing of his people . . . know[s] himself to be ordained for them, and they not for him" (p. 55), he stated that a king is accountable to God alone. Like the author of "An Homily Against Wilfull Disobedience and Rebellion,"[5] James insisted that princes are ordained by God, so that people must endure even an evil prince (p. 70). While it will never be possible to prove that Shakespeare was responding to information about James's interpretation of the role of king in *2 Henry IV*, it is certainly possible that the views James expressed could have provoked the deliberation with which act 5, scene 2 is handled.

Whether or not James influenced Shakespeare, it can be said that the constitutional balance Shakespeare dramatizes at the end of *2 Henry IV* and confirms in *Henry V* reflects more closely the constitution of his own times than the late medieval constitution of the times of Henry V. Through the nine English history plays that he wrote before Elizabeth's death, Shakespeare gives less attention to feudalism in the last four plays than in the first four, even though the first four were about a period closer in time to Shakespeare's England and thus further removed from feudal traditions. The best explanation I can find for this difference between the two tetralogies is that Shakespeare is more concerned with contemporary constitutional developments than with developments in the periods covered by the plays.

Those scholars who found a statement of the theme of the English history plays in Ulysses' speech on degree (*Troilus and Cressida*, 1.3.109–37) need not have looked outside these plays for a summary if, in fact, submission to "degree" is the theme. In *Henry V* Exeter says:

While that the armed hand doth fight abroad,
Th' advised head defends itself at home:
For government, though high and low and lower,
Put into parts, doth keep in one consent,
Congreeing in a full and natural close,
Like music.

(1.2.178–83)

Then the Archbishop of Canterbury adds:

Therefore doth heaven divide
The state of man in divers functions,
Setting endeavour in continual motion;
To which is fixed, as an aim or butt,
Obedience. . . .

(1.2.183–87)

The Archbishop then gives an elaborate description of the ends of government. He cites the familiar Renaissance example of the society of honeybees that "teach/The act of order to a peopled kingdom" (1.2.188–89). The honeybees have equivalents of a king and officers such as magistrates, merchants, soldiers, masons, citizens, porters, a "sad-ey'd justice," and so on. His conclusion, however, does not imply the sort of absolute obedience of the homilies or of Ulysses's speech:

I this infer,
That many things, having full reference
To one consent, may work contrariously. . . .

(1.2.204–6)

But just as in *Troilus and Cressida* Ulysses' speech, as L. C. Knights suggests, "appears as something other than the expression of an unquestioned standard," the Archbishop's speech does not appear to be unquestioned in *Henry V*.[6] The Archbishop is urging Henry to go to war so that the investigations into the Church will end; he uses this speech to show Henry that though he may depart for foreign

wars, yet many parts of the realm can cooperate toward the
goal of defending England:

> Therefore to France, my liege.
> Divide your happy England into four;
> Whereof take you one quarter into France,
> And you withal shall make all Gallia shake.
> If we, with thrice such powers left at home,
> Cannot defend our own doors from the dog,
> Let us be worried and our nation lose
> The name of hardiness and policy.
>
> (1.2.213–20)

When the first tetralogy opened, Shakespeare showed
that neither king nor people had any well-articulated expectations for the constitutional function of the monarchy until,
in Shakespeare's dramatization of the Wars of Roses, the
chaos of a king's ruling according to vague feudal assumptions of automatically owed allegiance and a nobility's
power struggle brought the country close to ruin. From the
repeated disasters of the civil war, Shakespeare shows both
kings and people perceiving that, to be ruled well, England
must have a king who demonstrates and can act upon respect for both the law and England's people; to this theme
Shakespeare then seems to have dedicated the second tetralogy. The theme was topical because of Elizabeth's advanced
age. In retrospect, knowing that constitutional difficulties
were almost immediately apparent with the arrival of the
new monarch, one can see that the theme had great urgency.
It probably took no special insight to realize the danger to
the constitutional equilibrium even before Elizabeth's death.
The less-than-wholly-joyous atmosphere of the reigns of
Henry IV and Henry V testifies, however, to how little is
achieved even by kings seemingly dedicated to the law and
their people. I find the conclusion of *Henry V* to be ultimately pessimistic about the fate of men in society. For
despite Henry's doing and saying the right things in terms
of the sixteenth-century constitution, his life was brief, his
achievements were shortlived.

Henry the Sixth, in infant bands crown'd King
  Of France and England, did this king succeed;
Whose state so many had the managing,
  That they lost France and made his England bleed. . . .

(Epil., ll. 9–12)

NOTES TO CONCLUSION

1. Catharine Drinker Bowen, *The Lion and the Throne* (Boston: Little, Brown and Co., 1957), p. 178.
2. J. P. Kenyon, ed., *The Stuart Constitution 1603–1688, Documents and Commentary* (Cambridge: At the University Press, 1966), pp. 27–42.
3. *2 King Henry IV*, ed. A. R. Humphreys (London: Methuen; Cambridge, Mass.: Harvard University Press, 1966), p. xiv.
4. D. Harris Willson, *King James VI and I* (New York: Oxford University Press, 1956), p. 131 gives the month of publication. Quotations are taken from Charles Howard McIlwain, ed., *The Political Works of James I*, 1918, reprint (New York: Russell and Russell, 1965).
5. *Certain Sermons or Homilies Appointed to be Read in Churches in the Time of Queen Elizabeth I (1547–1571)*, 1623, 2 vols. in 1, facsimile reprint (Gainesville, Fla.: Scholars' Facsimiles and Reprints, 1968), p. 280. This sermon has no status as a constitutional document even though it was "approved" by Elizabeth. The very need that such a sermon be preached annually may suggest the administration's insecurity about this subject.
6. L. C. Knights, "Shakespeare's Politics, with Some Reflections on the Nature of Tradition," *Proceedings of the British Academy* 43 (1957):119.

Selected Bibliography

1. PLAYS

Famous Victories of Henry the Fifth. In *Chief Pre-Shakespearean Dramas,* edited by Joseph Quincy Adams. Cambridge, Mass.: Houghton Mifflin Co., Riverside Press, 1924.

Heywood, Thomas. *The First and Second Parts of King Edward IV.* Edited by Barron Field. London: Shakespeare Society, 1842.

King Edward III. Pseudo-Shakespearian Plays. Edited by Karl Warnke and Ludwig Proescholdt. Halle, Germany: Max Niemeyer, 1883.

Marlowe, Christopher. *Edward the Second.* Edited by M. Moelwyn Merchant. London: Ernest Benn Limited, 1967. The New Mermaids, Philip Brockbank and Brian Morris, general editors.

Peele, George. *Edward I.* Edited by Frank S. Hook. In *The Dramatic Works of George Peele,* edited by Frank S. Hook and John Yoklavich. New Haven, Conn.: Yale University Press, 1961.

Shakespeare, William. *The Complete Works.* Edited by G. B. Harrison. New York: Harcourt, Brace and World, 1952.

———. *King Henry IV.* Edited by A. R. Humphreys. Parts 1 (1960) and 2 (1966). London: Methuen; Cambridge, Mass.: Harvard University Press.

———. King Henry V. Edited by John H. Walter. London:

Methuen; Cambridge, Mass.: Harvard University Press, 1954.

――――. *King Henry VI*. Edited by Andrew S'. Cairncross. Parts 1 (1962), 2 (1957), and 3 (1964). London: Methuen; Cambridge, Mass.: Harvard University Press.

――――. *King John*. Edited by E. A. J. Honigmann. London: Methuen; Cambridge, Mass.: Harvard University Press, 1954. Edited by John Dover Wilson. Cambridge: At the University Press, 1936.

――――. *King Richard II*. Edited by Peter Ure. London: Methuen; Cambridge, Mass.: Harvard University Press, 1956. Edited by John Dover Wilson. Cambridge: At the University Press, 1st edition, 1939; reprint, 1961.

――――. *King Richard III*. Edited by John Dover Wilson. Cambridge: At the University Press, 1st edition, 1954; reprint, 1968.

――――. *Troilus and Cressida*. Edited by Alice Walker. Cambridge: At the University Press, 1969.

Woodstock. Edited by A. P. Rossiter. London: Chatto and Windus, 1946.

2. LITERARY CRITICISM

Adams, Barry B., ed. *John Bale's "King Johan."* San Marino, Calif: Huntington Library, 1969.

Alexander, Peter. *Shakespeare's "Henry VI" and "Richard III."* Cambridge: At the University Press, 1929.

Altick, Richard D. "Symphonic Imagery in *Richard II*." In *Twentieth Century Interpretations of "Richard II,"* edited by Paul M. Cubeta, pp. 65–81. Englewood Cliffs, N. J.: Prentice-Hall, 1971.

Armstrong, William A. "The Elizabethan Conception of the Tyrant." *Review of English Studies* 22 (1946): 161–81.

――――, ed. *Shakespeare's Histories, An Anthology of Modern Criticism*. Middlesex, England: Penguin Books, 1972.

Arnold, Aerol. "The Recapitulation Dream in *Richard III* and *Macbeth*." *Shakespeare Quarterly* 6 (1955): 51–62.

Ash, D. F. "Anglo-French Relations in *King John*." *Etudes Anglaises* 3 (1939): 349–58.

Barber, C. L. *Shakespeare's Festive Comedy.* Princeton, N. J.: Princeton University Press, 1959.

Barish, Jonas A., ed. *Ben Jonson: Sejanus.* New Haven, Conn.: Yale University Press, 1965.

Barroll, J. Leeds. "Shakespeare and Roman History." *Modern Langauge Review* 53 (1958): 327–43.

Battenhouse, Roy. "Falstaff as Parodist and Perhaps Holy Fool." *PMLA* 90 (January 1975): 32–52.

———. "Tudor Doctrine and the Tragedy of *Richard II.*" *Rice University Studies* 60 (Spring 1974): 31–53.

Berman, Ronald. "Anarchy and Order in *Richard III* and *King John.*" *Shakespeare Survey* 20 (1967): 51–59.

———, ed. *Twentieth Century Interpretations of "Henry V."* Englewood Cliffs, N.J.: Prentice-Hall, 1968.

Bevington, David. *Tudor Drama and Politics, A Critical Approach to Topical Meaning.* Cambridge, Mass.: Harvard University Press, 1968.

Black, M. W. "The Sources of Shakespeare's *Richard II.*" In *Joseph Quincy Adams Memorial Studies,* edited by James G. McManaway et al, pp. 199–216. Washington, D.C.: Folger Shakespeare Library, 1948.

Bradbrook, M. C. "Shakespeare and the Structure of Tudor Society." *Review of National Literatures* 3 (1972): 90–105.

Brockbank, J. P. "The Frame of Disorder—Henry VI." In *Early Shakespeare,* edited by J. R. Brown and B. Harris, pp. 73–100. Stratford-Upon-Avon Studies 3. New York: St. Martin's Press, 1961.

Bromley, John F. *The Shakespearean Kings.* Boulder, Col.: Colorado Associated University Press, 1971.

Brooke, Nicholas, ed. *Shakespeare: "Richard II." A Casebook.* London: Macmillan Press, 1973.

———. *Shakespeare's Early Tragedies.* London: Methuen and Company, 1968.

Brown, J. R., and Harris, B., eds. *Early Shakespeare.* Stratford-Upon-Avon Studies 3. New York: St. Martin's Press, 1961.

Bullough, Geoffrey. *Narrative and Dramatic Sources of Shakespeare.* Vol. 3 (1960): vol. 4 (1962). London: Routledge and Kegan Paul; New York: Columbia University Press.

Bush, Douglas. *English Literature in the Earlier Seventeenth Century (1600-1660)*. 2d ed. Oxford: Clarendon Press, 1962.

Cairncross, Andrew S., *First Part of King Henry VI* (1962); *Second Part of King Henry VI* (1957); *Third Part of King Henry VI* (1964). London: Methuen; Cambridge, Mass.: Harvard University Press. Arden Edition.

Campbell, Lily Bess. *Shakespeare's "Histories"—Mirrors of Elizabethan Policy*. San Marino, Calif.: Huntington Library, 1947.

Champion, Larry S. "The Function of Mowbray: Shakespeare's Maturing Artistry in *Richard II*." *Shakespeare Quarterly* 26 (Winter 1975): 3–7.

Chapman, Raymond. "The Wheel of Fortune in Shakespeare's Historical Plays." *Review of English Studies* NS1 (1950): 1–7.

Clemen, Wolfgang H. *Development of Shakespeare's Imagery*. London: Methuen, 1951.

————. "Tradition and Originality in Shakespeare's *Richard III*." *Shakespeare Quarterly* 5 (1954): 247–57.

Cohen, Eilleen Z. "The Visible Solemnity: Ceremony and Order in Shakespeare and Hooker." *Texas Studies in Literature and Language* 12 (1970–71): 181–95.

Cubeta, Paul M., ed. *Twentieth Century Interpretations of "Richard II."* Englewood Cliffs, N.J.: Prentice-Hall, 1971.

Dean, Leonard F. "From *Richard II* to *Henry V*, A Closer View." In *Twentieth Century Interpretations of "Richard II,"* edited by Paul M. Cubeta, pp. 58–65. Englewood Cliffs, N.J.: Prentice-Hall, 1971.

Elliott, John R. "History and Tragedy in *Richard II*." *Studies in English Literature* 8 (1968): 253–71.

————. "Shakespeare and the Double Image of King John." *Shakespeare Studies* 1 (1965): 64–84.

Ellis-Fermor, Una. *The Frontiers of Drama*. 2d ed. London: Methuen and Company, 1964.

Forker, Charles R. "Shakespeare's Chronicle Plays as Historical-Pastoral." *Shakespeare Studies* 1 (1965): 85–104.

Friesner, Donald Neil. "William Shakespeare, Conservative." *Shakespeare Quarterly* 20 (1969): 165–78.

Gaw, Allison. *The Origin and Development of "1 Henry VI" in*

Relation to Shakespeare, Marlowe, Peele, and Greene. University of South Carolina Studies, first series, 1 (1926).

Gilbert, Allan. "Patriotism and Satire in *Henry V.*" In *Studies in Shakespeare,* edited by Arthur D. Matthews and Clark M. Emery, pp. 40–64. Coral Gables, Fla.: University of Miami Press, 1953.

Goddard, Harold C. *The Meaning of Shakespeare.* 2 vols. 1951. Reprint. Chicago and London: University of Chicago Press, Phoenix Books, 1960.

Hamilton, A. C. *The Early Shakespeare.* San Marino, Calif.: The Huntington Library, 1967.

Hart, Alfred. *Shakespeare and the Homilies.* Melbourne, Australia: Melbourne University Press, 1934.

Honigmann, E. A. J., ed. *King John.* London: Methuen; Cambridge, Mass.: Harvard University Press, 1954. Arden Edition.

Humphreys, A. R., ed. *First Part of King Henry IV* (1961); *Second Part of King Henry IV* (1966). London: Methuen; Cambridge, Mass.: Harvard University Press. Arden Edition.

Jenkins, Harold. "Shakespeare's History Plays: 1900–1951." *Shakespeare Survey* 6 (1953): 1–15.

Jorgensen, Paul A. "A Formative Shakespearean Legacy: Elizabethan Views of God, Fortune, and War." *PMLA* 90 (March 1975): 222–33.

Kay, Carol McGinnis. "Traps, Slaughter, and Chaos: A Study of Shakespeare's *Henry VI* Plays." *Studies in the Literary Imagination* 5 (April 1972): 1–26.

Keeton, George W. *Shakespeare and His Legal Problems.* London: A. and C. Black, 1930.

―――. *Shakespeare's Legal and Political Background.* New York: Barnes and Noble, 1968.

Kelly, Henry Ansgar. *Divine Providence in the England of Shakespeare's Histories.* Cambridge, Mass.: Harvard University Press, 1970.

Kernan, Alvin. "The Henriad: Shakespeare's Major History Plays." *Yale Review* 59 (1969): 3–32.

King, L. "The Use of Hall's Chronicle in the Folio and Quarto Texts of *Henry VI.*" *Philological Quarterly* 13 (1934): 321–32.

Kingsford, Charles Lethbridge. *English History in the Fifteenth Century and the Historical Plays of Shakespeare.* National Home-

Reading Union Pamphlets. Historical Series, no. 1. London, 1915.

Knight, G. Wilson. "A Note on *Henry VIII.*" *Criterion* 15 (1936) : 228–34.

———. *The Crown of Life.* 1947. Reprint. London: Methuen's University Paperbacks, 1965.

———. *The Olive and the Sword, A Study of England's Shakespeare.* London: Oxford University Press, 1944.

Knights, L. C. "Shakespeare's Politics, with Some Reflections on the Nature of Tradition." *Proceedings of the British Academy* 43 (1957) : 115–32.

Law, R. A. "The Chronicles and *1, 2, 3, Henry VI.*" *Texas Studies in English* 33 (1955) : 13–32.

Lewis, Edward Thomas. *Images of Social Order: A Study of Shakespeare's Changing Concept of Society.* Denver, Col.: University of Denver Press, 1972.

Lindenbaum, Sheila Serio. "Shakespeare and the Social Contract: The *Henry VI* Plays and the Political, Historical, and Dramatic Background." Ph.D. dissertation, University of California at Berkeley, 1971.

Manheim, Michael. *The Weak King Dilemma in the Shakespearean History Play.* Syracuse, N.Y.: Syracuse University Press, 1973.

Marriott, J. A. R. *English History in Shakespeare.* London: Chapman and Hall, 1918.

———. "Shakespeare and Politics." *Cornhill Magazine* NS 63 (1927) : 678–90.

Matchett, William H. "Richard's Divided Heritage in *King John.*" *Essays in Criticism* 12 (July 1962) : 321–53.

Maveety, Stanley R. "A Second Fall of Cursed Man; The Bold Metaphor in *Richard II.*" *Journal of English and Germanic Philology* 72 (1973) : 175–93.

Merchant, W. M. "The Status and Person of Majesty." *Shakespeare Jahrbuch* 90 (1954) : 285–89.

Ornstein, Robert. *A Kingdom for a Stage, The Achievement of Shakespeare's History Plays.* Cambridge, Mass.: Harvard University Press, 1972.

———. "Historical Criticism and the Interpretation of Shakespeare." *Shakespeare Quarterly* 10 (1959) : 3–9.

Painter, Sidney. *The Reign of King John*. Baltimore, Md.: Johns Hopkins Press, 1949.

Palmer, David J. "Casting Off the Old Man: History and St. Paul in *Henry VI*." *Critical Quarterly* 12 (1970): 267–83.

Palmer, John. *Political and Comic Characters of Shakespeare*. London: Macmillan, 1965. *Political Characters* originally published separately in 1945.

Pierce, Robert B. *Shakespeare's History Plays, The Family and the State*. Columbus, Ohio: Ohio State University Press, 1971.

Phialas, Peter G. "The Medieval in *Richard II*." *Shakespeare Quarterly* 12 (1961): 305–10.

Phillips, Owen Hood. *Shakespeare and the Lawyers*. London: Methuen, 1972.

Pratt, S. M. "Shakespeare and Humphrey, Duke of Gloucester." *Shakespeare Quarterly* 16 (1965): 201–16.

Prior, Moody. *The Drama of Power*. Evanston, Ill.: Northwestern University Press, 1973.

Quinn, C. M. "Providence in Shakespeare's Yorkist Plays." *Shakespeare Quarterly* 10 (1960): 45–52.

Rabkin, Norman. *Shakespeare and the Common Understanding*. New York: Macmillan Company's Free Press, 1967.

Reed, Robert Rentoul, Jr. *Richard II: From Mask to Prophet*. University Park, Pa.: Penn State University Studies, no. 25, 1968.

Reese, M. M. *The Cease of Majesty, A Study of Shakespeare's History Plays*. New York: St. Martin's Press, 1961.

Ribner, Irving. *The English History Play in the Age of Shakespeare*. Princeton, N.J.: Princeton University Press, 1957.

————. "The Political Problem in Shakespeare's Lancastrian Tetralogy." *Studies in Philology* 49 (1952): 171–84.

Richmond, H. S. *Shakespeare's Political Plays*. New York: Random House, 1967.

Riggs, David. *Shakespeare's Heroical Histories: "Henry VI" and its Literary Tradition*. Cambridge, Mass.: Harvard University Press, 1971.

Rossiter, A. P. "Angel with Horns: The Unity of *Richard III*." In *Angel with Horns*, pp. 1–22. London: Longmans, Green & Co., 1961.

————, ed. *Woodstock*. London: Chatto and Windus, 1946.

Sanders, Wilbur. *The Dramatist and the Received Idea*. Cambridge: At the University Press, 1968.

Sen Gupta, S. C. *Shakespeare's Historical Plays*. Oxford University Press, 1964.

Sewell, Arthur. *Character and Society in Shakespeare*. Oxford: Clarendon Press, 1951.

Sheriff, William E. "Shakespeare's Use of Native Comic Tradition in his Early English History Plays." *Wisconsin Studies in Literature* 2 (1965): 11–17.

Spencer, T. J. B. "Social Assent and Dissent in Shakespeare's Plays." *Review of National Literatures* 3 (1972): 20–38.

Sprague, Arthur Colby. *Shakespeare's Histories, Plays for the Stage*. London: The Society for Theatre Research, 1964.

Spurgeon, Caroline F. *Shakespeare's Imagery and What it Tells Us*. New York: Macmillan, 1935.

Sternlicht, Stanford. "The Making of a Political Martyr-Myth: Shakespeare's Use of the Memory of Richard II in *1* and *2 Henry IV* and *Henry V*." Ball State University Forum 12 (1971): 26–38.

Stirling, Brents. *The Populace in Shakespeare*. New York: Columbia University Press, 1949.

Stoll, Elmer Edgar. *Poets and Playwrights, Shakespeare, Jonson, Spenser, Milton*. New York: Russell and Russell, 1965.

Talbert, Ernest William. *The Problem of Order: Elizabethan Political Commonplaces and an Example of Shakespeare's Art*. Chapel Hill, N.C.: University of North Carolina Press, 1962.

Tillyard, E. M. W. *The Elizabethan World Picture*. 1943. Reprint. London: Chatto and Windus, 1960.

————. *Shakespeare's History Plays*. 1944. Reprint. London: Chatto and Windus, 1956.

Traversi, Derek A. *An Approach to Shakespeare*. 3d ed. Garden City, N.Y.: Doubleday, 1969.

————. *Shakespeare from "Richard II" to "Henry V."* Stanford, Calif.: Stanford University Press, 1957.

Ure, Peter, ed. *King Richard II*. London: Methuen; Cambridge, Mass.: Harvard University Press, 1956. Arden Edition.

Utterback, Raymond V. "Dramatic Perspectives on Shakespeare's History Plays: A Review Article." *Studies in the Literary Imagination* 5 (1972): 141-62.

Waith, Eugene M., ed. *Shakespeare—The Histories; A Collection of Critical Essays.* Englewood Cliffs, N.J.: Prentice-Hall, 1965.

Wallerstein, Ruth. *King John in Fact and Fiction.* Philadelphia: E. Stern and Company, 1917.

Walter, J. H., ed. *King Henry V.* London: Methuen; Cambridge, Mass.: Harvard University Press, 1954. Arden Edition.

Weiss, Theodore. *The Breath of Clowns and Kings: Shakespeare's Early Comedies and Histories.* New York: Atheneum, 1971.

Whitaker, Virgil K. *Shakespeare's Use of Learning, An Inquiry into the Growth of his Mind and Art.* San Marino, Calif.: Huntington Library, 1953.

White, Edward J. *Commentaries on the Law in Shakespeare.* St. Louis, Mo.: F. H. Thomas Law Book Company, 1911.

Williamson, Marilyn L. "The Episode with Williams in *Henry V.*" *Studies in English Literature 1500-1900* 9 (1969): 275-82.

Wilson, F. P. *Shakespearian and Other Studies.* Edited by Helen Gardner. Oxford: Clarendon Press, 1969.

Wilson, John Dover, ed. *King John.* Cambridge: At the University Press, 1936.

———, ed. *King Richard II.* 1939. Reprint. Cambridge: At the University Press, 1961.

———, ed. *King Richard III.* Cambridge: At the University Press, 1st edition, 1954; reprint, 1968.

———. "The Political Background of Shakespeare's *Richard II* and *Henry IV.*" *Shakespeare Jahrbuch* 75 (1939): 36-51.

Winny, James. *The Player King.* New York: Barnes and Noble, 1968.

Zeeveld, W. Gordon. "*Coriolanus* and Jacobean Politics." *Modern Language Review* 57 (1962): 321-34.

———. *Foundations of Tudor Policy.* Cambridge, Mass.: Harvard University Press, 1948.

———. *The Temper of Shakespeare's Thought.* New Haven and London: Yale University Press, 1974.

3. PRIMARY SOURCES OF LEGAL,
CONSTITUTIONAL, AND SOCIAL HISTORY

Ascham, Roger. *The Scholemaster.* 1570. Reprint. New York: AMS Press, 1966.

Aylmer, John. *An Harborowe for Faithfull and Trewe Subjectes.* . . . 1559. Facsimile reprint. Amsterdam, the Netherlands: Theatrum Orbis Terrarum, 1972.

Baldwin, W., ed. *A Myrroure for Magistrates.* See Campbell.

Bracton On the Laws and Customs of England. 1256. Edited by George E. Woodbine. Translated and revised by Samuel E. Thorne. 2 vols. Cambridge, Mass.: Harvard University Press, 1968.

Calendar of State Papers, Domestic Series, of the Reign of Elizabeth 1581–1590. Edited by Robert Lemon. 1865. Reprint. Nendeln, Liechtenstein: Kraus Reprint, 1967.

Campbell, Lily B., ed. *The Mirror for Magistrates.* 1559–87. 1938. Reprint. New York: Barnes and Noble, 1970.

Certain Sermons or Homilies Appointed to be Read in Churches in the Time of Queen Elizabeth I (1547–1571). 2 vols. in 1. 1623. Facsimile reprint. Gainesville, Fla.: Scholars' Facsimiles and Reprints, 1968.

Dewar, Mary, ed. *A Discourse of the Commonweal of This Realm of England Attributed to Sir Thomas Smith.* 1581. Charlottesville, Va.: University of Virginia for Folger Shakespeare Library, 1969.

Elton, G. R., ed. *The Tudor Constitution, Documents and Commentary.* Cambridge: At the University Press, 1960.

Elyot, Thomas, *The Boke Named the Governour.* 1531. Reprint. Edited by H. H. S. Croft. New York: B. Franklin, 1967.

Fortescue, John. *The Governance of England: Otherwise Called the Difference Between an Absolute and a Limited Monarchy.* Ca. 1471–76. Edited by Charles Plummer. Oxford: Clarendon Press, 1885.

Foster, Michael. *A Report of Some Proceedings on the Commission of Oyer and Terminer and Goal Delivery for the Trial of the Rebels in the Year 1746 in the County of Surrey, and of Other*

Crown Cases to Which are Added Discourses Upon a Few branches of the Crown Law. Oxford: Clarendon Press, 1762.

Franklin, Julian H., trans. and ed. *Constitutionalism and Resistance in the Sixteenth Century, Three Treatises by Hotman, Beza, and Mornay.* New York: Pegasus, 1969.

Glanvill, Ranulf de. *The Treatise on the Laws and Customs of the Realm of England Commonly Called Glanvill.* Ca. 1187–89. Edited by G. D. G. Hall. London: Nelson for the Selden Society, 1965.

Hall, Edward. *Chronicle Containing the Histories of England.* 1548–1550. London: J. Johnson et al, 1809.

Harrison, William. *The Description of England.* 1587. Edited by Georges Edelen. Ithaca, N.Y.: Cornell University Press for Folger Shakespeare Library, 1968.

Holinshed, Raphael. *Chronicles of England, Scotland, and Ireland.* 1587. [Edited by Sir Henry Ellis]. Vol. 2 (1807) ; vol. 3 (1808). London: J. Johnson et al.

Hooker, Richard. *Works.* 1597. Edited by J. Keble, revised by R. W. Church and F. Paget. 3 vols. 7th ed. Oxford: Clarendon Press, 1888.

James I, King of Great Britain. *Political Works.* Edited by Charles H. McIlwain. 1918. Reprint. New York: Russell and Russell, 1965.

John of Salisbury. *The Statesman's Book.* 1159. Translated by John Dickinson. New York: Alfred A. Knopf. 1927.

Kenyon, J. P., ed. *The Stuart Constitution 1603–1688, Documents and Commentary.* Cambridge: At the University Press, 1966.

Mirror for Magistrates. See Campbell.

Parsons, Robert. *A Conference About the Next Succession to the Crowne of Ingland.* Published by R. Doleman, 1594. Reprint. University Microfilms, *English Books Before 1640*, Reel 387, S.T.C. no. 19398.

Plowden, Edmund. *The Commentaries or Reports of Edmund Plowden, of the Middle Temple, esq; An Apprentice of the Common Law.* Ca. 1571–78. London: Printed by his Majesty's Law Printers, for Edward Brooke, 1779.

Ponet, John. *A Short Treatise of Politic Power.* 1556. Facsimile reprint. Yorkshire, England: The Scolar Press, 1970.

Ralegh, Walter. *The History of the World.* 1614. Edited by C. A. Patrides. Philadelphia: Temple University Press, 1971.

Rotuli Parliamentorum ut et Petitiones et Placita in Parliamento Tempore 1278–1532. [Edited by John Strachey. London: 1767–1777?]

Saint German or Germain, Christopher. *Doctor and Student: Or, Dialogues Between a Doctor of Divinity and a Student in the Laws of England.* 1518. 17th ed. Edited by William Muchall. London: A. Strahen and W. Woodfall, 1787.

Smith, Thomas. *De Republica Anglorum.* 1583. Edited by L. Alston. Cambridge: At the University Press, 1906.

————. See Dewar.

Tanner, J. R. *Tudor Constitutional Documents, 1485–1603.* Cambridge: At the University Press, 1922.

Welsby, Paul A., ed. *Sermons and Society, An Anglican Anthology.* Middlesex, England: Penguin Books, 1970.

4. SECONDARY SOURCES ON GENERAL POLITICAL BACKGROUND

Allen, J. W. *A History of Political Thought in the Sixteenth Century.* London: Methuen, 1928.

Bagehot, Walter. *The English Constitution.* Garden City, N.Y.: Doubleday Dolphin Books, n.d.

Baumer, Franklin Le Van. *The Early Tudor Theory of Kingship.* New Haven, Conn.: Yale University Press, 1940.

Bean, J. M. W. *The Decline of English Feudalism 1215–1540.* New York: Barnes and Noble, 1968.

Bellamy, J. G. *The Law of Treason in England in the Later Middle Ages.* Cambridge: At the University Press. 1970.

Bingham, Caroline. *The Making of a King.* Garden City, N.Y.: Doubleday, 1969.

Black, J. B. *The Reign of Elizabeth (1558–1603).* 2d ed. Oxford: Clarendon Press, 1951.

Bowen, Catherine Drinker. *The Lion and the Throne.* Boston: Little, Brown and Company, 1957.

Brown, A. L. "The Reign of Henry IV: The Establishment of the Lancastrian Regime." In *Fifteenth-century England 1399–1509, Studies in Politics and Society*, edited by S. B. Chrimes et al., pp. 1–28. Manchester, England: Manchester University Press, 1972.

Chrimes, S. B. *English Constitutional History*. 3d ed. London: Oxford University Press, 1965.

———. *English Constitutional Ideas in the Fifteenth Century*. Cambridge: At the University Press, 1936.

———. *Lancastrians, Yorkists, and Henry VII*. 2d ed. London: Macmillan and Company, 1966.

Chrimes, S. B. et al., eds. *Fifteenth-century England 1399–1509, Studies in Politics and Society*. Manchester: Manchester University Press, 1972.

Cooper, J. P. "The Supplication Against the Ordinaries Reconsidered." *English Historical Review* 72 (1957): 616–41.

De Bofarull Y Romañá, Manuel. *Las Antiguas Cortès El Moderno Parlamento El Regimen Representativo Organico*. Alcala De Henares, 1945.

Elton, G. R. *The Reformation 1520–1559. The New Cambridge Modern History*. Vol. 2. Cambridge: At the University Press, 1958.

———. "The Tudor Revolution: A Reply." *Past and Present* 29 (December 1964): 26–49.

Ferguson, Arthur B. "The Tudor Commonweal and the Sense of Change." *Journal of British Studies* 3 (1963–64): 11–35.

Fussner, F. Smith. *The Historical Revolution—English Historical Writing and Thought 1580–1640*. New York: Columbia University Press, 1962.

Ganshof, F. L. *Feudalism*. Translated by Philip Grierson. 2d English ed. New York: Harper and Row, 1961.

Glenn, Garrard. "Edward Coke and Law Restatement." *Virginia Law Review* 13 (1931): 447–60.

Goodman, Anthony. *The Loyal Conspiracy—The Lords Appellant Under Richard II*. Coral Gables, Fla.: University of Miami Press, 1971.

Gray, Charles M. *Renaissance and Reformation England 1509–1714*. New York: Harcourt Brace Jovanovich, 1973.

Harriss, G. L. "Medieval Government and Statecraft." *Past and Present* 25 (July 1963) : 8–39.

Hinton, R. W. K. "English Constitutional Theories from Sir John Fortescue to Sir John Eliot." *English Historical Review* 75 (1960) : 410–25.

Holdsworth, W. S. *A History of English Law.* Vol. 4 (1924) ; vol. 5 (1927). Boston: Little, Brown and Company.

Hudson, Winthrop S. *John Ponet (1516?–1556).* Chicago: University of Chicago Press, 1942.

Ives, E. W. "The Law and the Lawyers." *Shakespeare Survey* 17 (1964) : 73–86.

———. "The Reputation of the Common Lawyer in English Society 1450–1550." *University of Birmingham Historical Journal* 7 (1960) : 130–61.

Jay, Winifred. "The House of Commons and St. Stephen's Chapel." *English Historical Review* 26 (1921) : 225–27.

Jenkins, Elizabeth. *Elizabeth the Great.* New York: Coward-McCann, 1959.

Jones, Richard H. *The Royal Policy of Richard II: Absolutism in the Later Middle Ages.* Oxford: Basil Blackwell, 1968.

Jones, W. J. "The Crown and the Courts in England 1603–1625." In *The Reign of James VI and I*, edited by Alan G. R. Smith. London: Macmillan, 1973.

Judson, Margaret A. *Crisis of the Constitution.* New Brunswick, N.J.: Rutgers University Press, 1949.

Kantorowicz, Ernst H. *The King's Two Bodies, A Study in Mediaeval Political Theology.* Princeton, N.J.: Princeton University Press, 1957.

Keir, Sir David Lindsay. *The Constitutional History of Modern Britain Since 1485.* 8th ed. Princeton, N.J.: D. Van Nostrand Co., 1966.

Kingsford, Charles Lethbridge. *English Historical Literature in the Fifteenth Century.* Oxford: Clarendon Press, 1913.

Lea, Henry C. *Superstition and Force.* 3d ed. Philadelphia: Henry C. Lea, 1878.

Levine, Mortimer. "A Parliamentary Title to the Crown in Tudor England." *Huntington Library Quarterly* 25 (1961–62) : 121–27.

————. *Tudor England 1485–1603*. London: Cambridge University Press, 1968.

Lewis, P. S. "The Failure of the French Medieval Estates." *Past and Present* 23 (1962) : 3–24.

Lovejoy, Arthur O. *The Great Chain of Being, A Study of the History of an Idea*. Cambridge, Mass.: Harvard University Press, 1942.

Maitland, Frederic William. *English Law and the Renaissance*. Cambridge: At the University Press, 1901.

Major, Russell. *Representative Institutions in Renaissance France, 1421–1559*. Madison, Wis.: University of Wisconsin Press, 1960.

McIlwain, Charles Howard. *Constitutionalism Ancient and Modern*. Ithaca, N.Y.: Cornell University Press, 1940.

————. *The High Court of Parliament*. New Haven, Conn.: Yale University Press, 1910.

Manning, Brian. "The Nobles, the People, and the Constitution." In *Crisis in Europe 1560–1660*, edited by Trevor Aston, pp. 247–69. New York: Basic Books, 1965.

Morrall, John B. *The Medieval Imprint, The Founding of the Western Europe Tradition*. New York: Basic Books, 1967.

Mosse, George L. *The Struggle for Sovereignty in England, From the Reign of Queen Elizabeth to the Petition of Right*. East Lansing, Mich.: Michigan State College Press, 1950.

Neale, J. E. *Elizabeth I and Her Parliaments 1559–1581*. London: Jonathan Cape, 1953.

————. *Elizabeth I and Her Parliaments 1584–1601*. London: Jonathan Cape, 1957.

————. *The Elizabethan House of Commons*. New Haven, Conn.: Yale University Press, 1950.

Pickthorn, Kenneth. *Early Tudor Government—Henry VII*. Cambridge: At the University Press, 1934.

Plucknett, Theodore F. T. *A Concise History of the Common Law*. 4th ed. London: Butterworth and Company, 1948. See also *Taswell-Langmead*.

Pocock, J. G. A. *The Ancient Constitution and the Feudal Law*. 1957. Reprint. New York: W. W. Norton, 1967.

————. *Politics, Language and Time*. New York: Atheneum, 1971.

Pound, Roscoe. "Puritanism and the Common Law." *American Law Review* 45 (1911): 811–29.

Prall, Stuart E. "The Development of Equity in Tudor England." *American Journal of Legal History* 8 (1964): 1–19.

Pugh, T. B. "The Magnates, Knights and Gentry." In *Fifteenth-century England 1399–1509, Studies in Politics and Society,* edited by S. B. Chrimes et al., pp. 86–128. Manchester: Manchester University Press, 1972.

Randall, H. J. "The Beginnings of English Constitutional Law." *Illinois Law Review* 13 (1919): 462–99.

Read, Conyers. *Bibliography of British History, Tudor Period (1485–1603).* 2d ed. Oxford: Clarendon Press, 1959.

Rowse, A. L. *The England of Elizabeth, the Structure of Society.* New York: Macmillan Company, 1951.

Sabine, George H. *A History of Political Theory.* 3d ed. New York: Holt, Rinehart and Winston, 1961.

Schramm, Percy E. *A History of the English Coronation.* Translated by G. W. Legg. Oxford: Clarendon Press, 1937.

Slavin, Arthur Joseph. *The Precarious Balance, English Government and Society.* New York: Alfred A. Knopf, 1973.

Smith, Alan G. R. "Constitutional Ideas and Parliamentary Developments in England 1603–1625." In *The Reign of James VI and I,* edited by Smith. London: Macmillan, 1973.

————, ed. *The Reign of James VI and I.* London: Macmillan, 1973.

Taswell-Langmead's English Constitutional History. 11th ed. Edited by Theodore F. T. Plucknett. London: Sweet and Maxwell, 1960.

Tawney, R. H. *Religion and the Rise of Capitalism.* 1926. Reprint. New York: Mentor Books. 1961.

Thorne, E. S. *English Law and the Renaissance.* Florence, Italy: Leo S. Olschki, 1966.

Wilkinson, B. *The Coronation in History.* London: George Philip for the Historical Association, 1953.

————. "The 'Political Revolution' of the Thirteenth and Fourteenth Centuries in England." *Speculum* 24 (1949): 502–9.

Williams, Penry. "The Tudor State." *Past and Present* 25 (July 1963): 39–58.

Williamson, George. *Seventeenth-Century Contexts.* London: Faber and Faber, 1960.

Williamson, James A. *The Tudor Age.* 3d ed. New York: D. McKay, 1964.

Willson, D. Harris. *King James VI and I.* New York: Oxford University Press, 1956.

Wilson, Woodrow. *Congressional Government, A Study in American Politics.* 1885. Reprint. New York: Meridian Books, 1956.

Wolffe, B. P. "The Personal Rule of Henry VI." In *Fifteenth-century England 1399–1509, Studies in Politics and Society,* edited by S. B. Chrimes et al., pp. 29–48. Manchester: Manchester University Press, 1972.

Wolin, Sheldon S. *Politics and Vision, Continuity and Innovation in Western Political Thought.* Boston: Little, Brown and Company, 1960.

Woolley, Reginald Maxwell. *Coronation Rites.* Cambridge: At the University Press, 1915.

Wright, Louis B. *Middle Class Culture in Elizabethan England.* Chapel Hill, N.C.: University of North Carolina Press, 1935.

Index